THE POWER OF PERSONALITY

OF

PERSONALITY

How Introverts and Extroverts can Combine
to Amazing Effect

DR SYLVIA LOEHKEN

First published in Germany in 2014 by GABAL Verlag GmbH

This edition published in 2016 by John Murray Learning

Copyright © GABAL Verlag GmbH

Translated by Helen Roberts and Jackie Jones

Translation © Hachette UK Ltd

The right of Dr Sylvia Loehken to be identified as the Author of the Work has been asserted by her in accordance with the Copyright, Designs and Patents Act 1988.

Database right Hodder & Stoughton (makers)

The *Teach Yourself* name is a registered trademark of Hachette UK.

British Library Cataloguing in Publication Data: a catalogue record for this title is available from the British Library.

Library of Congress Catalog Card Number: on file.

ISBN 9781444792829

eISBN 9781444792836

1

Typeset by Cenveo® Publisher Services.

Printed and bound in Great Britain by CPI Group (UK) Ltd., Croydon, CR0 4YY.

John Murray Learning policy is to use papers that are natural, renewable and recyclable products and made from wood grown in sustainable forests. The logging and manufacturing processes are expected to conform to the environmental regulations of the country of origin.

John Murray Learning
Carmelite House
50 Victoria Embankment
London EC4Y 0DZ
www.hodder.co.uk

Contents

Acknowledgements   V

About the author   VII

Foreword by Anne M. Schüller   IX

Foreword by Hans Uwe L. Köhler   XI

Preface   XIII

Introduction   XVII

PART I: INTROVERTS – EXTROVERTS – CENTROVERTS

1. Introversion and extroversion: facts and myths   3

2. From 'I' to 'we': how the community shapes us   49

3. A meaningful life: feeling comfortable in alien territory   89

4. A chapter just for centroverts (finally!)   117

PART II: DIFFERENCES BETWEEN INTROVERTS AND EXTROVERTS IN PRACTICE

5. Same results – different methods   127

6. Management   155

7. Selling   195

8. Stressful encounters: status games   217

9. Being special together   267

Appendix   271

Notes   274

References and bibliography   281

Online resources   291

Index   292

THE PRIVILEGE OF A LIFETIME IS TO BECOME WHO YOU TRULY ARE.

C.G. JUNG

ACKNOWLEDGEMENTS

A book is rarely created in a bubble of solitude – even when it is written by an introvert. My final words are therefore dedicated to those who helped to ensure that this volume would ever reach your hands.

The staff of GABAL-Verlag, my German publisher, have stood by me with their professionalism and warmth since the *Quiet Impact* (Hodder & Stoughton, 2014) days. Ursula Rosengart and Ute Flockenhaus have also supported *The Power of Personality* from the start, venturing into unknown territory as a result. We were in agreement that it was high time to place the interaction of different personalities in the limelight.

It was a pleasure having professional support from Hodder & Stoughton in addition. Specifically I would like to thank Iain Campbell, Lyndsey Ng, and Antonia Maxwell.

While I was working on this book, talking to intelligent, exciting, supportive people – introverts, extroverts and centroverts – demonstrated to me better than all the mountains of books how much we learn from one another and can achieve together. I remember with pleasure my discussions with Dr Andrea Baare-Nair, Timo Braun (of the very cool Pink University), Stéphane Etrillard, Claudia Kimich, Hans Uwe L. Köhler, Dr Isabell Lisberg-Haag, Professor Dr Maria Parr, Lars Schäfer, Ulrike Scheuermann, Jochen Wieland and the wonderful mistress of Zen and communication Dr Fleur Wöss.

My thanks also go to the competent men and women from so many walks of life who illustrated some of the important things with their own expertise and experience at many different points. That helped a great deal more than many theories did.

The extrovert–introvert dialogue became a format in its own right on the 'noisy-quiet sofa' which Margit Hertlein and I do together. You can see for yourself how wonderful and productive being different can be at youtube.com/user/LeiseMenschenTV. Thank you, Margit!

My dialogue with Anne M. Schüller became particularly valuable to me. As a marked extrovert, she has captured the introverts' gifts of writing and razor-sharp analytical thinking – a phenomenal combination!

Dr Michael Meinhard is not only a good friend, but also the best of all illustrators. He listens, reflects and gets in touch when one of his stunning introvert ideas has matured. Thank you, Michael!

I live my personal extrovert–introvert–introvert life with John D. Kluempers, Ph.D. and my son. They tolerated the inception of this book patiently and with an occasional roll of the eyes (as they did for my previous book). That initial phase included mountains of books, extremely delicate scheduling and an unequal distribution of laundry and kitchen duties. I have to thank them for relaxing evenings around the card table as well. Men, you're incredible.

ABOUT THE AUTHOR

Dr Sylvia Loehken is an (introvert) wordsmith: she gives speeches, writes books and academic articles, leads seminars and coaches interesting people. Her big topic is the question: how can we best shape our lives on the basis of the personalities that we have?

Much in demand as an expert in introvert and extrovert communication, Sylvia Loehken helps quiet and not-so-quiet people to understand themselves and others better and to be successful with the package they have: at universities and research institutes, in boardrooms and at congresses, in conference rooms and when living with others.

With a background in academia as well as in science management and international collaboration (between Germany and Japan), Sylvia Loehken is familiar from many years of experience with the hurdles that can arise between introverts and extroverts when working together and communicating with each other – and likewise with the opportunities that blossom when the differences are understood, lived out and put to use.

The German version of Sylvia Loehken's book *Quiet Impact* (Hodder & Stoughton, 2014 [published by GABAL-Verlag as *Leise Menschen – Starke Wirkung*]), became a best-seller which received major media attention and helped to establish the *petit différence* between introverts and extroverts in the German-speaking world. It has become an important topic for public debate in many channels, and concerns and engages many people personally. *Der Spiegel* made 'The power of the quiet people' its cover story in August 2012 (Kullmann, 2012). In the same year, Sylvia Loehken was honoured as *Vortragsrednerin des Jahres* (Speaker of the Year) from the German speakers' platform *Vortragsredner.de*.

Sylvia Loehken lives with her husband and son between Bonn and Berlin, and between German and American culture. She likes to surround herself with good books, people who have more questions than answers and a mantle of tranquillity.

Contact Sylvia Loehken via:

leise-menschen.com

youtube.com/user/LeiseMenschenTV

twitter.com/LeiseMenschen

FOREWORD BY
ANNE M. SCHÜLLER

'You're like a wild horse. You run off ahead of everyone, don't even look around. You keep everyone on their toes. You always have something new on the go. Take a break now, keep quiet and give the others a chance.' The person who said this was presumably describing an extrovert. And it seems that people did have a fair bit of trouble with me! I once ripped a colleague to shreds in front of everybody at a boardroom meeting, someone I valued very much for his sound opinions: 'Say something for once. You just sit around here and never open your mouth. But you could contribute so much.' This particular colleague was presumably an introvert!

All this is a very long time ago. And of course it couldn't happen to me now. I have learned a great deal since then, have written books myself and also read a great deal in the process. I am particularly fond of one book: Sylvia Loehken's last book (*Quiet Impact* Hodder & Stoughton, 2014) about quiet people and their strong impact. In it, she tactfully shows the loud ones among us all what the quiet ones have to offer and how useful this is for the community, the working world and our existence together. And she shows this to the quiet ones among us too. However, her greatest achievement is this: she has given the quiet people a stage and placed them in the limelight. The wave of media attention in the press reflects the importance of this for the many, many wonderful introverts out there.

In her latest book, *The Power of Personality*, Sylvia Loehken takes us deeper into the subject:

1 By highlighting the importance of introversion and extroversion as personality traits, Sylvia Loehken demonstrates their right to a place in the discussion of diversity in the workplace.

2 The book helps readers to analyse themselves from an interesting perspective. It shows what introverts and extroverts need, what they are good at and what they need to watch out for. And because people

are rarely 100 per cent one or the other, but mostly a mixture of the two, the middle ground occupied by centroverts is also scrutinized.

3 The book shows how knowledge about introverts, extroverts and centroverts can be used effectively in people management and selling. Success is not determined by the homogeneity of a group but by members having different points of view and these being used correctly – particularly today in our increasingly complex, brave new business world.

As a scientist, Sylvia Loehken explores the various myths about introverts and extroverts in depth. Professionally, she shows how people with very different skills, inclinations and characteristics can interact and benefit from one another. As a human being, she makes a plea for tolerance and esteem for 'quiet' and 'not-so-quiet' characteristics – in the way we perceive ourselves and the way we perceive others. And almost by the way, she finally makes the implications of 'status signals' clear to us all (see Chapter 8). Enjoy.

Anne M. Schüller
Keynote speaker, best-selling author, business consultant

FOREWORD BY
HANS UWE L. KÖHLER

'Sometimes this world is too noisy for me, too agitated, and everything is always so terribly important!' This highly personal statement will perhaps amaze you as a reader, particularly when you discover that most people who know me (Hans-Uwe L. Köhler) as a speaker think of me as an extrovert.

When I first met Sylvia C. Loehken, we talked about exactly that point. 'Oh, you know, I'm really not like this – but I so rarely get to be me!' Sylvia answerd me quite incredulously: 'But you're not an introvert either!'

Are extroverts and introverts poles apart, like the colours white and black? Do they stand alone? No. They sit on a spectrum with the most wonderful shades of grey connecting them!

And if I were to give you one reason to read this book, it would be this: this book does not just provide explanations, it enables you to discover the 'spaces in between'. Anyone who focuses solely on simple opposites sees black-and-white solutions. It's only, however, possible to mature when considering the grey areas in between.

If you as a reader should find that you tend to go in one direction or the other, then you might be pleased by this insight – or you could, if you wanted to, get really cross about it. In actual fact, the status of your knowledge should encourage you to be curious about understanding the 'other' side. Then Sylvia Loehken's intentions with this book will be fulfilled, and the world in which we all live together might be made a little bit better.

And should it turn out that you don't fully belong to one side or the other, you won't be dismissed as some strange 'hybrid'. This book introduces us to a third group, the centroverts. You might be lucky and belong to that group, the sort that gets on well everyone! And you'll also know what makes Hans-Uwe L. Köhler tick!

Dear readers, in this book you can look forward to an instructive and inspiring read. Sit back, relax and enjoy this voyage of discovery …

Bon voyage!

Hans-Uwe I. Köhler
Keynote speaker and best-selling author on sales

PREFACE

This book explores how introverts and extroverts can communicate with each other successfully.

When I wrote *Quiet Impact* (Hodder & Stoughton, 2014) my aim was to fill a gap. Up until then there was no manual to help introverted people discover their strengths and communicate successfully. Because this gap was so wide, I decided initially not to address the perspective and characteristics of extroverts. The ambiverts, or centroverts as we will call them here, who are positioned in the middle, shared this fate: although they were mentioned, I focused mainly on the introvert perspective. I then searched for a long time to learn more about the other personalities, and found that while there are now quite a few manuals and textbooks for and about introverts, centroverts and extroverts haven't generally been catered for in the same way.

The book you are now reading is intended to fill this second gap. Considering the strengths and inclinations of introverts, extroverts and centroverts alongside one another, as well as the hurdles they face when dealing with each other, isn't just a matter of fairness, but also a necessity in the real world: because we don't live in introvert capsules and extrovert capsules. The reality is the hybrid team: in partnerships and the family, with friends and colleagues, with superiors and employees.

Many specialists consider that the degree of introversion or extroversion is one of the key differences between people. Psychologist James Dee Higley speaks of the 'north and south of the temperament' (Gallagher, 1994); C.G. Jung, who was the first to use the terms systematically, saw introversion/extroversion as the dominant personality factor. But we are only gradually beginning to think about the needs implied by this other *petit différence* – around 100 years after it became 'official' for the public at large, courtesy of Jung. That's astonishing, because other distinctions – young and old, local and immigrant, men and women, the disabled and the non-disabled – have been part of our social awareness and the debate on diversity for a long time. But although most personality tests include this distinction, some myths persist about what makes someone an introvert or an extrovert. In addition, interaction between introverts and extroverts still doesn't form part of the diversity debate, although this may be gradually changing. One indicator of this is the fact that the flagship publication *Der Spiegel* brought the debate to the public in a cover story (Kullmann, 2012). In addition, I experience this first hand in interactions with readers and clients.[1]

But the contents of this book are not intended to create a policy on diversity. The primary aim is to be of practical use to you. I will therefore simplify or summarize a lot of the science. If you would like to study individual areas in more detail you will find further explanations and recommended reading in both the notes and bibliography. However, the important points will be easy to understand without referencing these notes.

Part I of the book will give you a good look at the differences, strengths, priorities and needs of introvert and extrovert people – and you will understand what it means to be in the middle as a centrovert.

Part II shows what the differences mean in everyday life and ways in which introverts and extroverts can handle themselves and others. I have selected diverse areas of life, ranging from sport and learning to communication for managers, selling and status communication, but they all have one thing in common: they are the areas that my clients, readers and customers most frequently have in mind when they confront the topic of introversion and extroversion. I hope you will find issues and topics in this selection that are relevant to your own particular interests.

How to use this book

You will find real-life examples and stories throughout the book, but I have hidden the true identity of the people concerned. In order to help you identify the personality type under discussion, two simple methods have been used. First, the following icons have been used to distinguish the three main personality types:

 Extroverts

 Introverts

Secondly, the people involved have been given names starting with I or with E. Other icons in the text include:

 Questions for you to work on to help you in your journey of self-discovery

 The key points of the chapter in brief to help you consolidate your understanding of your new learning.

INTRODUCTION

The three factors of personality

Introvert or extrovert – it's only one motif in the highly complex jigsaw puzzle that makes up the human personality. This jigsaw determines how we develop, what we like, how we experience emotions. And there is a special rule for us when completing this jigsaw: we can only do it together with other people.

Three factors shape us here – our biological heritage, our social environment and the quest for our individuality.

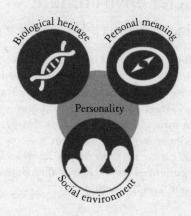

Factor 1: biological heritage

Our personality is shaped within very different areas. Our biological heritage is what we 'are given' when we come into the world. Over the last few years, progress in neuro-science has led to much of the research into personality being devoted to the structure of our brain, its processes and the substances involved in them such as neurotransmitters and hormones.

Studies show that differences between babies at the age of just four months allow reliable predictions as to whether the child will develop into an introvert or an extrovert. An important distinguishing feature here is sensitivity to environmental stimuli: 'introvert babies' have a more sensitive nervous system and therefore react more strongly (and more negatively) than 'extrovert babies' to bright lights, loud noises or strong odours. This corresponds as life goes on to the risk of over-stimulation for introverts, which drains their energy and significantly disturbs them (see long-term studies in Kagan, 2004)

However, this is just one piece of the complex jigsaw that forms a human being's personality.

Factor 2: social environment

For many years, scientists have argued over whether personality is influenced more by biological predisposition (nature) or social environment (nurture). Today, we know that the two areas are interconnected. More specifically, our biological predisposition influences the way we communicate with our environment. Yet this process is a two-way street like any other communication, because our environment, in turn, changes our brains throughout our lives. Although the development of a young brain is exposed to more and stronger change processes than that of an older one, we can all change. Our life experiences continuously alter both the structures and the metabolism of our 'thinking equipment'.

 Key idea

We don't arrive in this world as the finished article.

None of us is born with our 'equipment' complete. Part of what we're made up of, our 'second nature', comes from living with other human beings. We are all born into a social group and cultural context. The relationships with which we grow up constitute the second part of our equipment. They influence the way in which a growing child's brain develops. Relationships shape not only our language but also our preferences and the decisions we make. In short, it isn't enough to have a brain. A personality with all its facets can only develop in an exchange with other people – even purely biologically, because the neural connections in the brain are not formed until after birth. This only happens when we have mentors and they communicate with us, and is effected by the enormous adaptability to very different environments that characterizes humans. David Brooks (2011, p. 77) says that it is not the case that we first develop and then enter into relationships, we are born into relationships and these relationships are predominantly what make us into people in the first place.

Our social and cultural environment on the one hand and biological make-up on the other interact. So the question is not 'nature or nurture?' but more 'how do nature and nurture interact in the course of a person's development in such a way that a personality develops from it?' Our adaptability to our environment is a particular strength of our biological make-up. It enables us to thrive in all kinds of environments.

 Key idea

Our social and cultural environment on the one hand and biological make-up on the other interact: we have an effect on our environment and in turn the environment changes the structure and metabolism of our brains.

We are all born with introversion and extroversion as biological and measurable characteristics. But this is only the beginning of a person: at a specific time at a specific place and with specific people. It is the interaction between natural processes and social and cultural influences that shapes our personality – and therefore our introversion and extroversion as well. Our mentors, models, cultural expectations, the things that people expect of us – all these factors help to determine whether we live 'from the outside inwards' or 'from the inside outwards'.

Factor 3: the quest for meaning

The third factor that shapes our personality is also the one that exerts the strongest pull on us: it is our ability to make decisions about our lives, that appear to us meaningful and significant, of our own free will. These decisions are quite likely to result in introverts displaying extrovert behaviours or extroverts experiencing introvert periods. This can lead to a harmony-loving introvert reacting to a personal attack during a meeting by putting a colleague in his place. It may lead to an extrovert going on a week's silent retreat in a monastery. It may even mean that we pursue a career which on the face of it does not match the personal characteristics that have resulted from our predispositions or our 'second nature' – because the job in question fits better with our own image of ourselves. In other words, we should and must bond with others during our development in order to become people. However, we become true personalities through self-realization: finding our own values and goals.

 Key idea

Our personality develops and changes through the interaction of our biologicial make-up, social environment and the decisions we make.

It is this third factor that gives the development of our personality that certain something: the ability to make our own decisions gives us what we call freedom. We cannot choose either our biological make-up or our social environment. However, there is one thing we can do: choose for ourselves what gives our lives meaning and value. This may mean that in certain situations we opt to behave in one particular way when our personalities would normally suggest a different course of action.[2]

Yet in spite of all the freedom we enjoy, we cannot entirely shed our innate characteristics and the social conditions that have shaped our personalities. The different areas interact: for example, we know nowadays that social ties play a major role in our decision making because they influence our unconscious minds. What we ultimately do is only partly the result of deliberate consideration.[3]

You will discover in the first part of this book how you can handle challenges that might seem 'unnatural' to your type as an introvert or extrovert. You will also find a more detailed explanation of all three factors – biological predisposition, social environment and meaning-related decisions as you read through.

I hope that one thing in particular from what I have said so far is clear: personality has many facets. Neither introverts nor extroverts are controlled entirely by their biological predispositions – just as the behaviour of men and women is not controlled by their gender. What makes us people is the interplay of innate and acquired characteristics – and the freedom to go against our inclinations at times and 'steer against the wind' when we think it's important.

 Key idea

Introversion and extroversion may shape us, but they're not a straitjacket. That's why successful introvert and extrovert personalities are to be found in every walk of life.

The following table takes a cross-section of nationalities across the ages to show people who have decided to do what's important to them – introverts or extroverts who have successfully followed a vocation, shaped it and become influential in their chosen field. This overview is intended to encourage you: personality traits like introversion and extroversion may have a deep influence on us, but they're the whole story. It is our privilege to decide how we use our personalities.

Successful introverts and extroverts

	![Introvert] Introvert	![Extrovert] Extrovert
World changers	Eleanor Roosevelt, USA Mother Teresa, Albania	Martin Luther King Jr., USA Socrates, Greece
Intellectual stars	Simone de Beauvoir, France Isaac Newton, United Kingdom	Johann Wolfgang von Goethe, Germany Karl R. Popper, Austria/United Kingdom
Writers	Franz Kafka, Czech Republic Joanne K. Rowling, United Kingdom	Karen Blixen, Denmark Thomas John Boyle, USA
Scientists	Niels Bohr, Denmark Jane Goodall, United Kingdom	Alexander von Humboldt, Germany Daniel Goleman, USA
Politicians	Angela Merkel, Germany Barack Obama, USA	Gerhard Schröder, Germany Boris Johnson, United Kingdom
Businesspeople	Mark Zuckerberg, USA George Soros, Hungary	Richard Branson, United Kingdom Steve Jobs, USA
Fashion professionals	Anna Wintour, USA Tom Ford, USA	Heidi Klum, Germany Karl Lagerfeld, Germany
Musicians	Ludwig van Beethoven, Germany Annie Lennox, Scotland	Franz Liszt, Austria-Hungary Udo Lindenberg, Germany

	Introvert	Extrovert
Visual artists	Vincent van Gogh, The Netherlands Leonardo da Vinci, Italy	Frida Kahlo, Mexico Pablo Picasso, Spain
Stars of the cinema, TV and stage	Woody Allen, USA Tilda Swinton, United Kingdom	Jack Nicholson, USA Oprah Winfrey, USA
Athletes	Lionel Messi, Argentina Nico Rosberg, Germany	Usain Bolt, Jamaica Christiano Ronaldo, Portugal
Entertainers	Jerry Seinfeld, USA Terry Gilliam, USA/UK	Eddie Murphy, USA Mel Brooks, USA
Fictional figures	Charlie Brown, *Peanuts*, USA Hamlet, *Hamlet*, (Shakespeare), United Kingdom	Lucy van Pelt, *Peanuts*, USA Papageno, *The Magic Flute*, (Mozart/Schikaneder), Austria

PART I

Introverts – centroverts – extroverts

1.
Introversion and extroversion: facts and myths

Introverts and extroverts: the biological differences

The first big difference between introverts and extroverts derives from neurobiological factors: extroverts usually cope well with impressions received from the outside world; i.e. stimuli perceived by their sensory organs. What is more, extroverts also derive much of their energy and quality of life from these external stimuli and from exchanges with other people.

 Key idea

Different brain structures are the cause of the difference between extroverts and introverts. Extroverts place greater value on external impressions, while introverts place greater value on intense inner processes.

Extroverts like activity and initiative; many extroverts are enthusiastic travellers and love variety. They are generally sportier and have more contacts and more sexual partners than introverts (see Cain, 2011, p. 231). Introverts become engaged without these external stimuli. Their activities are different from their extrovert counterparts as they are more reflective. Even an apparently inactive person can be operating at full speed inside. The result of this difference is that introverts are more easily overstimulated than extroverts.

Introverts value and need quiet periods for themselves – quite literally. Not too loud, not too bright, preferably without anyone else, at most with very few people. They derive their energy from periods of low stimulation without company. Extroverts can also behave like this after stressful periods. However, introverts are inherently dependent on this need to escape and quietly recharge their batteries.

Hypersensitivity is closely associated with this. Hypersensitive people are also easily overstimulated – and although the majority of them are introverts, American psychologist Elaine Aron (1999) concludes that 30 per cent of extroverts are also hypersensitive.

Space doesn't permit a close look at this here, but what is certain is that overstimulation can be a problem for both introverts and the hypersensitive.

The second difference between extroverts and introverts is that extroverts like to take a chance and while introverts prefer to play it safe.

This can also be attributed to neurobiologically measurable differences. In the brains of introverts and extroverts, different parts of the neural emotional centre are active. Introverts have a more sensitive anxiety centre, while extroverts react more strongly to the prospect of reward. The concentrations of the different neurotransmitters also vary. Introverts have a higher level of acetylcholine, which is responsible for concentration, memory, learning and assessing.[4] Extroverts on the other hand have a higher level of dopamine in their brains. This neurotransmitter promotes exercise, curiosity, the search for variety and striving for reward and exciting activities.

 Key idea

'No risk – no fun!' or 'Safety first!' The biological differences between extroverts and introverts mean that they also need different experiences to make them happy.

This small difference has definite consequences for the personal inclinations of introverts and extroverts. Introverts prefer to distance themselves, need space to process their impressions and also have a strong self-preservation instinct. Acetylcholine especially ensures a relatively high need for safety. Introverts actually have fewer accidents and are more alert than average. Extroverts on the other hand value variety and activities which promise a reward. Dopamine means that extroverts accept challenges, take risks and sometimes even put themselves in danger to reach their desired reward. The need for stimulating variety and rewards is so strong that some extroverts will put relationships or possessions on the line that are actually really precious to them. Extroverts certainly have a bigger social and professional network but they are more inclined to put long-term partnerships at risk by engaging in other sexual relationships; they also have more of a tendency to gamble and even commit more crimes.[5]

Our choice of clothes is a clear example of how we express our tendency towards safety or risk. After all, we choose them to reflect our personalities. According to fashion expert Susanne Ackstaller, there are definite differences between introverts and extroverts.

 ## Your appearance shows what sort of person you are

Susanne Ackstaller, texter and blogger

When it comes to questions of fashion and style, reality in fact matches our expectations. Introverts tend to dress in a classical, simple style, choose subdued colours and patterns and use make-up discreetly. But extroverts go the whole hog. They dress to impress, their business outfits are pepped up with striking accessories and instead of lip gloss they wear bright red lipstick. As for brand names, introverts prefer Jil Sander while extroverts are more likely to choose Escada.

Although I have certainly seen introverts with really wild shoes, the basic idea seems valid!

The impressive thing about extroverts is their capacity for enthusiasm and delight: this may range from deep longing to euphoria. These positive feelings are also a consequence of the high dopamine concentration in the brain and the very active nucleus accumbens (see later in this chapter). Enthusiasm and euphoria are reactions when something important has been achieved or an attractive target has been reached, resulting in a kind of reward doping in the brain.[6] Introverts rarely tend towards exuberant feelings such as extreme excitement or wild joy. For those extroverts looking on pityingly, this does not in any way mean that their quality of life is any lower. It is just different. For example: where an extrovert might light a firework, an introvert will warm up in front of a coal fire.

 Key idea

Where an extrovert enthusiastically lights a firework, an introvert warms up contentedly in front of a coal fire.

The flip side is that if there is no stimulus from the outside world, boredom and tedium can set in more quickly for an extrovert than for an introvert. This can lead to the under-stimulated extrovert taking unnecessary or excessive risks and suffering harm in order to reach a dopamine high – and other people usually suffer along the way. Overestimating yourself and behaving in a socially damaging way are also believed to be dopamine side-effects. Criminal behaviour or devastating financial crises are two key effects which give you an idea of the range of possible risks.

But the introvert's neurotransmitter, acetylcholine, also has its disadvantages: caution, reflection and evaluation, which are encouraged by this neurotransmitter, often lead introverts to delay or to forget to act. Many brilliant ideas remain unrealized because the introvert brain baulks at the risk of putting ideas into action or has too many doubts.

Biological differences and their consequences: overview

Introverted: inward-looking	Extrovert: outgoing
Higher inner activity level, relatively high sensitivity to stimuli, little need for external impulses for energy or quality of life	Higher outer activity level, relatively low sensitivity to stimuli, more need for external impulses for energy or quality of life
Greater need for safety	Greater need for reward

Strengths – and hurdles

Now that you know something about the differences between introverts and extroverts, one question suggests itself: exactly what use is this knowledge? This question is both justified and important. The answers are the key to leading a 'natural' life where we value and benefit from the differences between introverts and extroverts in all areas.

Neither introverts nor extroverts are 'better' people. They are just plain different in what they can do well and what stresses or challenges them. This means that an extrovert approaches a goal or network-building differently from an introvert, whether that be taking a specific career step or even just organizing an everyday routine.

! Key idea

Introverts and extroverts are not the same – but they are worth the same, and they can each enjoy success in their own right.

The differences make introverts particularly strong in certain areas and extroverts in others. But they also bring with them certain hurdles and specific needs and difficulties. In this section you will become familiar with ten typical strengths and ten typical hurdles. You will also get a first glimpse of how introverts and extroverts sometimes perceive each other in terms of their strengths and hurdles. Anything 'different' is not always attractive, even if it is actually a strength. First of all, there are two important points which you should bear in mind as you read on.

1 The following two lists detailing strengths and hurdles are neither exhaustive nor are they intended to offer a complete psychological profile of introvert and extrovert personalities. They include characteristics which can be important for interpersonal communication. In other words, they provide a basis for getting along with both introverts and extroverts in your professional and private everyday life. And yes, you can also learn something about your own ability to communicate with the outside world.

2 In real life, there is no neat division between introvert and extrovert characteristics. First of all, we are all a mixture of introvert and extrovert. Secondly, there are no exclusive rights to strengths and hurdles. However, trends can be observed – such as the way very many introverts enjoy writing, an introspective activity which fosters an inner discussion on content. Conversely, many extroverts will prefer talking to writing because it is quicker, more direct and spontaneous and allows direct contact with other human beings. Nevertheless, there are of course excellent extrovert authors and excellent introvert speakers. Just not quite so often …

Now to the characteristics themselves. For clarity you will find them paired side by side as introvert and extrovert characteristics in two summary lists (strengths and hurdles) with a brief explanation. As you read on, you will be able to glance back at the lists.

You will also be encouraged to ask yourself questions as you read.

? Strengths and hurdles

Q. What strengths and hurdles do you observe in yourself?

This question will be revisited at the end of this chapter – with space for your notes.

Introvert and extrovert strengths

Strength pair 1: caution and courage

Many introverts tend to be cautious, i.e. they have an ability to perceive and weigh up risks. The cautious avoid risks that cannot be calculated and where the outcome is uncertain.	Many extroverts are bold. They are prepared to take risks to achieve an attractive goal. They prefer to take a gamble rather than hang around.

The high concentration of acetylcholine (for safety) in introvert brains and dopamine (for reward) in extrovert brains is the biological basis for caution or boldness. The two strengths directly correspond with the concentrations of these neurotransmitters, assisted by the different activities in the anxiety centre (amygdala, more active in introverts) and the reward centre (nucleus accumbens, more active in extroverts).[7]

Many introverts are for this reason consistent, plan ahead and think carefully before acting. This is advantageous in stress-free periods when it's not necessary to fight. Caution is also an important early warning system when handling risks that creep up on you – dangers that do not make their presence felt immediately, but can have enormous effects in the long term. Examples here are climate change, global distribution of resources, food quality and data security.

On the other hand, boldness causes many extroverts to act decisively and energetically, even to the extent of taking a risk with regards to comfort or safety if it seems necessary. They take a chance or gamble with money or relationships if it seems important for their purpose. Avoiding pain is less important for them, with their lower sensitivity, than for introverts who tend to be sensitive to stimuli. Extrovert boldness can be useful for example in uncertain, dangerous times when it is necessary to open up new territory and find new resources.

Consequences for communication: Cautious people communicate carefully the information they want to pass on. They are discreet and use what they have seen and heard to gauge correct the words and behaviour to use as best they can. They are often diplomatic.

Bold people break out of accepted rituals and shake things up. They dare to speak out and fight for a cause. They take a chance on the consequences, which may not always be good for their relationships.

Cautious people prefer to avoid pain, risk and difficulty more than bold people. In exchange with others, the cautious may easily mistake bold for reckless. And to bold people, cautious people can appear to be scaredy-cats or at least doubting Thomases.

Strength pair 2: substance and enthusiasm

Introverts are always busy processing their impressions by comparing, filtering and evaluating. This is the basis of substance: when an introvert says something, it often has a specific significance, depth or quality	Extroverts are often inspired and enthused by impressions. They can become euphoric and carry others along in their enthusiasm.

People with substance strive to extrapolate a deeper dimension to subjects, events or questions. The preferred inner activity of introverts is the consideration, evaluation and comparison of information, and is a good basis for exploring issues indepth.

As an introvert, a compelling reason for wanting to be an extrovert is their enthusiasm, which can sometimes escalate to euphoria. The introvert neurotransmitter acetylcholine is less conducive to this heady emotion – the extrovert neurotransmitter dopamine is much more so! Extroverts are more likely than introverts to become enthusiasts who infect others with their energy and may spur them into action.

Consequences for communication: You will have realized by now that one of the main reasons why many introverts have an aversion to small talk is that they find it too shallow. Even though an introvert may be fully aware that small talk is predominantly a means of building up basic trust and good relationships, it provides too little stimulation for the abundant inner life of a typical introvert. On the other hand, most introverts very much appreciate a conversation with depth. In such a conversation their strength of 'substantial thinking' can be indulged. Sophia Dembling (2012, p. 26f) mentions another reason for cherishing true conversation:

> Studies show that a deep conversation with an argument about the content is better than small talk for a sense of wellbeing; small talk merely serves as reassurance of the relationship level but it is rather threadbare in terms of subject matter.

> But extroverts bring a glow to communication. They can create inspiring, amusing and motivating moments by infecting others with their pleasure in their surroundings, in new ideas and in interesting activities. That often makes them irresistible.

> Those who prefer substance may easily consider enthusiastic people superficial or over-emotional. Enthusiasts often consider people of substance dull or cold. In their view, any emotional sparkle is missing.

Strength pair 3: concentration and flexibility

Introverts seem to find it easy to focus intensely and pour their energy into the matter in hand.	Flexible extroverts find it easy to adjust their thinking and actions or react quickly to new situations.

Introverts like getting to the bottom of things and going the extra mile. If they can avoid overstimulation and sudden interruptions, they will work on a project for hours. They best use their energy by focusing on what they consider to be meaningful (see Strength pair 2). This can produce astounding results, especially in combination with their perseverance (see Strength pair 8). Almost all successful scientists and inventors have strong powers of concentration.

But extroverts have flexibility on their side. They not only tolerate but even value a variety of outside stimuli, so it does not matter to them if their everyday life is fast moving, taking surprising twists and turns or entailing unexpected appointments and tasks. This agility allows them to be less sensitive to interruptions than introverts. What is more, extroverts draw energy from flexibility, as this supplies additional stimulation.

Consequences for communication: In exchanges with others, introverts are able to give all their attention to their counterparts. This is probably the most valuable currency in human communication (apart from trust) and can lend an introvert a very intense presence. Introverts are especially convincing when they show how thoroughly they know their subject and can deal with questions and comments – even in public situations such as lectures or discussions.

With nimble-footed agility, extroverts are able to lend a conversation wit and pace. They can change tack effortlessly and spontaneously and include new information in their thought processes. This is particularly useful in negotiations and wherever improvisation is needed; an extrovert will make reference to something someone else has said or something that has happened in the interim. For extroverts, written drafts are often a bit like trampolines: they bounce off them in whichever direction takes their fancy.

Focused people who like to concentrate tend to consider flexible people inconsistent, unreliable or vague. Flexible people sometimes find focused people inflexible, fixated or boring.

Strength pair 4: listening and presenting

Many introverts filter out important information from what they see or hear in dealings with others, managing to extrapolate points of view and requirements.	Many extroverts are especially successful in putting forward their own position and presenting themselves as skilful, assertive and effective.

With their capacity for putting themselves and their position forward, extroverts are good advocates for their own point of view and requirements. This is especially true if they are good speakers (Strength pair 9). Because they are less sensitive to external stimuli, extroverts often appear more 'cool', i.e. more relaxed and laid-back, than easily overstimulated introverts. That gives them another advantage in (self-) presentation, as they radiate power and authority.

While many introverts are masters of the underestimated craft of genuine listening, extroverts are able to find the right words and deliver them. If necessary, they can usually do this very quickly as well!

It is worth mentioning one particular type of listening here: most introverts are particularly practised in listening to and observing *themselves*. They use this 'self-monitoring' to adjust to the social demands of specific situations.[8]

Consequences for communication: Many introverts actually listen and observe well. They are experts in processing and absorbing the resulting information. They can filter out important messages from the material gathered through their eyes and ears to feed into further dialogue. Like concentration, listening gives the impression to the communication partner that the other person is extremely approachable and highly attentive. Many introverts follow up to get more detail and ask for explanations, referring to what they have just heard. This usually has a very positive effect. Introverts also often recognize subtleties or nuances in what they hear or observe, and notice unvoiced conflicts between those present or a sudden change in mood or atmosphere. This can be invaluable when diplomacy and tact are needed.

The strength of extroverts relates to the other part of this communication. Extroverts often manage to convey meaning confidently and convincingly and are energetic advocates. They are also quick to include what they have just heard in new strategies, particularly by drawing on their great flexibility (see Strength pair 2).

A good listener may consider such a 'speaker' type as egocentric or lacking in substance. A good speaker may consider a 'listener' type as passive or lacking in momentum. But don't forget that extroverts need stronger stimuli than introverts to be able to listen well – introvert masters in this field should take that into account (see Cain, 2011, p. 235)!

Strength pair 5: calm and speed

Inner calm in introverts leads in the best cases to concentration, relaxation and clarity.	For extroverts, speed in the best case leads to speedy action without lengthy consideration.

For introverts, outer calm is important, as it ensures protection against the risk of overstimulation. But calm is not just an aid – it is also a strength. If you manage to achieve inner calm – as introverts frequently do by avoiding overstimulation – you will gain several advantages. The main positive consequences are the ability to differentiate between important and insignificant stimuli, a feeling of inner peace, better concentration and therefore greater performance capabilities, consequences which can be measured in people who meditate regularly.

Quiet people are often perceived by those who are less calm as docile – but also as considerate if they have an ability to listen (Strength pair 4) or empathize (Strength pair 10).

Extroverts have another trump card up their sleeve: compared to introverts, they have shorter neural pathways in their brains and are more resilient to high doses of stimulation, so they are able to react quickly to external stimuli. In risky or dangerous situations, this inbuilt reflex which causes extroverts to act quickly can be a crucial coping mechanism.

Consequences for communication: A calm communication partner is less aggressive and has greater powers of concentration. Such people also have particular advantages in negotiations or conflicts because they do not rush around frantically but deal with one thing at a time, understanding how to make use of the power of a pause or of silence. In the hustle of our times that is a great, rare and beneficial asset.

Extroverts are able to convert new information and ideas quickly into speech and action in delicate situations such as disputes and in difficult negotiations. As they are generally more prepared to take a risk than introverts, they are less likely to hesitate – although there is of course a greater risk of misjudging such situations.

Quiet people sometimes find fast communicators frenzied and exhausting. Quick people think that quiet communicators may be lacking in drive, or that they are arrogant or unimaginative.

Strength pair 6: analytical thinking and drive

Introverts with their tendency towards analytical thinking can break down difficult interrelationships, give structure to complicated tasks and plan systematically.	Energetic extroverts act whenever they consider it necessary. Once an action has been identified they want to implement it straight away and bring about changes in their environment or among their colleagues.

Introverts are different from extroverts in that their mental processes are running continually. They also like to organize their lives to be predictable. Manageable structures and careful planning help them relax, as surprises are tiring, cost energy and easily lead to overstimulation and loss of energy. This lifelong practice provides many of them with a crucial strength: the capacity to think along organized pathways, get to grips with difficulties and save energy.

Their drive is perhaps the main indication of the 'outward strength' that many extroverts have in abundance. Many extroverts are known as 'doers', pragmatists who tackle things courageously and implement while others are still hesitating and considering. Many extroverts also like trying things out as a form of learning because they like the immediate stimulation of exchange with the environment and are less unsettled by risk than the average introvert. Like speed, an extrovert's drive can put him on top form in crisis situations, but involves more risks in the event of failure.

Consequences for communication: The analytical thinking of introverts means it is easy for them to come back to the main thrust of an argument and can therefore lend structure to a discussion and ensure results. Introverts feel secure when they have preparatory information available in difficult situations. That information may be the agenda for a meeting, received by email in advance – or even a visit to the room where an important presentation is to be held. If it is possible to avoid surprises and to be able to plan procedures and develop ideas in peace, introverts with their analytical thinking are at their best because they can then invest more energy in the actual communication.

Extroverts with their drive generally have the upper hand where the need in communication is to get things done. It is often they who deal boldly with projects, insist on actual decisions in meetings and speak with a refreshing bluntness in plain terms to bring considered and planned matters to the implementation stage.

People with drive sometimes consider analysers to be worriers or 'eggheads'. On the other hand, strong analytical personalities often see the behaviour of 'go-getters' as being that of a 'bull in a China shop' or frantic histrionics.

Strength pair 7: independence and emotional warmth

Many introverts like being independent and not too dependent on others. They like to live according to their own principles. They are happy to be on their own.	Many extroverts like working in a team and to be in the company of others. They like to provide and receive positive feedback.

Extroverts are like wind turbines in that they need interaction with their environment. Feedback from their surroundings is usually important. They also like to give something in return in the form of affection for those whose company they value. When extroverts sense the esteem of the team members, they will invest energy in the success of the group and feel generally happy, as will those around them. That has a positive effect on any team. They 'throw themselves into any campaign in which they are involved'.[9]

Introverts are similar to batteries, less dependent on feedback from their environment. They are also less receptive to rewards than extroverts. In many cases this independence enables them to distance themselves from the opinions and attitudes of others. Provided they have reached a certain maturity, they are also less likely to focus on themselves, their own impact and their own needs. This distancing effect allows introverts to think 'outside of the box' and produce a notable performance. This strength may mean that they can be surprisingly non-conformist and can be liable to question things which appear to be self-evident. Independence can make even cautious introverts into rule breakers who can set off a quiet revolution. One example of this was the great introvert Mahatma Gandhi, who achieved Indian independence by passive resistance. Another example is the quiet Black American Rosa Parks, who in 1955 refused to give up her seat on the bus to a White during segregation – and sparked off the African-American civil rights movement.

Consequences for communication: The extrovert strength of emotional warmth has a more direct impact than the introvert strength of independence. This is manifested as devotion and as a spark that may kindle warmth in others and generate enthusiasm and agreement in them. If you have ever heard good extrovert speakers on the stage, or an extrovert professional networker dealing with complete strangers, you know what an effect this capability can have.

Independent introverts can think and communicate outside conventional pathways, but they can also grant others this inner independence and leave them room to manoeuvre. This has a positive effect in everyday management, for example. You can find more on this together with relevant studies in Chapter 6.

Independent people sometimes find emotional warmth stifling or intrusive. To those who offer such warmth, independent people can easily seem distanced or indifferent.

Strength pair 8: tenacity and spontaneity

Tenacious introverts can stick at something patiently for a long time, even though success is not immediately forthcoming.	Extroverts can often change abruptly from one activity to the next. They find these switches stimulating and interesting.

Introverts are sceptical about quick solutions, not least because of their need for security. They tend to value tenacity, stamina and patience. Terms like these do not at first seem very 'sexy' – certainly not in a time when we have no time! But they enable extraordinary performance. The capacity to pursue something against all odds, a readiness to lock yourself away and get to the bottom of something without giving up, even if the interim results are frustrating, leads to amazing results – what about the development of the theory of relativity, series of successful novels or the discovery of the Northwest Passage? In science and literature, tenacity is important for good results – there is little scope here for shooting from the hip.

In the field of personality psychology, there is now a lot of talk about resilience – the capacity to stick to your guns no matter what the interruptions or obstacles. The mountains that can be moved by tenacity point to the enormous inner strength of introverts in the same way that drive is a particularly clear indicator of the outward strength of extroverts (Strength pair 6).

Tenacity is obviously also a successful (and seriously underestimated) prescription for a career. The psychologist Lewis Terman, developer of the Stanford-Binet intelligence test, was himself tenacious. He recorded the development of highly gifted pupils over 35 years. His conclusion was that tenacity has a greater effect on success than intelligence.[10] The psychologists Howard Friedman and Leslie Martin from the University of California (Riverside) referred back to the data of the Terman Study and established that tenacity even has a significantly positive effect on length and quality of life (Friedman and Martin, 2012).

The parallel extrovert strength is spontaneity. It relates to a capacity to change your actions depending on the situation and to spring into action at short notice if this appears attractive or sensible (or both). Spontaneity is an especially positive consequence of the high level of reactability which many extroverts have. The difference from flexibility (Strength pair 3) is that spontaneity means a swift redirection of activity on the spur of the moment when a situation changes. It can also be caused by a distraction. On the other hand, flexibility is to do with energy levels: variety and scope energize extroverts by providing additional stimulation and enable them to be particularly agile among a variety of actions.

Consequences for communication: Tenacious introverts always have the advantage if endurance is needed in discussions or for a written task. For example, in negotiations, diplomatic mediation and the medium you have in front of you now: books.

Spontaneity is a useful strength in communication where a courageous decision to act or a change in strategy is needed. A spontaneous extrovert can take the exchange to a different level with the question 'Can I ask you about something completely different?', or can save situations which seem to have become deadlocked. And extroverts can always spring a surprise if plans take a completely new direction. Spontaneous extroverts are seldom boring!

A tenacious person may consider a spontaneous person undisciplined, erratic or unreliable. A spontaneous person may perceive a tenacious person to be inflexible or behaving like a hamster in a wheel.

Strength pair 9: writing and speaking

TALKING EVEN WITH VERY INTELLIGENT PEOPLE IS DIFFICULT, BUT WHEN I READ THEIR BOOKS, I GET THE BEST CONSIDERED THOUGHTS IN A BEAUTIFUL AND EFFICIENT FORM. I LEARN FASTER FROM BOOKS THAN FROM A CONVERSATION WITH THE AUTHOR.

AARON SWARTZ (1986–2013), PROGRAMMER, AUTHOR, INTERNET ACTIVIST[11]

Many introverts prefer to write rather than speak. They find it easier to express themselves in writing than orally.	Many extroverts prefer to speak rather than write. They find it easier to express themselves orally rather than in writing.

The distinction 'introverts think in order to speak; extroverts speak in order to think' is reflected in this strength pair. Many introverts like to write and use the mental freedom and distance offered by this medium to take time to consider. Extroverts value an immediate exchange with their environment, a direct, fast route to their colleagues. They therefore often prefer the spoken word, which can be used spontaneously, flexibly and without lengthy preparation. This naturally does not rule out the possibility of extroverts writing well and introverts speaking well. Extroverts can benefit from writing just as introverts can benefit from speaking.

The psychologist Ulrike Scheuermann is a writing coach who has written some important works of reference on renowned writing experts in the German-speaking world.

Writing: different for introverts and extroverts

Ulrike Scheuermann, writing coach

'I continually find from my coaching that introverts definitely find writing easier than extroverts – writing is a mental activity done quietly, providing the inner, creative pleasure they crave.

'It is more of an effort for extroverts to take that step into quiet writing. They find it helpful to talk constantly about the topic they are writing about, to write in brief sections and write amongst other people, such as in a café or in a library' (Scheuermann, 2013b).

For those introverts who find it difficult to express themselves orally, it can help if they formulate their thoughts and strategies in writing beforehand, deciding who they want to meet at a conference, for example. This may make it easier for them to express their ideas confidently in an oral discussion. Sometimes it is enough to communicate a suggestion or an assessment by e-mail or in a written submission. But in that case follow up and talk to those concerned. If you put too much down on paper (even electronic paper) it won't necessarily lead to action.

Consequences for communication: Extroverts often have a strength-related home advantage in all areas of oral communication, such as meetings, negotiations and especially small talk.

Introverts score with their writing skills in everything that has to be considered and is most effectively produced on paper or on the computer. They shine at drafting and in writing e-mails, which they often prefer to telephone conversations.

If you like writing, it is often relatively stressful to participate in oral communication – especially if it takes a long time or it is unexpected. If you prefer talking, written texts can be a battle, especially if they are lengthy.

Strength pair 10: empathy and conflict management skills

Empathetic introverts are good at putting themselves in others' shoes. They highlight common interests in order to find a solution.	Extroverts can manage conflict and are willing and able to address awkward topics and problems to find a solution.

Introverts' particular gifts of observation and listening enable many to develop a particularly high ability to empathize. They can hear overtones of meaning and understand complicated mixtures of feelings. They are therefore better able to put themselves in someone else's place in many situations and include the result in their communication behaviour. Susan Cain (2011, p. 219 f.) points to studies which show that empathetic people also have a greater tendency to comply with moral standards. Whether that is true is uncertain – what we can fairly safely deduce from empathetic behaviour is a certain mindfulness in dealing with others. If you can imagine yourself in someone else's position, you will lend them your attention and concentration.

However, hurdles can reduce a capacity for empathy. If an introvert is overstimulated, anxious or avoiding contact, then their capacity for empathy usually fades.

With their strength of managing conflict, extroverts can ease strained situations. They have the confidence to address delicate sensitivities. Add to this the strengths of courage and drive and they have the best qualifications for dealing with trouble. Extroverts also find it less stressful for a relationship if there is some dispute now and again – they see tension as part of communication and can tolerate the higher dose of stimulation and risk associated with contention.

Consequences in communication: As a rule, introvert empathy is positively received by all parties to a discussion and ensures good solutions in negotiations and in controversies – especially if accompanied by strengths such as analytical thinking and substance. If caution is added, an ability to empathize can be of inestimable value for introverts in all situations requiring diplomatic intuition. People with an ability to empathize are more amenable and more agreeable than people who have only their own interests at heart and do not bear in mind those of others. Empathetic people find it relatively easy to find a compromise. They know that it's not just about them.

In introverted cultures, consideration of the feelings of others is often highly valued, and this is reflected in norms of communication. In Japan and China it is unheard of to snub anyone publicly so that they lose face. Even when discussing important matters, it is always borne in mind that the feelings of others are important and must be taken into consideration.

Extrovert conflict managers can intervene to save or restore a team's capacity to work, as conflict costs strength, resources and synergy. For introverts that creates a solid, predictable basis for their performance capability, as they suffer more under conflict and its uncertainties because of their need for safety.

In extroverted cultures such as the USA or France, the requirement of consideration for others is not valued in the same way as in introverted cultures. A readiness for conflict and to be alone against the world tends to be seen as an expression of autonomous individuality.

Empathetic people who need harmony often feel under pressure from those who can handle conflict because disputes put them under strain. Those who can handle conflict, however, sometimes find empathetic people annoying sensitive little plants and find them unapproachable if they are of a different opinion.

Introvert and extrovert strengths: overview

Introvert	Extrovert
1. Caution	**1. Courage**
Perceive and weigh up risks	Take risks in order to achieve something
2. Substance	**2. Enthusiasm**
Strive for meaning, depth and quality when thinking or communicating	Be enthused by impressions, carry others along

3. Concentration	**3. Flexibility**
Be able to stick with something	Be adaptable and able to adjust to new situations
4. Listening	**4. Presenting**
Gather and process information and draw conclusions from it	Convey information well and convincingly
5. Calm	**5. Speed**
Unimpressed by stimulation, seeks concentration, relaxation and clarity	Act quickly without thinking too much about it
6. Analytical thinking	**6. Drive**
Break down interrelationships, structure the complicated, plan systematically	Outward strength, act on insights, change the environment
7. Independence	**7. Affection**
Live independently according to own principles, be alone, allow others their independence	Be part of a community, give and take positive feedback
8. Tenacity	**8. Spontaneity**
Inner strength: pursue something patiently for a long time	Rethink a decision and change strategies if this seems necessary or attractive after new information
9. Writing	**9. Speaking**
Prefers written to oral communication and finds the former easier	Prefers oral to written communication and finds the former easier
10. Empathy	**10. Conflict management skills**
Put themselves in other people's shoes and highlight commonalities	Able to address awkward topics and problems to find a solution

Introvert and extrovert hurdles

Introverts and extroverts do not just have specific strengths on their side. Their different characteristics also bring a tendency towards specific hurdles which can make some undertakings and forms of communication difficult.

This section covers the most common hurdles that introverts and extroverts have to face. They may not seem like good news to you – we associate hurdles with disadvantages, difficulties and pressure points. But although risks and disadvantages may arise from them, individual hurdles are also important waymarkers as they indicate the particular needs that introverts and extroverts have in their interactions with each other.

In the following I will not go into the way introverts and extroverts perceive the hurdles in others. Using Hurdle pair 1 as an example, it is quite easy to predict what anxious and careless people will think of each other. When dealing with a hurdle, the mutual perception of very different personalities is even more critical than with the strengths, where it was worth spelling out the issues to sharpen the awareness of the other type of personality.

Hurdle pair 1: anxiety and carelessness

Introverts may be too cautious when dealing with others or chancing a risk. This can block decision-making or action.	Extroverts may take careless risks and suffer losses which may be painful.

Both anxiety in introverts and carelessness in extroverts can be fairly directly attributable to differences in brain physiology as described earlier in the chapter.

Introverts have a more active amygdala and therefore have to cope with stronger anxiety stimuli than extroverts. The neurotransmitter acetylcholine causes a particular need for safety. That means anxiety is a more frequent companion for introverts than for extroverts. Although this more intense perception of anxiety is biologically more likely, in the end, it is only what we introverts make of our tendency towards anxiety that counts. For this purpose we have other important areas of the brain that make sure anxiety doesn't stop us from doing things that are important to us. The main area is the cerebral cortex where we do our conscious thinking. As Susan Cain (2011, p. 201) says, the latter is more difficult in times of stress than when we are relaxed and our energy reserves are charged up. Too much pressure in the form of anxiety and stress evidently blocks our conscious thinking and causes the emotional switch points of our brain to take command. But the more we consciously leave our comfort zone because there is something to do which is important to us, the less our anxiety becomes an obstacle. Let us then acknowledge this hurdle if we have it – and practise crossing boundaries in its company.

Extroverts have their own biological probability. Their active nucleus accumbens and the higher level of the neurotransmitter dopamine make them especially receptive to possible rewards and attractive experiences of all kinds. They will underestimate a risk taken in order to achieve a result, as it appears small compared to the reward and its attractiveness, so the extrovert is all too prone to acting without realizing the actual situation. Extroverts also tend more than introverts to overestimate their own capabilities and act hastily. More or less as a side-effect of the dopamine, they are more inclined to accept risks for these two reasons and find they have actually gone beyond their capabilities or capacities.

This is what constitutes recklessness, staking too much when the laws of probability are not in your favour. This can happen on both a large and a small scale. Examples range from hazardous financial transactions to risky games of chance and dangerous climbing expeditions.

Consequences for communication: Anxiety can lead to avoidance of all situations where the outcome is uncertain, such as confrontation, conflict, negotiation and very rapid dynamic discussions such as debates. Anxious people often give off low-status signals (see the section in Chapter 8).

Recklessness can lead extroverts to other risks, pushing their luck too far in salary negotiations, unprepared or offensive approaches in sensitive situations, flippant behaviour in dialogue with sensitive partners. Damage or tension may easily arise between people here.

Hurdle pair 2: attention to detail and superficiality

Introverts sometimes get lost in the detail. It is then easy to lose sight of priorities and the big picture.	Extroverts sometimes occupy themselves only cursorily and not thoroughly enough with people and matters that deserve more attention.

Introverts who are always processing information intensely get lost easily in the myriad data that inundate everyday life. Paying attention to every little bit of information makes it difficult to see the big picture. Introverts who tend to concentrate on the detail can consciously learn to concentrate and pay attention to what is key. These often very clever people can then keep on track more easily (Strength pairs 2 and 3).

Superficiality is the extreme flipside of attention to detail. Apparently unimportant details are swept aside and a trust in gut feeling leads to rash decisions or premature actions for which they may pay a high price: the more complex the decision, the better it is to be cautious. One detail can tip the crucial balance.

Consequences for communication: Because of an attention to detail, introverts can lose ground in exactly those areas where they are capable of scoring points with good specialist knowledge and structured thinking, such as in discussions or negotiations. If you lose sight of the key focus and cannot get to the point, you pay a high price in such situations.

But extroverts who fail to make an effort to delve deeper into a topic also lose in communication. If you reveal gaps in your knowledge about your own product in a sales pitch or show a definite lack of knowledge in a debate, you lose credibility and trust. A very extreme example is the former American vice-presidential candidate Sarah Palin, who has been ridiculed because of her lack of knowledge of foreign policy.

Extroverts often find it trying when introverts go into too much detail. They lack the patience and sometimes the desire to find out more – whereas they may enjoy small talk, more than introverts, where the topic is apparently 'superficial' but the relationship level is being built up and nurtured. For their part, introverts often think little of extroverts who do not pay detailed attention to the matter in hand or think about it carefully enough.

Hurdle pair 3: overstimulation and impatience

Many introverts feel overloaded by too many, too loud or too fast impressions.	Many extroverts are bored and seek alternative stimulation if they have to wait too long for something, boredom sets in or nothing changes.

Introverts are easily overstimulated for biological reasons. External impressions overtax them in such cases and sap their energy. They become irritated, tired and even lose strengths, such as concentration (Strength pair 3) and calm (Strength pair 5).

Rest periods and time out can significantly reduce overstimulation.

With their make-up, extroverts are more likely to be challenged when there are insufficient impressions. The hurdle is impatience: if anything is going too slowly or is too boring, extroverts easily become restless (or irritated) and look for other potential sources of stimulation. In the worst case scenario, impatience leads to actions or decisions which are not always the best. 'As long as you yourself are talking, you will not find out anything,' Austrian writer Marie von Ebner-Eschenbach (1830–1916) once said. And she was right. Speakers predominantly expect that others will learn something from them – by listening to them. This expectation does not often apply in reverse: extroverts in particular tend to be already considering their next remark while lending a cursory ear and only appearing to be listening. They learn little by that approach.

Consequences for communication: For introverts who tend to be easily overstimulated, certain situations are more difficult; perhaps a reception where conversation partners are always changing, or there is a noisy background or a raucous, strident flock of guests. Communication with large groups is also usually particularly stressful for introverts. However, this does not include public appearances – because of their predictable rituals, such events are not necessarily overstimulating. A conversation with ten people is more so!

At the same reception, impatience can put some extroverts at a disadvantage. I have even met extroverts who interrupt others because they already know how the sentence ends. But if you send out restless signals while your quiet manager is describing how a decision came to be made at a meeting, this does not bode well for a good relationship.

It goes without saying that easily overstimulated introverts and easily impatient extroverts can certainly stress each other out …

Hurdle pair 4: passivity and self-dramatization

Introverts tend to stay in the same situation. They avoid taking the initiative, even if that may have negative consequences for them.	Extroverts tend to put themselves forward at the expense of others in order to gain attention.

By 'passivity' I mean the dark side of calm: a refusal to do something – feeble, dull, stubborn, indifferent or frozen by anxiety. Passive people prefer to tolerate sufferings rather than becoming active and changing something about the situation. The darkest side of passivity is a refusal to shape your own life. Instead, passive people allow others to take control of a situation.

Extroverts are especially dependent on feedback from their environment. Self-dramatization can become a temptation here, i.e. an excessive tendency to put oneself forward too forcibly – even at the expense of others – in order to gain recognition. In brief: where passive people do too little, the self-dramatist does too much. The latter goes too far and has no qualms about the need to elbow others out of the way.

Consequences for communication: The apparent lack of drive demonstrated by passive people can also be heard in the voice, in its volume and intonation. Extroverts particularly tend to underestimate passive people. Because of the lack of vigour, they place too little weight on what is being said or they lose interest in listening – especially if they are impatient (see Hurdle pair 3). If in addition utterances are too rare or too slow, this can lead to serious misjudgements – even to the assumption that the person they are speaking to is not the most intelligent of beings. This misconception often goes uncorrected. Passive people set boundaries less often and less emphatically in difficult situations or during verbal onslaughts and represent their position in debates with less commitment. They also send out low status signals (see Chapter 7) and easily represent themselves as inferior in relation to others.

A self-dramatist can be similarly stressful to an introvert, as to quiet people they are exhausting and pushy. Their communication style and behaviour might be described as being 'full of hot air' or 'a chatterbox'.

Hurdle pair 5: flight and aggression

Some introverts withdraw into themselves if they are under stress or there are problems, instead of facing up to the situation.	Some extroverts go on the offensive if they are under stress or there are problems, and attack others instead of getting to grips with the situation.

Flight is a movement, and in this sense it is different from passivity, with which we have already dealt. If you run away you are avoiding stress by doing something else. People might flee in order to save energy or to avoid stress, problems or risks. They deflect the issues, do something else or run away. Unfortunately, distancing yourself does not eliminate stress – not on the inside, where the pressure remains, nor on the outside, where it is rare for anything to be resolved by escape.

Extroverts tend to use a counter-reflex response if they are under stress or suffering problems. They go on the offensive and attack. This corresponds with the fact that extrovert energy spreads outwards rather than inwards. The hurdle does not arise as a result of the associated drive (Strength pair 6) but because of the aggressive element which can appear confrontational to others, or may snub or hurt them. Aggression can prevent any real handling of a dispute and often leads to the people involved concentrating mainly on attack and defence.

Consequences for communication: The two hurdles have an especially negative effect where the aim is to overcome 'tricky' communication – i.e. situations which are difficult because the subject matter or the relationship (which is even more 'tricky'!) is under strain. A typical example is conflict dialogue. In such cases neither 'stonewalling' by the person in flight nor the fighting energy of the aggressive partner is especially helpful – less than ever if they are on opposing sides.

Hurdle pair 6: intellectualization and impulsiveness

Introverts sometimes tend to neglect or underestimate the value of emotions and overestimate the rational aspect.	Extroverts sometimes tend to ignore the voice of reason and instead give their feelings free rein.

Impulsiveness represents a hurdle for extroverts in instances where they react too quickly to external impressions. Reward centre and sensory impressions then quickly lead to emotional reactions, even if these are not sensible. One example is eating unhealthy food which smells or looks good (just think here about your own favourite tasty but unhealthy food).[12]

The introvert hurdle of being too rational (intellectualization) is closely linked with the strength of analytical thinking (see Strength pair 6). This strength becomes a hurdle and a disadvantage if rational thinking is given too much weight and blocks access to the emotions. That can happen so that control is apparently maintained: the rational is clearer and appears more manageable than the irrational! But at the same time perception is reduced as are options for good communication with others. A straightforward exchange of facts is rarely sufficient. The apparent gaining of control leads to a loss of control.

Consequences for communication: Intellectualized people are more predictable in interaction than impulsive ones. They are also reliable when it comes to facts but can be boring and inflexible – and unpleasant if attention to detail is also a hurdle for them (Hurdle pair 2).

Impulsive people, on the other hand, bring energy, colour and surprise to the proceedings. However, they are often stressful for introverts and can also be diverted and easily lose the thread.

Rational people consider impulsive ones to be unpredictable and unreliable. Impulsive people often think rational people are obsessively controlled or have a reduced quality of life.

Hurdle pair 7: self-denial and self-centredness

Introverts sometimes deny their own characteristics and needs – or evaluate them negatively.	Extroverts sometimes make their own characteristics and needs into a point of orientation and demand that their environment accommodates them.

Someone in self-denial neglects their personal needs and characteristics. They suppress or devalue them. Many quiet people tend to self-denial because they receive signals in some environments which portray extroversion as a desirable norm, with comments such as 'Get over yourself!', 'Don't be so stand-offish', or 'Just go with it!'

An introvert who listens to such signals of criticism may internalize them and get the impression that they don't 'fit in'. Two things can happen: they either isolate themselves socially ('I don't want to be like that') or go into self-denial ('I'll never be like them'). Neither variation is good for living confidently and autonomously.

Self-centred extroverts have difficulty in a diametrically opposed area. They tend to measure everyone against themselves and expect to be treated accordingly by other people. They fail to empathize with the needs of others and consider their own attitude to be absolute. The result is isolation which they really don't want – as an affinity with their environment is something they particularly rely on.

Of course, even introverts can be self-centred. An extrovert's special hurdle is that their self-centredness, which is typical of their 'outgoing' personality, is communicated with lots of energy, while self-centred introverts usually seem to proceed less conspicuously.

Consequences for communication: Those introverts with the hurdle of self-denial may have difficulties expressing their needs and priorities in an exchange with others. Communication can be stressful when introverts do not express their concerns directly and only signal their dissatisfaction.

Of course communication with self-centred extroverts can also be extremely stressful, particularly for very reserved introverts, when they put much energy and emphasis on claims for their own needs. They might say things like, 'Wait a minute – this is about what *I* want.' From an introvert's perspective, such a statement easily comes over as unpleasant and even rude, leading to thoughts such as, 'He thinks he's the centre of the universe!'

Extroverts may also have problems motivating people if they have difficulty looking at the needs of others rather than their own. Motivation based on what the 'motivator' wants fails to grasp the different factors which may drive people. This can have as much of a negative impact in everyday management as in bringing up children or being in a relationship.

Hurdle pair 8: fixation and distraction

Introverts may tend to be inflexible when interacting with others. They stick to a position or suffer it if they cannot live or act as they are accustomed.	Sometimes extroverts find it difficult in interaction with others to concentrate on the matter in hand. Instead, they keep switching between one thing and another.

Extroverts have problems with under-stimulation. Hurdles that follow from this include not only impatience (Hurdle pair 3) but also distraction. If extroverts spend too long on one thing or have to deal with a long-term project, the extrovert brain often demands more stimuli (unless the matter itself is fascinating). The main consequence is the proverbial procrastination. Why spend more than an hour over concept draft when there are so many new posts on Facebook? Why learn to play a musical instrument bit by bit if your friends are outside asking you to join in their exciting activities?

In contrast, easily overstimulated introverts suffer under too high a dose of external impressions. They prefer to direct their energy towards internal processes and prefer the stress of too much external activity to be at least kept within certain bounds. These include sudden changes of direction and new decisions (which flexible extroverts with Strength pair 3 may well like). To some extent, then, fixation is a means of acquiring energy. But fixation is not good. It is the frozen form of the tenacity which you read about in Strength pair 8. Introverts who struggle with this hurdle find it difficult to do something unaccustomed or change their routines.

Consequences for communication: Extroverts who are easily distracted often find it difficult to concentrate, especially in long conversations or when creating complex written communication – writing is indeed, compared to speaking, the second choice for many extroverts. Easily distracted people may also be led astray in negotiations and discussions if too much time is spent on just one point.

The hurdle of fixation means that introverts feel uncomfortable if flexibility is demanded of them, for example, in a discussion in an unusual setting or with new contacts, or if a new structure in the working environment is introduced. In negotiations and discussions, the temptation for fixated introverts is the direct opposite of what it is for distracted extroverts. Those who are fixated often find it difficult to distance themselves from their point of view and then like to persist with one point. When combined with the hurdle of too much attention to detail this can lead to continually going round in circles, which becomes very stressful.

Hurdle pair 9: contact avoidance and self-avoidance

Many introverts like to limit themselves to just a few contacts but this can lead to the risk of social isolation.	Many extroverts tend to draw on the resonance from the outside world in assessing themselves.

Like fixation, avoidance of contact is an energy-saving strategy. Interaction with others costs energy. Many introverts feel comfortable with just a few attachment figures – and that's fine. However, avoiding people because they cause stress or become too much like hard work is the hurdle of contact avoidance – and it can come at a high price. In extreme cases it leads to social isolation.

The difference from flight (Hurdle pair 5) lies in what is avoided. The escapee evades action, the contact avoider gives people a wide berth.

Do not confuse contact avoidance with shyness. This is important, as introverts are often described as 'shy'. But shyness is not a personality trait. It is based on an anxiety about social evaluation and there are targeted means to overcome this. There are also shy extroverts! Introversion on the other hand is a personality trait of healthy people, and contact avoidance is one of the hurdles in the normal range.[13]

With outward-looking extroverts, a more likely hurdle is self-avoidance. This leads to the person concerned evading any self-analysis, instead focusing their attention on the outside world. A self-avoider will place the emphasis on their own impact. Gifted self-presenters also have self-dramatization (Hurdle pair 4) in their repertoire.

The problem is that self-avoiders lack independence because of their need for resonance from others – even fleeting acquaintances.

Consequences for communication: The lack of intercourse with others also leads to a lack of stimuli for contact avoiders. They stew in their own juice and fail to exploit the opportunity to develop ideas or solve problems with others. In complex circumstances this can mean mediocre performance. No one can be an expert in everything these days! If for example you do not communicate with others in science, you do not have access to the knowledge of colleagues which will often provide a different view on the subject of your own research.

The way others perceive you may well also suffer: if you constantly avoid them, people may start to think of you as difficult, odd, arrogant or (see above) shy.

Extroverts with a tendency towards self-avoidance are heavily dependent on the feedback of others. If others think they are great, they feel great. This filtering of perception through others can make extroverts susceptible to emotional blackmail. You want to seem good, successful, attractive and convincing to others and may therefore react sensitively if you are left hanging and denied feedback. This can lead to enormous pressure in a negotiation or a conflicted discussion.

Hurdle pair 10: conflict avoidance and overpowering force

Some introverts tend to go out of their way to avoid conflict even if the situation becomes stressful or escalates as a result.	Some extroverts tend to use their energy to pressurize people in order to pursue their own aims or interests.

The basic extrovert tendency to turn energy outwards can be truly overpowering for other people. When the overpowering force is coupled with the hurdle of aggression (Hurdle pair 5) or self-centredness (Hurdle pair 7), the effect can be like a steamroller. The extrovert's energy is used solely for asserting himself intensely, loudly and clearly. This occurrence is usually associated with external high status signals: consuming energy, space and time (see Chapter 7) and powerfully pursuing one's aims is not a bad thing in itself. Only when the interests of others are unheeded and your own are pursued with no regard for casualties does the situation become critical. Furthermore, it is disproportionate if every discussion in a meeting (or every decision at home around the breakfast table) is used to start an argument. In the long term it not only saps your strength but also has a negative effect on the quality of relationships.

Conflicts are particularly stressful for introverts who are easily overstimulated and safety-orientated. Conflicts are however a part of life: wherever people are together, there will be incompatibility in their thoughts, feelings or actions. It is enormously important to overcome such differences in order to make a functioning communal life possible. For both introverts and extroverts, though, addressing conflict is associated with many uncertainties. Shying away from conflict is an especial hurdle for anxious introverts (see Hurdle pair 1). Another factor fostering this hurdle is the high energy cost associated with awkward situations. Even analytical thinking (Strength pair 6) is only of limited use in overcoming it, because emotions are unpredictable.

Consequences for communication: In status disputes, especially in competition or confrontation, an extrovert's high level of energy can exert enormous pressure – and thus stress – on an introvert. When an overbearing extrovert meets a conflict-avoiding introvert, it is hard for the latter to be assertive, but it is possible by using your own instincts and keeping a cool head. You can find more specific information on confrontation between introverts and extroverts in Chapter 8.

On the surface, introverts often have fewer conflicts with others than extroverts. This is partially because extroverts express their opinions more loudly, and with their capacity for conflict management (Strength pair 10) they have the capacity to indicate clear boundaries. But conflict avoidance is another reason for this perception.

But introverts have just as many tensions and problems with others as extroverts – and these do not resolve themselves. The consequence of conflict avoidance can be that the affected introvert becomes very worried and concerned, wrings his hands, goes round in circles and invests a great deal of energy and attention in the matter – especially because conflicts have a tendency to escalate and are very rarely resolved by disregarding them.

You now have a picture of all the most common hurdles for introverts and extroverts. An overview list is given below.

Introvert and extrovert hurdles: overview

Introvert hurdles	Extrovert hurdles
1. Anxiety Action and decision-making are blocked as a result of excess caution	**1. Recklessness** Taking a gamble on something important by taking unnecessary risks and over-estimating themselves
2. Attention to detail Getting lost in the detail, losing sight of major interrelationships and priorities	**2. Superficiality** Cursory dealing with people and things, not being thorough enough
3. Overstimulation Being overtaxed by too many, too loud or too fast impressions	**3. Impatience** Getting bored for lack of impressions
4. Passivity Lingering in a situation even if this has negative effects	**4. Self dramatization** Drawing attention to yourself at the expense of others to gain attention
5. Flight Avoiding difficult situations by retreating	**5. Aggression** Avoiding difficult situations by attacking
6. Intellectualization Neglecting emotions, overestimating the rational intellect	**6. Impulsiveness** Letting the emotions run wild, underestimating the intellect
7. Self-denial Denying your own characteristics and needs or evaluating them negatively	**7. Self-centredness** Using your own characteristics and needs as a point of orientation and being demanding

Introvert hurdles	Extrovert hurdles
8. Fixation Inflexibility in interaction with others, relying on habits for wellbeing	**8. Distraction** In interaction with others, moving quickly back and forth between topics or impressions, lack of concentration
9. Contact avoidance Favouring a small number of contacts, putting oneself in danger of social isolation	**9. Self-avoidance** Making one's self-assessment dependent on evaluation by others
10. Conflict avoidance Not dealing with difficult situations actively and accepting stress	**10. Overpowering force** Putting pressure on others to pursue own aims and interests

[?] Your strengths and hurdles

Think about your strengths and hurdles. Have some of the points you have read here struck a chord with you? Enter your thoughts here.

1. Which of the strengths do you recognize in yourself?

Your introvert strengths	Your extrovert strengths

2. Which of these hurdles do you recognize in yourself?

Your introvert hurdles	Your extrovert hurdles

Myths about introversion and extroversion

Now you have a good insight into the differences between introverts and extroverts. To end this chapter, let's look at four assertions about the two personality types which are so common that you will certainly be familiar with some of them. Only they're not true.

Myth 1: Extroverts are more socially accessible than introverts

This myth is a favourite. It is a ghostly presence in many texts – even very clever people like Steven Reiss have adopted it (2010, p. 215f): the saying is that the main thing which differentiates introverts and extroverts is their accessibility to other people. There is a preconception that introverts avoid contact and extroverts enjoy it.

Neither assumption is quite right. For example, there are shy extroverts who suffer anxiety when making social contacts. (Remember, shyness is different from introversion – see contact avoidance earlier in this chapter) And there are extroverts who seem very much quieter than their introvert contemporaries (my husband is one of these, so I know what I'm talking about!). There are also socially accessible introverts who like dealing with people and are barely distinguishable from extroverts to an outsider. Extroverts are not even necessarily more lively than introverts – what is crucial is that their focus lies outside their own personality (see Olsen Laney, 2002, p. 21).

If we look closer we can see that social accessibility has little to do with the depth of relationships. Those who make contacts easily and know a lot of people do not automatically have good friends. And if someone opens up gradually to people, that person may well have a few deep, trusting relationships that will last a lifetime and continue to develop.

It is true that we all need people around us – some more, some less. What makes us introverts or extroverts is the way our brain responds to stimulation, processes information – and how we regenerate when we are tired. That is perhaps why extroverts prefer to be at the centre of things more than introverts on social occasions and at work. They also like to make new contacts faster.

But that provides a counterbalance to introverts, who may have fewer friendships developed over many years. Many introverts also have a gift for holding a proper conversation going far beyond small talk – and creating a completely different pleasurable and bonding experience. Sometimes they also like getting all the attention, but it is not as important for their sense of wellbeing as it is for extroverts who usually blossom when they get the attention of those around them.

In short, interest in other people, intact relationships and bonding are not the sole preserve of either introverts or extroverts. There are just different styles – as in swimming!

Myth 2: Introverts are less assertive than extroverts

This is another widespread myth that is easily refuted. Living examples to prove the opposite are assertive and successful introverts such as Warren Buffet, Angela Merkel, Simone de Beauvoir and Mark Zuckerberg.

Being ambitious, having the will to influence your own environment or striving for positions of power are personal traits which are more or less pronounced in all of us. Introversion and extroversion have little to do with it.[14] This does not rule out the fact that the two personality types have their own strategies and preferred modes of action to achieve these aims, as can be clearly observed in high-profile figures.

Extroverts like Steve Jobs or Bill Clinton had the ability to enthuse others and built up and extended their area of influence by this means. Power-conscious introverts like Angela Merkel and Barack Obama have other characteristics enabling them to achieve and secure their influence, such as clear strategies, tenacity and focus *en route* to their goals and the ability to bind loyal followers to them.

Chapter 8 deals with how introverts and extroverts differ from each other when they communicate claims to power and status in everyday life.

Myth 3: Introverts and extroverts are just not compatible

It is obvious that neither extroverts nor introverts have been 'weeded out' in the course of human history – the ratio between them is about as even as that between men and women.

Introverts and extroverts are different. And yet they live and work together, marry each other, hire each other and form mixed teams in families, at work and in leisure activities ranging from skittles clubs to charities. Everything that makes these people different in terms of strengths, needs and priorities makes introversion and extroversion an aspect of diversity – just like the differences between genders, cultures or generations.

The truth is that introverts and extroverts complement each other. An introvert with a quiet, empathetic manner can make conversation easier for a shy extrovert.

Extroverts encourage introverts to venture something new to achieve their aims. Introverts warn extroverts about taking risks too casually. An extrovert can encourage an introvert friend to present brilliant research results at a conference. Introverts and extroverts can be very,

very successful together! You can find more about this in Chapter 5. And in the rest of the book as well for that matter.

Myth 4: We are extroverts or introverts depending on the situation

An introvert is sometimes the life and soul of the party. Sometimes an extrovert is addicted to a subject and will bury himself behind piles of books. Introverts can behave in an extrovert manner in social situations – to the extent that they are sometimes taken for extroverts (that happens to me a lot). Conversely, extroverts may behave in an introvert manner under certain circumstances.

Luckily, people are not that predictable in what they do, which makes them exciting and fascinating. It is important not to confuse behaviour with far deeper personality traits.

Certainly, introverts can behave like extroverts and extroverts can behave like introverts. The closer they are to the middle of the introvert/extrovert continuum, the easier the excursion to the 'other side' becomes. But this behavioural agility does not alter the structure of our personality. Our ability to adapt our own role and our actions to the situation in which we find ourselves corresponds to the original meaning of the term 'person'. *Personare* is literally 'to speak through' and refers to the actors of Greece and Rome who declaimed their roles through masks. We are all able to mask our behaviour in various ways. But this has little to do with our substance, the fixed characteristics of our personality.

The reverse view is interesting: whether we are introverts or extroverts, consciously or unconsciously we seek out situations that match our particular personality.[15] The extrovert physicist Richard Feynman was a regular visitor to bars and enjoyed the company. This provided him with energy and a wealth of ideas. An introvert on a pub crawl with his friends on a Saturday night, in contrast, will unlike his extrovert friends probably spend his Sunday recharging his batteries by taking long walks on his own or reading for hours. Saturday evening could well be his only social event in weeks.

Key idea

The situation does not make the person: the person seeks the situation.

Gilbert Dietrich cleverly summarizes his current research in his blog geistundgegenwart.de: 'From the point of view of personality psychology (...) it is not crucial whether a person is one thing or another on occasion, but what he or she *usually* or *mostly* is.'[16] The conclusion to be drawn from this is that we will keep encountering certain experiences, certain preferences, certain relationships and even problems in spite of situation-dependent fluctuations. In the words of Dietrich: 'The situation cannot determine the personality trait; the personality seeks the situation for itself.' Daniel Nettle (2009) calls this relationship 'situation selection'.

One thing is important: if you frequently leave your personal comfort zone on the introvert/extrovert scale, make very sure that you regenerate in your own way from time to time. The extrovert scientist should treat himself to social occasions or dynamic sporting activities to balance things out – just as a certain introvert British Crown Prince tends to his plants. Our personal comfort zone is ultimately the place where we regain our energy.

 And now you ...

Have you worked out where your own characteristics lie? If you want to make sure, do the test in the Appendix now. Then take another look at the description of strengths and hurdles in this chapter, and complete the following overview for your own findings.

Overview: Your personality with strengths, hurdles and personal priorities

| I am | An introvert ☐ | An extrovert ☐ | A centrovert ☐ |

(Centroverts: see Chapter 4 also)

1. My perceptions from the overview and according to the test (if completed):

2. These characteristics seem to me to be particularly pronounced:

3. Overview of my strengths and hurdles		
Strengths	Hurdles	Initial conclusions

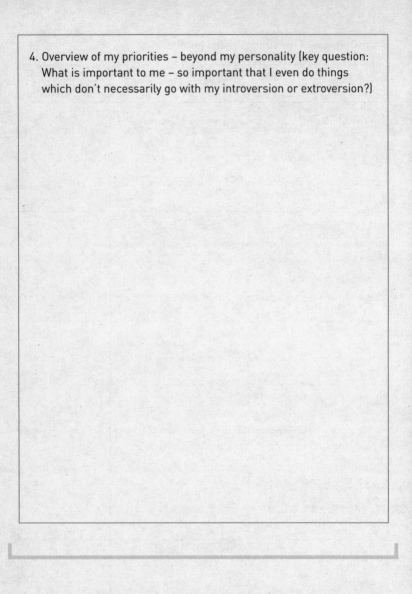

4. Overview of my priorities – beyond my personality (key question: What is important to me – so important that I even do things which don't necessarily go with my introversion or extroversion?)

Now you have identified your strengths and hurdles and taken the first step in identifying your personal concerns, you can apply this knowledge in the next few chapters and learn about how these characteristics may affect your life and your interactions with others.

Key points in brief

1. There are prejudices and stereotypes which characterize the image of introvert and extrovert personalities. On closer inspection, you will find that both personality types are many faceted, and the differences between 'introverts' and 'extroverts' lie in areas quite different from those you might normally expect.

2. Neither extroversion nor introversion is good or bad, better or worse. Both personality types are a mixture of advantages and disadvantages, strengths and weaknesses.

3. Specific strengths related to personality type are to be found particularly frequently in both introverted and extroverted people. These strengths help in dealing with oneself and with others, in pursuing goals and shaping one's own environment.

4. Introverts and extroverts will typically be faced with their own particular hurdles. These hurdles form the particular needs and challenges facing the two personality types. It is important to know them in order to face up to any problems, and avoid wasting energy or struggling with communication problems in difficult situations.

5. As personalities in the middle of the introvert-extrovert continuum, centroverts have some advantages which allow them both flexibility and stability simultaneously. Nevertheless, in this middle and less specific position the centrovert is still faced with the task of spelling out their own individual and social needs.

2.
From 'I' to 'we': how the community shapes us

HOW DO I KNOW WHAT I AM THINKING WHEN I CANNOT HEAR WHAT I AM SAYING?

MARGIT HERTLEIN, EXTROVERT, HUMOUR WORKSHOP TRAINER

In the previous sections, you have encountered introverts, extroverts and centroverts as individual personalities with specific characteristics. You are also now familiar with the biological differences which make people introverts, extroverts or centroverts, and know that humans are very much more exciting and complex beings than just the result of chance neural characteristics. If we want to understand ourselves and our personality characteristics better, then we should look also at the communities in which we grow up and live. For it is only by living with others that our personality develops and finds its expression. The social environment is therefore the focus of this chapter.

The social environment

How exactly hereditary and acquired factors interact in the development of personality still remains rather uncertain. But one thing is clear: the association is so close that psychologists often describe the social part of our personalities as our 'second nature'.

Introversion and extroversion are only 40 to 50 per cent based on genetic disposition.[17] Against this background, what does our social environment in which we grow up and live mean for our introvert and extrovert traits? And what is the significance of diversity in our community? This chapter deals with these questions.

Let us first take a look at the big picture: at the individual people and the significance of the crowd.

Introverts: the principle of community

Everyone is dependent on social relationships from the cradle to the grave. As babies we are incapable of surviving by ourselves. It's a long time after birth before the human brain is 'ready'. Neural connections are not formed until we begin to communicate with the people around us – and do not become permanent until they have been used repeatedly. This only happens when others pay attention to us: when we receive abundant stimulation and encouragement, warnings, advice and appraisals from our surroundings; and when the people around us help us to develop rules, structures and processes in our lives. The main currencies in our development are affection and trust – we need affection and can only thrive if we can rely on others. In addition to these currencies, our social environment ideally gives us stability (and with it security), as well as new impulses (and with them possibilities for development).

! Key idea

Our social environment ideally provides us simultaneously with stable conditions and new impulses.

A child's personality is developed by its relationship with its surroundings and by its communication with them, sending and receiving signals through all its senses. These impressions gained in interaction with others shape the brain structure.The influence of the social environment is a condition for the emergence of an awareness of self.

Other people are after all a prerequisite for us gaining a sense of our own identity. It is in development that the sense of a social counterpart first begins, a 'you'.

That is also why our first utterance is typically 'Mummy!' or 'Daddy!', not 'I!'. Only after that does an awareness of self and saying one's own name occur. This emotional bond with others provides a child with an early and strong understanding of the social community to which it belongs.[18]

Gerald Hüther (2013, p. 44) gets to the heart of the interplay between biology and social environment:

IN ALL THOSE AREAS WHERE IT DIFFERS FROM THE ANIMAL BRAIN, THE HUMAN BRAIN IS FORMED AND STRUCTURED BY RELATIONSHIP EXPERIENCES WITH OTHER HUMAN BEINGS.

OUR BRAIN IS THEREFORE A SOCIAL PRODUCT AND AS SUCH IS OPTIMIZED FOR THE CREATION OF SOCIAL RELATIONSHIPS. IT IS A SOCIAL ORGAN.

The phases of growing up, development and, later, adult life follow. In these phases too, the people in our environment remain important to us and at the same time provide a sounding board for our own opinions. On the one hand we want to belong and adapt – we learn from childhood to fit in – and then in the end, with the enormous flexibility unique to humans, we are able to 'pass' as adults into our social environment.[19]

On the other hand, we differentiate between 'others' and 'ourselves'. What is interesting is that what we call 'our self' or 'our personality' is largely the product of impressions – feelings, rules, assessments and orientations – which are handed on to us by others. First our families then our peer groups set us an example of what we should know, what is good or bad, what 'a good life' looks like and what we should do or what would be best left alone.

We take these standards on board in a learning process and we manage this particularly easily when dealing with people who have a role model function for us. And then intriguingly we think our judgements, inclinations and decisions are our own: that is the effect that the 'we' of the community has on the coming into being of the 'I'.

In other words, in our development we internalize external impulses in a continuous process, and what we make of them remains more or less permanently in our neural system. As a result we fit perfectly into our environment, which can look very different, depending on geographical situation, culture and social position.

In difficult situations, support from others is an important anchor and provides security and assurance. But we also really only enjoy the good things – from a terrific success to a new built-in cupboard to beautiful holiday experiences – properly if we can share these experiences with others. This does not mean that the continuous presence of other people is necessary for us to feel good – and I'm not just saying that as an introvert: a broad-based study shows that the mere awareness of living among firm friendships is a key factor for personal happiness and even increases the probability of surviving a serious illness. Physical closeness or the frequency of direct contact is *not* key, as the authors expressly state.[20]

The basic relatedness to fellow human beings is deeply embedded in us. This means that we are designed for a life in groups. We are only happy when we know we are at least to some extent part of a community. The American social psychologist Roy Baumeister summarizes it as follows: 'Whether someone is part of a network of stable relationships or alone is a much more reliable objective predictor of the happiness of the person concerned than any other' (Brooks, 2011, p. 300)

Growing up as an introvert or extrovert

The way in which we develop as introverts or extroverts also depends on the people with whom we grow up: our parents and siblings, later our own children, but also friends and confidants. They all form the close circle or our 'group', which makes a deep impression on us. Let us take the extrovert Elliot as an example:

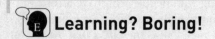 **Learning? Boring!**

Elliot is clever. He was always one of the best: in kindergarten and in primary school at any rate. At secondary school it gradually became more difficult. Learning vocabulary, tedious homework, then later essays and projects – that was just not his thing. Instead, he met up with his friends, played guitar in a band, played sport and organized class parties and city trips for himself and his friends.

There was not much room in Elliot's life for quiet learning – and that brought a few risks because his performance in the sixth form would count towards his A-levels. The fact that he and his friends were 'cool' did not really help him.

Elliot found it difficult to grapple with schoolwork by concentrating on his own. He soon became understimulated. But he had had an enormous starting advantage since early childhood: caring parents and grandparents who always supported him and accepted him for what he was – a rather boisterous, extrovert boy who threw himself enthusiastically into his environment. Curious, eager for life and friendly, his parents made sure that their young whirlwind deployed his energy outwards in a socially acceptable manner (sport, friends, music with others) and kept his impulsiveness under control where necessary.

 Key idea

Social factors control key development stages in the brain.

Elliot had acquired something which David Brooks (2011, p. 104 ff.) describes as 'safe restraint' in a summary of several studies. As a result of his protective, encouraging, loving environment, Elliot learnt to approach his environment optimistically and without anxiety. His brain also developed its full potential as a result of his good environment. In his frontal lobes, Elliot developed the capacity to control his impulses within a socially appropriate framework, develop orientation and make plans. He was also able to develop his reward centre fully – unlike children with less favourable parameters – and was able to enjoy the nice things in life to the best of his ability (remember the reward centre, or the nucleus accumbens, which is especially active in extroverts, from Chapter 1). His social environment also allowed his biological features to mature.

But there was something else: Elliot was also lucky enough to have an environment which supported him and helped him to compensate for his weaknesses when his personality did not make it easy for him to learn on his own.

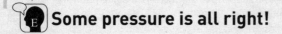

Some pressure is all right!

Elliot's parents were worried about their son. They had recently sought advice on how they could support him in working towards his A-levels. They sat down with him and helped him to organize a work and study schedule.

The plan left enough space for Elliot's other activities – but it also encouraged something else that Elliot himself did not have much of: the learning of discipline.

His mother had a good idea which motivated Elliot better. She encouraged him to set up some working groups with some of his friends for his 'difficult' subjects. They met regularly to sort out difficult tasks. She also encouraged him to get some of the best in the year group on board, even if they were not part of his close circle of friends. She explained: 'It's a win–win situation for everyone: you get to know more and the newcomers to the group get more status by spending time with you cool boys.'

Elliot knew that just being with his friends would not get more knowledge into his head. He found his mother's idea of inviting along real whizz-kids ideal. And off his own bat he used his intrinsic strength and began to put "Operation A-level" into action the very next day.

It is evident in a wide range of areas that social success is increased when members of a community help each other and even out each other's weak spots. Here it is the family which supports Elliot, but political parties, companies, citizens' initiatives and professional associations can all support their members and help them make progress. Without a supporting social base, comparatively few people manage to be more than moderately successful.[21]

Introvert children need an accordingly different sort of support: they benefit from quiet moments and protection from overstimulation and disturbance. If they are particularly cautious, they can learn with the encouragement of their environment to calculate risks and even to take risks in order to achieve something important. Above all, however, it helps them if they are already learning at home that they have a value of their own and specific advantages on their side, even in a 'loud' environment or culture. This self-reliance is inestimable asset for a life in mixed teams.

With the aid of his parents, Elliot is well on his way to becoming a powerful, successful young man. If he manages to control his distractibility by concentrating and avoiding tempting distractions, he will probably get good A-level results. And yet he will always seek situations which are particularly attractive to him because they match his personality.

 Key idea

Introverts and extroverts often seek social situations as they grow up which match their disposition.

Elliot is certainly not alone in that. According to recent studies, people who have an inborn tendency towards certain characteristics are inclined to seek social situations which match these characteristics. This applies to both introverts and extroverts.

 I'll get round to it later!

Ivy is Elliot's older sister. As an introvert, she spends her free time quite differently when she can. Ivy is about to take her A-levels and is stressed by the examination situation. Nevertheless she is regularly preparing the material systematically and knows that she is as well prepared as she can be. She is particularly good at Maths and Physics and is contemplating a career as an industrial engineer (although she has so far only told a few people this). She does not mind spending long periods reading or revising – as long as she is not disturbed, because disturbance quickly tears her away from her concentration. With her analytical head she likes cracking complex problems – and in her way then feels just as good as her brother when he is applauded after a successful guitar solo.

Ivy chooses quite different activities from her brother. While Elliot prefers to spend time with his friends and band members and to take part in exciting experiences, she values the inner pursuit of topics which interest her. This is an important aspect of living with others: it is not just that a community shapes the individual person – the individual person also helps to shape his community with his preferences in the medium term.

 ## Finding your own place in the community

At the usual loud, jolly family parties, Ivy likes going for a walk in the fresh air from time to time with a quiet uncle. Elliot is usually somewhere with his cousins, where the laughter is loudest and there is most going on.

As adults, Ivy and Elliot will have plenty of practice in areas they themselves have been able to choose – so they can in the best case scenario not only live out their predispositions and develop the particular strengths associated with them, but will also be able to enrich their own communities with what they are good at and be successful in that way. Their environment will benefit when perhaps Elliot sets new trends as a music manager or Ivy gives new momentum to industrial engineering as an academic. A legacy for the next generation will also benefit the community. If both siblings and their partners later encourage their offspring to develop their own strengths, this will also have an ongoing positive effect on the future.

Nevertheless, it can be difficult if the adolescent child's personality type deviates from the norms of its environment. These days, more and more people are aware that an introvert child is completely normal – but even when the general culture is not as extrovert as in the USA or Brazil, there may still now and again be friction and misunderstandings. School can be a case in point: Elliot and Ivy will not grow up in Finland (an introvert culture) or the USA (an extrovert culture), but in Germany, which is more or less a centrovert country somewhere between the two.

 Key idea

The community shapes the person – and the person shapes the community.

The challenges for different personality types as they grow up are maybe somewhat less difficult these days compared to what they were in the past. After all, we live in a time when nerds and geeks from Harry Potter to Mark Zuckerberg and Edward Snowden can become icons. Nevertheless, the attitude of the parents to their offspring is crucial. Those who do not have as much luck as Ivy and Elliot will perhaps get signals from father, mother or siblings which indicate: 'It would be better if you were more outgoing. You don't really fit in the way you are!' Many introverts who grew up in characteristically extrovert environments can tell you a thing or two about that. But extroverts as well who grow up amidst a majority of sensitive introverts are sometimes viewed negatively.

In such cases, introverts and extroverts may still learn later on to accept themselves and their own strengths. But of course it is best if they learn from an early age to say: 'I'm fine just the way I am!'

If you would like to read more on how best to support introvert and extrovert children, look in Olsen Laney (2002), Cain (2011) and Loehken (2014).

Take a moment now to look back at the first part of your own life.

Your life

Looking back: who were the introverts, extroverts and centroverts who supported you as you grew up?

1. Who were the people to whom you related most closely? Note your assessment of the personality types as I (introvert), E (extrovert) or C (centrovert).

Name   I/E/C

....   ——

....   ——

....   ——

....   ——

....   ——

....   ——

2. In what way did these people affect you most? What especially did you learn and take on board from these individuals? Where were you encouraged in your strengths and where were you corrected in your hurdles?

Name	Learning experience
....	_____
....	_____
....	_____
....	_____
....	_____
....	_____
....	_____
....	_____

```
.........................................          _____
.........................................          _____
.........................................          _____
.........................................          _____
.........................................          _____
.........................................          _____
```

Community 2.0: Social media from introvert and extrovert perspectives

YOU CAN'T HUG A SOCIAL MEDIA PROFILE.

STEVE PAVLINA, BLOG ENTRY ON 31 DECEMBER 2012 AT STEVEPAVLINA.COM

Now you know how much the quality of human community depends on the type of communication and on how people get on with each other. The greatest innovation of the last few decades has been the arrival of the internet and – especially for the creation of community – social media. They have extended the opportunities for action and created new exchange channels. They also have attractive and less attractive sides for introverts and extroverts equally. Social media and its use are therefore the focus of this section.

Social media include all the internet platforms that offer channels for direct communication between users. Since their appearance the term 'community' has acquired a digital interpretation. Through blogs, contact forums and chat rooms, Facebook, LinkedIn, Xing and YouTube, we can now enter into a dialogue with people we may never meet in person. This dialogue is predominantly carried out in writing, even though pictures, videos and the spoken word are also used. Both introverts and extroverts use social media. They choose this type of communication in accordance with their own personality, i.e. they each use social media differently and also see quite different advantages in it. The following overview shows you the advantages that social media offer – depending on whether viewed as an introvert or an extrovert.

Advantages of social media (introvert and extrovert perspectives): overview

Introvert motives	Extrovert motives
Social media offer virtual instead of personal contact so being alone and social life can be neatly combined without much expenditure of energy.	Social media offer virtual contact in addition to existing personal contact so you can carry out an exchange with the same person through completely different channels.
The time and place of communication during exchanges is self-determined.	Whether you are at work or 'home alone', you can still connect to people via social media.
Social media allow written communication – and writing is, after all, an introvert strength. Some platforms (e.g. WhatsApp and Twitter) can to some extent replace a telephone conversation – and certainly e-mails.	Social media allow real-time communication – and spontaneity and speed are, after all, extrovert strengths.
The internet is a place full of information and therefore full of possibilities for extending your own horizon – pure joy for an introvert.	The internet is a giant adventure playground full of surprising discoveries and exciting impulses – pure joy for an extrovert.

But however much social media have to offer from either an introvert or an extrovert point of view there are, as with all good things, also temptations and risks in using them – especially when you spend a lot of time on the internet. There is a specific section on digital communication in your professional life in Chapter 6.

The following sections show the most common side effects' and these may look different for introverts and extroverts. There are also specific perspectives and advice for the two personality types.

 ## Social media for introverts: what you need to watch out for

Risk 1: *Over* estimating the benefits of social media.

Hurdles: flight, fixation. Profiles in social media are like shop windows. The contact that you only get online can scarcely ever be compared with personal contact – even though an interesting exchange online may lead to a personal encounter, or, conversely, a personal acquaintance can be continued online.

Tip: Do not replace physical encounters with digital communication. Do feel free to remain in your personal comfort zone: communicate in your virtual circles in the same way as you like to do in your 'real' meetings. Maintain a manageable number of contacts. Even on purely professional platforms such as Xing and LinkedIn, confirm only invitations from people you have also met or with whom you have a connection. If you don't communicate indiscriminately in real life, you shouldn't do so online either. Do not be pressured into being present: even in social media, occasional time-outs are quite acceptable.

Risk 2: *Under* estimating the benefits of social media.

Hurdles: contact avoidance, passivity. Older introverts in particular sometimes tend towards a negative assessment of digital activities because they are not 'real'. But contacts in social media can fill a gap and extend your scope. Via Xing, LinkedIn or Google+ you can easily stay in contact with colleagues or friends from college even if they move to a new job or a new town. In this respect, social media can be like an address book which continually updates itself – and you can easily keep up to date with who is going where.

With Facebook you can easily stay in contact with family members and other people who are important to you and are now abroad.

Tip: Extend your social media network cautiously. Consciously maintain the contacts you already have. Set yourself a time allowance for using social media for personal and professional use that you don't drop below if you can possibly help it. Think of regular updates as part of your networking strategy. Communicate directly as well – status posts are not enough for an interesting dialogue.

Social media for extroverts: what you need to watch out for

Risk 1: Too much time on the net

Hurdles: distraction, self-avoidance. Facebook, Twitter, etc. are an entertaining way to put off unpleasant work. Also, if you don't like being alone, or are seeking displacement activities for some other reason, you can spend a huge amount of time in online company without really doing anything in the end. A real extrovert temptation!

Tip: Set yourself an upper limit for the amount of time you invest daily in using social media. Consciously choose offerings with which you can best pursue your aims. You don't have to be on all the platforms. By limiting yourself to three or four, you will avoid getting bogged down. Deliberately close down all other windows on your screen if you are working on a draft or a longer text. But be kind to yourself: allow yourself some breaks to keep in contact – live or on the Web 2.0!

Risk 2: lack of caution

Hurdles: superficiality, impatience, impulsiveness. Friends and followers on social media are not real friends – as you know. However, this does not mean that encounters in social media must always be fleeting or superficial. But it does mean that you should not upload all your information onto the net.

Tip: Consciously maintain your online contacts – this can lead to sustainable professional and private relationships. That includes communicating regularly on your chosen platforms and also maintaining direct dialogues.

But be careful about divulging private information, even though exchanges on the net can quickly lead to a sense of closeness. Look at your user settings – do you have the privacy you want?

Never post internal matters from your professional life or your professional networks – that will destroy trust and damage your reputation.

If in doubt as to whether something specific should be posted, just ask yourself whether there is anyone in your workplace you would prefer not to have this information. Perhaps your arch enemy? And don't forget: cyber-bullying, reputation damage and identity theft all happen on the net too. Safety-oriented introverts know that and are accordingly cautious about where they put information. But extroverts need to know it too!

We will now look a bit closer at how you behave in the digital world and how you use social media.

 Your use of social media – why and how?

1. Why do you use social media?

   I want to stay in contact no matter where I am. ☐

   I see it as a good extension of personal encounters. ☐

   I like communicating like this. ☐

   I sometimes use a bit of trial and error. ☐

   I feel more or less forced to join in. ☐

2. Have another look at the temptations and risks for introverts and extroverts above. Where do you feel you fit in?

3. How can you deal with these temptations and risks to avoid the disadvantages and use your time and energy better?

Introverts and extroverts: together but different

Non nobis solum nati sumus.
(We were not born for ourselves alone.)

MARCUS TULLIUS CICERO

The opportunity: enrichment

Both introverts and extroverts need company. Even very withdrawn introverts do not necessarily avoid other people – they tend to avoid overstimulation and insecurity. They therefore concentrate on a few people with whom they may be closely associated.

In everyday life there are very different types of social communities which may benefit from variety. These communities exist side by side and are often tightly knit together. Besides our families, we also live in circles of friends and cooperate in our work place with bosses, colleagues and staff. According to statistics, 50 per cent of all couples have found their 'other half' in their family and friendship circles or among colleagues. There are similar numbers for those who set up small companies: half of the founders set up businesses with people from the same circles of family, friends or colleagues.[22] Of course, the existing trust makes commitment easier and more attractive. (There is a special chapter on networks, professional contacts, and introverts and extroverts living together as partners or family members in Loehken, 2014.)

Here the focus is a basic question: how can introverts and extroverts with their differences benefit from each other in a community – whether it is in the private or the professional environment? This question can be answered in three parts:

Recognize the differences

Level out the hurdles

Benefit from each other

Combine strengths

How introverts and extroverts can benefit from each other: three conditions

1. Know the differences!

Introverts and extroverts should know about their differences so that they are clear that they often have different needs, different priorities and different strengths and hurdles. You are at an advantage if you live according to your own needs and advantages and at the same time respect the needs and advantages of others.

Examples: It is a good thing when introverts know that extroverts often need conversational exchange in order to sort out their thoughts and develop their ideas. It is equally a good thing for extroverts to know that introverts develop their best ideas when they have peace and quiet (and perhaps a pencil or a keyboard).

As manager of Manchester United, Sir Alex Ferguson had to combine the talents of his louder protégés with those of his quiet stars to create one of the best clubs in international football. Bringing a team of introverts and extroverts together to achieve their best performance only works if the trainer knows the different needs of the players.

2. Level out the hurdles!

Introverts and extroverts can make sure that specific hurdles remain within manageable limits and do not cause any damage.

Examples: Introvert caution may balance out extrovert recklessness; extrovert drive, extrovert eloquence or extrovert courage can limit introvert flight or introvert passivity. This balance can be a salvation in difficult or risky situations.

This interaction is illustrated by the familiar Bible stories of the brothers Moses and Aaron. Aaron the eloquent extrovert accompanied the introvert Moses to negotiations with the Egyptian Pharaoh. And Moses for his part kept an eye on Aaron, as the latter had a tendency towards unconsidered actions in order to get stimulation and reward.

On the occasion when Moses was away on an important mission without Aaron (to receive the Ten Commandments), Aaron promptly organized the calamitous affair with the golden calf.

3. Consolidate strengths!

When introverts and extroverts consolidate what they can each do especially well or easily, they can achieve much more than if they only had their own strong sides available. This synergy can lead to an enormously creative and different performance.

Examples: The introvert strengths of concentration and substance can provide a solid basis for the spontaneity and speed of an extrovert because the latter then has his feet on bedrock instead of his head in the clouds. Extrovert flexibility and courage combined with introvert calm and caution can create the perfect basis for implementing something new in a controlled manner with sufficient security.

By contrast, the enthusiasm, eloquence and drive of an extrovert can make a product famous that is invented by an introvert with the strengths of tenacity, analysis, concentration and substance. This is exactly what Steve Jobs and Steve Wozniak did when they put Apple computers on the market.

The first condition (know the differences) is a prerequisite and the basis for the second and third, as introverts and extroverts need to know about each other. Even the best complementary abilities and the best team potential can fall at a hurdle of feeling that it is not a good thing to be different and in case of doubt 'birds of a feather should flock together'. Let's look at this a bit more closely.

The condition: understanding

If you look carefully in everyday life, you will easily see a discrepancy between the sweet promises of diversity and the reality. What applies to men and women, young and old, native inhabitants and people from foreign cultures, also applies to introverts and extroverts: however much they need each other, however much they can benefit from their differences, sometimes they are wary of each other. Very.

This is shown most vividly (and also rather dramatically) in what introverts and extroverts sometimes think of one another and the way they express this. Over the last few years I have compiled a collection of the negative terms used by both introverts and extroverts to describe the other personality type.

What introverts say about extroverts: Never know what mood they'll be in, chatterbox, clumsy oaf, over-emotional, hot-head, superficial, bulldozer, stupid, steamroller, diva, moody

What extroverts say about introverts: Boring, puts a spanner in the works, lame duck, sensitive flower, not too bright, wallflower, nit picker, bean counter, unsociable, professional worrier, unfriendly, unapproachable, reader, impractical, timid

However amusing some of these terms sound, they bear witness to the fact that the relationship between introverts and extroverts is in a sorry state. Seeing their own tendencies as 'natural', an introvert tends to think of an extrovert as shallow or stupid. Correspondingly, an extrovert tends to believes that an introvert is an unapproachable party pooper or a boring hanger-on.

Reactions to each other can be extreme: an introvert becomes surly if her (well-meaning) extrovert friend tries to coax her to a party full of strangers. Similarly, some extroverts may also not be too pleased if an introvert friend wants to talk all evening about a book they have just read – without even a third opinion or a television in the background. In short: there are things which we may find wonderful, but others may have a different view.

In psychology the tendency to see our own characteristics as positive and normal is described as 'self-hugging'.[23] This is when we consider the characteristics, preferences and behaviours linked to our personality to be natural, good and self-evident, but if other people demonstrate characteristics, preferences or behaviours which are completely different or even quite the reverse, we consider them as negative. From the point of view of the self-hugger, the world is perfect when it is just like him or her. The quiet introvert then appears inaccessible, detached, timid or arrogant, and the dynamic extrovert seems stressful, superficial, inconsiderate or even invasive.

Self-hugging may be part of our human nature, but it can easily become a problem – especially if the task is really to achieve something together or to solve a complex problem by a combined effort, instead of making value judgements about our differences. It becomes difficult when the participants are under stress – e.g. because of time pressure, because the task is complicated or if there is something else which is more important, i.e. the question of who is the strongest – a case of status dispute. You can find out in Chapter 8 how to behave in such a situation and (as an introvert or extrovert) keep a cool head. The most important thing here is that a rational understanding of the differences between introverts and extroverts can reduce purely impulsive reactions and make sympathetic behaviour easier.

The big task in introvert–extrovert cooperation is knowing, understanding and cherishing the differences.

So extroverts are misunderstood by introverts – and introverts are misunderstood by extroverts. The latter pattern is even more likely because withdrawn introverts who prefer to stay silent instead of clearing up a misunderstanding or expressing their needs leave a lot of room for interpretation. Imogen's example demonstrates this clearly:

Reunion

After several years, Imogen was looking forward to meeting Elsa again. The two lawyers had washed up on shores far apart from one another in the course of their lives. But there was a reunion on the agenda this New Year's Eve: a celebration with the extended circle of acquaintances from the time when they were students in Munich, to which the two friends and their families from China and the USA were travelling. Elsa was the organizer.

But anticipating the event had felt better to Imogen than what she actually experienced during the evening. Although Elsa greeted her warmly and cheerfully, she moved on to the next person after what felt like only 45 seconds. Imogen hoped for more chances to chat during the evening, which for her felt very long (of course, at New Year parties, you have to stay until after midnight ...). After all, they had both been through quite a lot and had only kept in touch now and again electronically.

But Imogen's wish was never fulfilled. When she went to her hotel with her husband and daughter in the early hours of the morning, she had only had the chance to exchange a brief few words now and again with Elsa. And because Elsa kept moving on so quickly, they only talked about what Imogen saw as 'chit-chat'. Did Elsa perhaps not want anything to do with her and was that what she was signalling that evening? Imogen slept badly – turmoil, Champagne and heavy thoughts are not good relaxants ... Imogen was disappointed – but neither before, during nor after the reunion did she express what was important to her and what she wanted. She therefore shared the responsibility for the situation. How was Elsa to know what she needed if Elsa did not need the same thing?

We are usually emotionally drawn to people who 'tick' in much the same way as we do. But we can use our rational side to learn to recognize and tolerate differences. We can also learn that our own characteristics are not absolute and should not be projected unthinkingly onto others. Even when people want the same thing, they often get there by different means. As they say, there's more than one way to skin a cat! Knowing, tolerating and valuing form the great art of introvert–extrovert cooperation.

What could Imogen have done based on the three conditions for introvert–extrovert cooperation earlier in this chapter?

 Two points of view – one friendship

1. Know the differences!

Imogen would have been less disappointed if she had known Elsa's needs, which were very different from her own. Elsa revelled as an extrovert in the reunion with many friends and was happy with this lengthy social stimulation – extensive conversations or longer concentration on a conversation with one person would have likely got in her way.

It is just as important that Imogen should have perceived her own needs and seen them as equally important. If she valued quiet conversations with old acquaintances, she could have made sure in advance that she would be able to find good opportunities for this. She could have started an exchange on Facebook, for example, or made arrangements to meet individual contacts.

But there was one thing that Imogen could have done above all others: she could have let Elsa know what she wanted. Introverts easily forget that their thoughts cannot be read off a teleprompter on their foreheads – especially by extroverts!

2. Level out hurdles!

With all the hectic to-ing and fro-ing Elsa did herself harm as well as good, even though she enjoyed it. As a result of her hurdles of impatience, distraction and impulsiveness, it may be that in the end some important experiences were missed. Imogen could have contributed her introvert strengths here. With empathy and by listening she could have found out beforehand what Elsa really wanted. Perhaps a reunion alone with a former admirer? Dancing to the old songs? This is easily done by a tenacious, analytical planner ... And Elsa would certainly have shown her appreciation. She is after all an extrovert.

Elsa for her part could have used her enthusiasm, drive and eloquence to help Imogen to get into conversation, possibly with people she didn't know all that well.

3. Combine strengths!

Elsa and Imogen could (and Imogen could have planned this beforehand) have revived their friendship by combining forces to do something to make the party a success. Organize a photo session with everyone? Set up a big story-telling session where all the former fellow students could contribute something? A meal with specialities from all the places that people came from?

Imogen's analytical planning and her capacity for written exchange could have made sure of the preparation. Elsa's presenting skills, courage and emotional warmth could have supplied some dazzling ideas.

And not least, the bond resulting from such a joint project would have been a real joy for Imogen.

Elsa's story shows one difference which is often observed between extroverts and introverts in the manner in which they prefer to conduct their social relationships.

Extroverts best enjoy being in human company. The stimulation which the contact itself brings does them good. But the social experience is also enhanced by the outwardness which characterizes extroversion.

A little exchange here and a new contact there shows extroverts like Elsa that they are connected to the world and the world can see them. Social exchange energizes them. Profound conversations and lengthy discussions are not necessary.

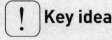

Key idea

Extroverts and introverts need the company of others in their own way.

For extroverts, any extension of their social network is pretty much welcome. It can be an invitation to a party, a network event or even a chance encounter. For them, being alone can easily lead to understimulation and then to boredom or restlessness. Without human company and at least exchanges via social media, extroverts also soon get the feeling that they are missing something or are lonely. The lack of outside stimulation makes the dopamine level drop and leads to frustration.

 Contact simulation

My extrovert husband switches on the radio every morning and leaves it on while he is drafting plans or communicating with customers. And for him it is a nice additional stimulation. As an introvert, however, all background noise is for me a horror when I'm working quietly. It too easily makes for overstimulation and stops me thinking.

Introverts on the other hand usually prefer to concentrate on a small circle of family members, familiar faces and colleagues. They often place particular value on the quality of conversations. They like having people around them in whom they can confide and with whom they can have long conversations. They invest time and energy in the select number of relationships which mean something to them. That is why introverts often find small talk stressful or at least dull.

This however makes no difference to their satisfaction – quite the opposite. Psychologist Matthias Mehl of the University of Arizona and his colleagues managed to find evidence that conversations make us happier and more satisfied. And interestingly, this satisfaction starts after the 'real' more in-depth conversations, not snippets of small talk (Mehl et al, 2010). However, it is not clear how many introverts were among his test subjects ... Introverts can also become stressed when social interaction demands too much 'outwardness' from them: a conversation which lasts too long or is continually re-starting, with too many people at too short intervals, easily leads to overstimulation for introverts, prevents quiet reflection and robs them of energy.

Introverted people feel lonely without company much less easily. They enjoy being alone and even need a quiet, low-stimulus environment to recover and restore their energy. Regularly being alone usually makes introverts satisfied and provides real recovery. Introverts know that alone is not lonely – and you can feel just as lonely in a crowd if there is no emotional or substantive bond.

 Company for thinkers

A good example is supplied by Immanuel Kant, the great philosopher of the Enlightenment and confirmed introvert. Indeed, Kant went for a daily walk on his own and worked many hours alone, but went to the coffee house after his lectures. He liked having regular company at lunchtime as well and discussed his ideas with friends, colleagues and scholars. His principle was: 'Eating alone is unhealthy for a philosophizing scholar.'

Introverts like being among people as well. But they need fewer social contacts and enjoy them in different proportions. And they often fill their encounters with other ideas of quality.

The possibility: the power team

IT'S NOT THAT INTROVERTS AREN'T GOOD TEAM PLAYERS. WE JUST DON'T NEED TO BE IN THE SAME ROOM AS THE REST OF THE TEAM AT ALL TIMES.

SOPHIA DEMBLING (2012, P. 158)

In this section you will get an overview of various possibilities and examples of good professional cooperation between introverts and extroverts. The perspective is that of a team member – if you are a manager, there is a special section in Chapter 6 on good interaction between introverts and extroverts in teams.

Here are the three conditions again which form the basis for productive introvert–extrovert cooperation.

1. Know the differences!

For introverts	For extroverts
Use your own advantages.	**Use your own advantages.**
You are not very dependent on outside feedback so you also do well without being patted on the back.	Group situations and the spoken word suit you.
Let your bosses know about your good results or get input to make headway. By doing so, you use your strengths in one-to-one conversation and confidently demonstrate your performance without demanding too much of your bosses' time or energy.	Take over moderating tasks, coordinate different areas, discuss ideas and concepts with team members. Help to create a 'we' feeling in the team.
Respect your own needs: work alone without being disturbed.	**Respect your own needs: cooperation with others.**
Establish communication-free periods during the working day. If need be, come in early in the mornings or work late. Or better still: arrange times when you can work at home. Even if you share your office or travel about, seek out somewhere where you can be undisturbed for at least a couple of hours for complex tasks such as drafts or strategies. Wherever possible, try to avoid telephone calls, email or the internet at such times.	Develop ideas and concepts together with others. For this you should use the ways of communicating that especially suit you, such as brainstorming, a casual exchange of ideas, meetings or social media. If you cooperate with introverts as well, you will get the best input if you allow them time to prepare.

(Continued)

The second best option if there is no empty conference room available anywhere or working in your home office is not an option is to use noise-suppression earplugs or headphones for limited periods.

Peace and quiet

On social occasions or when working in large groups make sure you have low-stimulation periods or 'alone time' in between.

At conferences and events, make appointments with individuals or small groups. Skive off a talk or a 'social' now and again and go for a walk. Or take a snooze.

And the last opportunity to catch your breath is still the cubicle in the washroom ...

Meetings in big groups: speak with individual participants before the meeting. Find some allies to your cause and plan a strategy for the meeting.

Stimulation.

Make sure that you regularly get variety and new experiences. Change activity when you get bored or feel restless.

Spread pending telephone calls or short meetings with colleagues (be careful with introverts) between phases of cogitating. You will find it better to work in shorter periods on a project – and keep coming back to it. Minimize distractions in concentrated work phases – changing activity after 45 minutes is better than continually going back and forth between the internet and the draft paper.

Contact

Limit the time you spend alone sitting in front of the computer. Relax with others – enjoy lunch with others in the team and outside it. That's how you get new ideas and interesting information, meet cool people and manage your network as well.

Writing

Prepare bullet points for discussion beforehand in writing – if you do that your information will be well thought out and on hand. Please don't forget to refer to it as well!

Reward

Feed your reward centre: Keep your eye on what attracts you to a task.

Have you shown a contract you have concluded successfully to your line manager? Might your

Volunteer for written tasks which best show what you are capable of. That will reduce the likelihood of you being allocated unpleasant tasks and increase your visibility with things you are good at. (Exceptions: be cautious about protocol – and a low status jobs; see Note X).

Keep to the point in oral interactions: Target individual bosses and colleagues, plan the content, summarize the key points in conversations.

Collect all large and small successes in writing. That will strengthen your self-confidence and your memory – which might be useful for salary negotiations!

work on the project recommend you for some more exciting tasks? Is there a chance of an extra commission ?

If you do not see anything stimulating in your task, reward yourself after you have achieved some of your important goals. And if you find yourself in this situation too often, start looking around for a more attractive job

Respect the differences.

Extroverts charge up their energy reserves when they chat in the kitchen with others. (They are not lazy.)

Many extroverts love travelling for work or having a number of appointments on one day. This is how they get variety and can generate a fresh wellspring of ideas together with others. (They are not avoiding work. It is their favourite way of working.)

Extroverts talk a lot and discover ideas when brainstorming.

Respect the differences.

Introverts replenish their energy reserves before the next working day when they don't go to the bar with the team after dinner but take their leave. (They are not spoilsports.)

Many introverts love having working days without any appointments so that they can work undisturbed on their projects. (They are not unsociable. It is their favourite way of working.)

Introverts value it if you do not burst unannounced into the office but make an appointment.

2. Level out hurdles!

Introverts: Help from extroverts!	Extroverts: Help from introverts!
Invisibility.	**Recognition junkies.**
Introverts often feel passed over or robbed by extroverts in the recognition of performance – no matter how good the work they deliver may be, only those who manage to deliver the team results are identified with them and extroverts seem to manage that with relatively little effort. Learn from your extrovert colleagues to stand up for your efforts and present them if that is appropriate.	Don't believe everyone who gives you nice feedback. Being able to speaking well does not mean that you deliver the goods. Being liked does not give you an aura of competence.
Learn by watching how they self-confidently and energetically represent their own interests. That is sometimes a problem for you when you realize with the strength of empathy what others want or expect. That can lead to a type of group pressure to which you feel exposed.	If you want to know how good your work really is, then ask a clever introvert team member the following question: "How can I get better?"
	Learn from introverts that the best form of success is when other people notice it without your having to rub their noses in it.
	Look also at how they manage to work out the needs of others by listening and paying attention.
	In many situations that can be inestimably valuable for you.
PR reluctance.	**Out of sight – out of mind.**
Extroverts know that good performance will only be rewarded if it is appropriately communicated.	Introverts keep what is important in their heads – not just what is right in front of their eyes or what is suddenly urgent. They are just less dependent on immediate stimulation.

If you cannot score points in spontaneous group situations, seek a private conversation with your bosses – show what ideas you have and where you want to take on responsibility. With extrovert team members, consider how that can best be realized.

Consult with introvert colleagues now and again about the question of which activities or people at work should have priority.

You will see that you will get answers which you would never give yourself.

Lazy speech.

Do not use your capacity for expressing yourself in writing as an alibi for avoiding talks or presentations. If you are properly prepared with notes (think first, then speak – completely in accordance with introversion), then you may be very much better in front of the board of directors than some extroverts.[24]

Audacity.

Yes, you are bold and like accepting a dare when the goal appears attractive. Nor do you shy away from radical steps, and you know that that's what it takes sometimes to make progress. But the whole team will bear the consequences – positive and negative.

Watch extroverts as they make a presentation. What do you like? What can you make use of? What would you prefer to do differently? There may be a chance of a sales pitch which you can present with an extrovert so that you get through to both the introverts and the extroverts on the customer's side. For example, you could let the extrovert take on the welcome and create the mood and do the factual part yourself.

And with your eyes on the glittering prize at the end of the road you may sometimes miss the dangers at the edge of the path.

So you should discuss your plans with your cautious introvert colleagues as well as with other bold extroverts. You will get a more realistic assessment of the upcoming risks.

3. Combine strengths!

Introverts: Score points with extroverts!	Extroverts: Score points with introverts!
Division of work. Forge strategic alliances with extrovert colleagues. Can they for example do the question and answer session during the meeting (stressful for you) while you do the state of the project presentation? By listening quietly can you find out what the boss wants while the extrovert colleague deals with implementation in the team afterwards? Make it clear that you consider both tasks equally important.	**Division of work.** Forge strategic alliances with an introvert colleague. For example, can she do the draft that you are both keen on while you try to convince potential supporters to back it? Can you convince your boss that your project needs a bigger budget if the introvert colleague puts together the figures and arguments? Make it clear that you consider both tasks equally important.
Make use of extrovert energy. Be glad of the power which extroverts have available when they get sufficient stimulation. Leave things for the extrovert team colleagues to do which sap your energy but will give them strength: perhaps negotiating with colleagues from other departments about the budget or looking after relations with customers who like to talk. You can then save your quiet strength for strategically important long term activities.	**Make use of introvert endurance.** Be glad of the quiet endurance that introverts have available when they pursue important matters – even without any immediate feedback. Leave things for the introvert team colleagues to do which sap your energy but will give them strength: structuring a meeting, compiling and fine tuning complex drafts on their own and in peace and quiet or solving complicated customer problems. Use your energy to make sure that the drafts find acceptance.

Celebrate success.	**Address conflicts.**
Sometimes it is OK to party – celebrate project and team successes together. Combine your capabilities with those of extrovert colleagues. Who's doing the planning? Who's doing the invitations? How can it become a really nice get-together? And which head of department should be invited from a PR point of view?	Use your own strength of openly addressing conflicts – but plan your course of action with an introvert colleague who will support you with the strengths of caution, listening and analytical thinking. That will reduce the risk of escalation and increase the chances of a settlement.

 Find your own opportunities

The examples you have read in this chapter should encourage you to find your own creative opportunities. Read the following questions and note the ideas that come into your head here.

1. Which of your introvert or extrovert strengths can you use in your team in your daily work?

2. Which of your characteristics will be of benefit when the introverts and extroverts in your environment balance them out?

The advantages of diversity in the community

Evolution has evidently not preferred either introverts or extroverts. On the contrary. Independently of whether a culture prefers introverted or extroverted forms of communication, the ratio between introverts and extroverts in a population is about even. The proportion of introverts is estimated in the literature at 30–50 per cent. There is a reason for this balance: obviously, both personality types contribute major and different strengths to the success of the community and to the survival of humanity. Throughout history it has certainly been useful that there have been as many risk-ready extroverts to shout 'Let's attack! We've got to get out of here; otherwise they'll smoke us out of the cave!' as there are safety-oriented introverts who caution 'It's too dangerous – visibility is too poor! Let's wait until the sun comes out!.'

But even today we need introverts and extroverts to overcome the demands of modern societies and global problems. We need people who calculate coolly and weigh up the possible benefits just as much as people who encourage others to leave their comfort zone in favour of the prospect of something better. We need hands-on dynamic people who roll up their sleeves as much as quiet thinkers who use their energy for inner reflection.

! Key idea

We need introverts *and* extroverts to overcome the demands of modern society and global problems.

Man's outstanding capability is to maintain a body of knowledge and pass it on to future generations, allowing progress, insight and development. For this we need patient, tenacious, systematic introverts. Furthermore, in order to weigh up risks and keep within sensible bounds, humanity needs safety-conscious, focused, substantive introverts – whether on a flight across the Atlantic, in the building of atomic power stations or in the development of corporate finance strategies.

On the other hand, when we need to conquer new ground and defend our own community even in the face of danger, when short-term action is urgent even without full information, then extroverts are an advantage as they will boldly and courageously take the helm with an eye on attractive rewards. Not least, in our complex world with the myriad data available to us, many creative achievements are not possible unless introverts and extroverts with their own vantage points and capabilities work together and do what they each do best. Innovation is often produced by combining contrasts to form something new, by melding quite diverse matters, traditions or ways of working (see Brooks (2011, p. 241f.) for more on this). Here is a practical example:

The book as an introvert–extrovert product

Dr Petra Begemann, ghostwriter of business text books/manuals

The majority of my clients like the stage and making a 'big entrance' and are rather 'extrovert'. I am the analyst in the background who goes through the contents, makes sure they follow a clear thread and that everything is crisply phrased. It augments things wonderfully when each side recognizes the strengths of the others – then 1 + 1 actually do make 3! For me that means embarking on something with an awareness that my opposite number will want to develop ideas further in conversation and will not come along with the finished article. For my customers it means putting up with someone who keeps probing and asking questions until in the end we get the full deal.

This principle also applies to the great stages of business and show business: 1 + 1 = 3. The extrovert Steve Jobs and the introvert Steve Wozniak founded Apple together (with Ronald Wayne) and laid the foundation stone for the success of the company. The extrovert Mick Jagger and the introvert Keith Richards together projected the Rolling Stones into musical history. The introvert Hillary and the extrovert Bill Clinton were with their combined strengths as much of a political power couple as the introvert Barack Obama and his extrovert wife Michelle. Something astounding can obviously happen when introverts and extroverts combine their special capabilities.

 ## Key idea

External focus combined with inner processing can lead to great creative achievements.

Just as men and women, young and old and people from different cultures can achieve a great deal together with their diverse perspectives and priorities, introverts and extroverts can also benefit when they adapt to one another and pursue their aims together, professionally and privately. And it always extends the personal horizon when we spend time with people who have something to add to our perspective and have learnt to value and appreciate this other perspective.

In my own work, I have often had the privilege of exchanging ideas with extrovert colleagues. Here is an example of one of the most creative exchanges, which resulted in the production of a completely new video format.

 ## The noisy–quiet sofa: an extrovert–introvert project

My colleague Margit Hertlein is as pronounced an extrovert as I am introvert. We both give talks to other people – but in completely different ways. We both travel a lot – with quite different ideas about what is nice and what you have to put up with.

Together we have brought to life the 'noisy–quiet sofa': Once a month we offer five minutes exchange of ideas about the differences between 'loud' and 'quiet' people. We film on a bright orange sofa (Margit's colour of course) in a Berlin back yard and use our two different personalities to demonstrate the contrast we are talking about. We both have a penchant for conversation. To show the dialogue between extrovert and introvert whilst talking about extroverts and introverts is a good example as far as I am concerned of how exciting it can be when different personalities work together.

But have a look for yourself. You'll find all the available videos from the 'noisy–quiet sofa' on my YouTube channel by following the link http://www.youtube.com/user/LeiseMenschenTV .

It is not until you know yourself and take your own needs into account that you can live and work optimally in company with others. And of course you will want to live your own life with different kinds of people and groups.

And that is what the following chapter is about.

Key points in brief

1. Personality – including introversion and extroversion – can only develop and take shape in association with others.

2. The social environment ideally gives children and young people stable conditions and new impulses for their development as they grow up.

3. Children and young people develop their personalities to fit in with their environment, and by communicating with it, and as they do so they internalize external impulses in a continuous process.

4. People are flexible in two respects: they can adapt to very different surroundings and they can choose their own attitudes and make their own decisions in a given environment.

5. Introverts and extroverts often seek social situations as they develop which match their disposition. It is important for both personality types that they are valued and supported in their environment for what they are.

6. Introverts and extroverts use social media differently but can both benefit from them – especially when they take into account the temptations that are specific to their personality type.

7. According to the principle of self-hugging, introverts and extroverts both tend to find people who are similar to themselves more attractive – and they find people who are different more difficult or less likeable.

8. But introverts and extroverts can get along perfectly well together under three conditions: when they understand the differences between the personality types, when the hurdles between them are levelled out and when they complement each other with their strengths.

9. The whole of society benefits from introverts and extroverts: they each contribute their own abilities to make living together successful. With their sometimes very different perspectives, introverts and extroverts can work together and through the association of contrasts and different characteristics create and achieve something new and extraordinary.

3.
A meaningful life: feeling comfortable in alien territory

I MUST ACT ACCORDING TO MY CONVICTIONS.

MARIE CURIE 1911, WHILE INSISTING ON ACCEPTING HER NOBEL PRIZE

So, you have worked out whether you are introvert, extrovert or centrovert. You have discovered the importance of your social environment for your personality. Does that mean your personality is forever set in stone by your biology and community? No. Our predisposition towards introversion or extroversion is only part of what becomes our story. There is a third factor involved in making up our personality: personal meaning.

Meaning: deciding on what's essential to you

More than the two factors already discussed in the previous chapters, the quest for personal meaning demonstrates what distinguishes us as humans from every other living being: the ability to make decisions of our own free will on how we want to shape our lives and what we want to do during our time on this Earth.

To do so, we need to have some conception of what is important and meaningful to our own lives. Our conclusions about what is important and meaningful to us may match the 'typical nature' of an introvert or extrovert: for example, the extrovert becomes a motivational speaker and the introvert a philosopher.

Often, however, what we consider meaningful is not congruent with what we think of as 'typical' environments for our personality type. That's when it gets interesting: we may have to square up to ways of living and behaving that just don't look ideal for the introvert or extrovert that we belive are. It's no problem under some circumstances: our conception of what is truly important to us spurs us on to do things that are 'alien' to us and live under less than ideal conditions.

American scientist Brian Little explained this apparent paradox with his free trait theory.[25] He distinguishes between 'fixed' and 'free' traits in a personality. In addition to biological predisposition and the influence of the social environment, he too highlights the assumption of a third component which he calls 'third nature' – the level on which individual decisions, goals and projects take place. To be able to implement these decisions, says Little, we need 'free' traits, which are free because they are independent of nature and environment. And in some way they also *make* us free: from the genes and social environment that define so much of the person that we (and others) perceive ourselves to be.[26]

 ## The introverted mentor

Brian Little is a good example of someone who has shaped his personal story according to what is dear to his heart – even if it has sometimes gone against the grain of his introverted personality.

Susan Cain (2011, p. 319) describes Little as a passionate mentor, who during his active phase inspired his students with his brilliant lectures and personal care as a university teacher.

But Little always made sure of one thing: that he could withdraw at least for brief periods and regenerate undisturbed in peaceful surroundings.

The decision to live by these free traits may demand more energy – but since a person then experiences a life filled with meaning, the extra effort is worthwhile – in a fairly literal sense, it is a meaningful investment.

Describing Little's basic scientific assumption in visual terms, personality is to be understood as a multi-lane carriageway from which we can benefit. The third level, which forms the topic of this section, is the ability to set the indicator and change lanes in accordance with our own ideas.

Many years before Brian Little's time, another introverted psychologist, Victor Frankl, portrayed the search for personal meaning as man's central aspiration – and as the basis of his dignity. He was another man who demonstrated by his own life what this can mean.

 Meaning – a lifesaver!

Viennese psychiatrist Victor Frankel survived the Nazi concentration camps and during that period lost his wife, his brother and his parents. The ordeal he endured opened up an insight: according to Frankl, the will to survive, and therefore the chances of survival, depend on whether the person concerned thinks there is a point in continuing to live.[27] Frankl based his logotherapy on this insight. At the core of it is a call to set out on a journey leading to whatever gives our life significance on a very personal level, even if this is an arduous and difficult task. Frankl sees it as the only way to a fulfilled, self-determined life.

The search for personal meaning in life is the subject of many other studies, books and lectures. One thing is important here: when we pursue tasks and activities that appear meaningful to us, it not only gives us satisfaction, but also makes us transcend our innate and socially acquired characteristics. And like predisposition and environment, meaningful activity also plays a part in shaping our personality.

For example, extrovert Richard Feynman opted for a life of physics research, although the long hours of patient, painstaking work with no human contact undoubtedly were not right for his 'nature'. Yet it was his work that inspired him, that created meaning for him, that he found valuable and therefore fascinating – and that ultimately won him the Nobel Prize in Physics in 1965.

 Key idea

A personality needs two things: to connect with others and its own very personal values and goals.

Similarly, an introverted character like physicist Angela Merkel decided on a career in politics because conditions in her country and immediate environment were such that helping to shape the political structures was more meaningful and important to her than a 'natural' introverted life in research. So the quiet physicist set out on a course that took her all the way to leadership of the German government.

No one but you can seek out your personal 'meaningfulness factors'. What you perceive as important and meaningful is an entirely separate issue from whether you are introverted or extroverted. At the same time, depending on the nature of your job, you will occasionally become extroverted as an introvert and introverted as an extrovert. This doesn't mean you'll be transformed into the other personality type, but simply that you will use the scope of your free traits. At the end of this section onwards you will find questions and resources that you can consult on this point.

Going beyond your comfort zone

As mentioned earlier, an important type of human flexibility is the mobility to adapt to an environment.

 Key idea

Flexibility (1): How a growing child adapts to his or her community as he or she develops.

In connection with the search for personal meaning, a second type of flexibility comes into play. It, too, transcends personality and is therefore not the same thing as the extrovert strength of the same name. It is mobility of choice, which makes up a large part of our inner freedom.

! Key idea

Flexibility (2): The freedom to select your own attitudes in a given environment and to act accordingly.

Both definitions of flexibility given in this book are only very indirectly associated with the extrovert strength you were introduced to earlier. They are part of the basic outfit that comes with being human.

This mobility towards our own understanding of meaning leads in practice to two different areas: first, you have to use your own traits to fulfil the tasks that appear important and meaningful. Secondly, it is sometimes essential to accept the need to behave in a way that is pretty much foreign to your personality but that is required by the task in question.

! Key idea

Living outside your comfort zone:

1. Use your own personality to perform tasks
2. Do 'alien' things: accept aspects of a task that require behaviour that is foreign to your personality

We will now look at the best way to deal with these two areas. We will look in detail at *how* introverts and extroverts can use their intrinsic characteristics and do 'alien' things – both of them successfully – in Part II.

1. Use intrinsics

You already know that the first thing we do both in our development and in everyday situations is look for the 'intrinsic': our first impulse is to introduce our own traits into our environment, thereby using them and putting our stamp on our activities. The traits we have acquired by predisposition and social environment are open to us like a treasure chest – *and* you don't need much energy to be the way you are already.

The same applies to the areas that are particularly important to us: we tend – and it's a good thing – first of all to use what we have available and what partly determines our identity. Note X shows you how to work this out. You first have to get to know your own characteristics, the 'differences'.

You should know what your traits as an introvert or extrovert are, where your strengths lie and what hurdles you face. In this section, we can add the element of meaning to that initial aspect.

 Key idea

Recognizing differences means:

- *firstly* knowing the strengths, priorities and needs that are associated with your own personality.
- *secondly* knowing what areas of your life and what activities contain meaning and significance.

One good example of a famous German shows how far a person can go if he is clear about these two questions and attributes a significance of his own to his life.

Use intrinsics: Alexander von Humboldt

Alexander von Humboldt (1767–1835) was a scientist *pur sang*. He was willed with enthusiasm for getting to the bottom of things and making new discoveries. In contrast, he found life at Schloss Tegel, his family's ancestral home in Berlin, very hard to bear. He called it 'Schloss (Castle) Boring', spent as much time as possible outside in the open from an early age, and started collections of minerals, plants and insects even as a boy – something that was to make him famous later on in quite a different context. Field research, science that he could reach out and grab, suited him better than a traditional, classical education.

Following the death of his parents, his inheritance enabled Alexander von Humboldt to do what he really wanted. He resigned from the civil service and as a scientist of independent means he travelled the world: Latin America, the USA, Russia and Central Asia. He explored landscapes and natural resources in several adventurous expeditions, often under extreme conditions. He didn't want to tie himself down to one single discipline and produced important work in such diverse areas as chemistry and botany, oceanography and astronomy, physics, ethnology and demographics. His search for the new took him to extraordinary discoveries. More or less by the way, the enthusiastic networker developed young scientists, exerted political influence in favour of human rights and managed to acquire important sponsors and patrons – including the Czar of Russia and two Prussian kings. He was not averse to public fame and enjoyed his prominence.

Humboldt exploited his extrovert strengths quite deliberately in his brilliant achievements: his love of exploration and action, his courage and energy, his powers of description, his ability to form personal connections and give speeches as well as his flexibility even under adverse circumstances made the globetrotter one of the greatest nature explorers of all time. He was a teacher who aroused enthusiasm in a huge audience (including non-scientists) and a discussion partner esteemed by the most famous learned men of the day.[28] 'You couldn't learn from books in a week what he could tell you in a lecture in one hour,' wrote Goethe in a letter.

2. Do alien things

When the territory is more likely to be attractive for the other personality type, using your own strengths isn't enough in most cases. That's where Brian Little's 'free traits come into play (introduced above). You will then be in a role that demands elements foreign to your personality, behaving in an introvert manner in some situations as an extrovert personality, or in an extrovert way as an introvert personality.

 Do alien things: Alexander von Humboldt

When Alexander von Humboldt spent too long in an environment that bored him, he often fell ill. Unlike his introverted brother William (1769–1859) who was an excellent scholar, he found it hard to concentrate during his education. He wasn't too keen on sitting for hours pondering over abstract knowledge, and was considered far less gifted than his brother.

Nevertheless, Humboldt managed to publish 30 volumes of his worldwide research and travel reports (though they were never finished) and to sit at his desk for many hours: the subjects of his research fascinated him, as did everything new that he discovered. For their sake, he accepted periods that were extremely low in stimulation apart from in his mind – possibly a consequence of his peer group and of the classical education received in his youth. But the prospect of new projects and expeditions also gave him strength – and so undoubtedly did his extensive communications and many inspiring contacts, including the most exciting figures of his time.

You see, living in 'alien territory' takes energy. And it can entail a variety of risks and side-effects originating in the hurdles of the personality concerned.

 Alien territory: introverts and risks

Safety-oriented introverts may find it hard to take risks. Unlike extroverts, they don't get a stimulating kick out of experiencing danger and uncertainty in order to achieve an attractive goal, such things are more likely to activate their anxiety.

Facing up to this anxiety means expending energy – an outlay which, however, generally becomes less with increasing 'practice', as demonstrated by the actions of the 'quiet' revolutionary Mahatma Gandhi, for example. He was an introvert who repeatedly planned extremely risky campaigns involving thousands of people.

Conscious confrontation with your own feelings ('there is ultimately no such thing as security') and an analytical assessment of the risks can be very helpful in doing what is important even in the face of your own need for safety.

Importantly, fear can even become a productive driver: 'Fear has been one of humanity's greatest drivers from time immemorial,' says the broker and great industry transformer Harald Blumenauer in an interview with Jánszky and Jenzowsky (2010, p. 111).

 Alien territory: extroverts and focus

In contrast, extroverts often find it difficult to work on one thing on their own for hours. This also takes energy – and the discipline of patient persistence, which requires you to waive stimulation and reward, sudden impulses, hands-on action and human society, and is much more the home territory of the introvert.

Keeping your eyes on a reward 'greater' than momentary distraction helps here. Alexander von Humboldt showed how well this can work: a field so fascinating that it can rivet the attention of the extrovert, the goal of making all those discoveries available to contemporaries and posterity: this prospect is attractive and a reward of quite different proportions.

Caution: Energy management needed

Regardless of whether you're an introvert or an extrovert, make sure that you only act in an 'unnatural' way, i.e. to turn extrovert or introvert, when you really need to. Then if possible return to your comfort zone on the introvert–extrovert continuum to recharge your depleted energy.

Jung already pointed out that constantly living outside your own comfort zone can be exhausting and even make you ill.

It seems that finding our own niche is one of the biggest challenges imposed on us by life. Filling this niche demands our entire personality – and as we have seen, sometimes even something above and beyond that. Those who move into different territory for this purpose put themselves at risk and use more energy. But both extroverts and introverts may decide to do something that appears alien or unaccustomed at first glance – because it's important to them. And that, in turn, is energizing.

Let's look at a few typical examples of how extroverts use their intrinsic characteristics and do alien things in introvert territory and vice versa – and very successfully, at that.

The extrovert in 'introvert territory'

Typical introvert territories are fields of action that work 'from the inside outwards' and therefore have a lot to do with ideas, conceptions and inner processing. These areas require the use of precise analysis and extensive reflection, conceptualization and the search for essentials, and carefully considered structuring.

Such areas can also be attractive to extroverts under certain circumstances. People who are stimulated by the analysis of conceptual models, for example, to whom acquiring knowledge is an adventure, and who find solving complex exercises and problems irresistible, may opt to conquer inner worlds, extrovert or no.

Let's take three examples.

Introvert territory 1: Science

THERE IS A RESTLESSNESS IN ME THAT OFTEN MAKES ME THINK I'M LOSING WHAT LITTLE REASON I HAVE. AND YET THE RESTLESSNESS IS SO ESSENTIAL IN ORDER TO WORK CEASELESSLY TOWARDS GOOD CAUSES.

ALEXANDER VON HUMBOLDT, IN A LETTER TO WILHELM GABRIEL WEGENER, A FRIEND OF HIS YOUTH

The extrovert Alexander von Humboldt (1769–1859) and his introvert
brother Wilhelm (1767–1835) are historical examples of how
differently introverts and extroverts approach science and conduct
research. On a more general level, some aspects can be summarized
that make it easier for extroverts to live as naturally as possible in the
'introvert territory' of science.

 Extrovert scientists: survival tips

- Make sure you get lots of stimulation and keep doing something
  different – this will give you ideas.
- Make sure you interact with colleagues so as to identify your own
  ideas more easily.
- Contribute actively to your discipline and give plenty of lectures – this
  oral interaction provides stimulation.
- For the same reason, attend conferences, colloquiums and lectures,
  make notes of your own thoughts as soon as possible or record them
  as spoken messages.
- Don't be afraid to pursue unusual, interdisciplinary and exotic ideas.
- View research as a kind of game – that's what Nobel laureate Richard
  Feynman is known to have done (see box below).
- Enjoy awards, distinctions, job offers, invitations to give keynote
  speeches and general fame as rewards and incentives.
- Benefit from science and research as international fields of activity
  in the form of trips, contacts abroad, international collaboration and
  projects.
- Always remember how cool/important/exciting/influential your
  academic activity is.

A recent example of an extrovert career in the top league of science is the life of one highly unconventional US American:

 The genius in the night club: Richard Feynman

Another illustrious extrovert scientist of the 20th century was physicist Richard Feynman (1918–1988). Like Alexander von Humboldt, he worked across disciplines; in addition to quantum field theory and quantum mechanics, for which he received the Nobel Prize in 1965, he was also interested in such diverse areas as molecular biology and computer technology. Feynman was a brilliant teacher and speaker – another parallel with Humboldt – and found original ways, for example in the Feynman Lectures, to acquaint a wide audience with his 'egg-head' subjects.

Feynman was one of the most creative intellects of his time and was careless of convention. His hobbies included bongo-drumming and life drawing – an activity he pursued in the nightclubs he visited almost every evening.

Since Richard Feynman was a man of the spoken word, he sometimes only put important facts and insights which he shared with colleagues on paper after the event.

Feynman detested the abstract as well as over-superficial thinking, and was famous for both his impatience and his sense of humour. His last words as he succumbed to cancer in 1988 were: 'I'd hate to die twice – it's so boring.'

Introvert territory 2: engineering

PEOPLE THINK WE'RE ECCENTRIC AND DULL.

EKKEHARD SCHULZ, ENGINEER AND EX-THYSSENKRUPP CHIEF (2010)
55 GRÜNDE, INGENIEUR ZU WERDEN [55 REASONS TO BECOME AN ENGINEER] *HAMBURG: MURMANNN*

Engineering is supposed to be typical introvert territory. I can confirm that from my own professional practice, but not without major caveats: my training programmes are often intended for engineers and I do see a majority of introverts there. However, a relatively large number of extroverts go for careers in engineering compared to science. This may be because the field offers a lot of scope for personal input. Scientifically-oriented, structured, focused thinkers and tinkerers (introverts) become engineers, and it seems as if this type has formed the image of the engineer. But hands-on pragmatists (extroverts) are also to be found – think of a technical engineer working in a team with other experts in the field of equipment servicing and maintenance. The comparison below is ideal-typical, but it illustrates relatively clearly what introverts and extroverts like to make of the profession of engineering. My impressions are based on ten years or so of regular training programmes with engineers.

Introverts and extroverts in engineering: moulding your professional life to your nature

Introverted engineers	Extroverted engineers
Are interested in mathematical and analytical content.	Are interested in interacting with others.
Like to tinker around, think and solve abstract problems.	Like to organize and solve concrete problems.
Like to work on their own.	Love teamwork and frequent communication.
Are often happiest as specialists; they like to deepen their expert knowledge in training and development.	Like management activities, and therefore choose combined study programmes such as industrial engineering and often invest in an MBA degree on top.
Love regular working hours and an everyday routine.	Find detachments abroad, consultancy work and a variety of projects in general exciting.

You can see from this list that extroverts can also find interesting careers in the apparently 'introvert territory' of the engineering profession that fit well with their personality type – without having to make too much of an effort.

Introvert territory 3: writing for a living

> THE DIFFERENCE BETWEEN THE RIGHT WORD AND THE ALMOST RIGHT WORD IS THE DIFFERENCE BETWEEN LIGHTNING AND A LIGHTNING BUG.
>
> *MARK TWAIN (LETTER TO GEORGE BAINTON, 1888)*

Writing is really an introspective activity: it only works if the writer thinks first and then gives his thoughts an externally visible form and structure. In addition, writing is an activity which, unlike speaking, is generally practised in solitude. Nevertheless, there are extroverts who love writing and write very successfully. However, they write in a different way – you'll soon realize how different when you read how a successful introvert author and a successful extrovert copywriter handle their favourite activity.

 How I work as an 'introvert'

Dr Matthias Nöllke, author and speaker

As an author, I need introvert and extrovert qualities. The proportion of introvert qualities that goes into creating a book increases more and more in the process. What I mean is, to begin with I seek an exchange with other people, to generate ideas but also to discuss my own thoughts with them. Sometimes they can persuade me out of some idea or another. In many cases it's also very useful for research to meet people in person (but that depends very much on the book project). However, the trend is unmistakable: there's an increasing progression towards introversion. In other words, discussions and interviews become more concentrated, and I myself am not all that keen to talk about the book in this period. This leads to the somewhat paradoxical effect that I talk a lot more about the book in the early phase, then at the time when I actually know *more* and would have more to say, I also have *less* of a pressing need to express it orally because by that time I'm writing.

A certain amount of interaction can continue into the writing period, but I do have a 'hard writing phase', sort of between three and six weeks long and ending with the – on-time – submission of the manuscript. At that time I become an 'ultra introvert'. Writing every day. Not wanting to be disturbed. Meeting my volume target. In complete peace and quiet. At this stage, I always prepare a writing schedule for myself. And every time, I fall drastically short of my own targets to start with. I know that will happen and I try to take it into account in my planning, but it's no help at all: first I get behind, I panic a bit, but as soon as I have half the manuscript together the book almost writes itself. It has been known for me to submit before the deadline although I started out trailing.

And that means daily, disciplined and lone work in the 'hard writing phase'. By the way, I always look at what I wrote the day before the following morning, to get back into it and get up speed for the new text, but also for revision. It's not all that uncommon for me to rewrite whole texts and sometimes end up with a volume for the day of minus three pages (five deleted, two written).

I don't really have fixed writing rituals. Tea helps me to write, but otherwise there's nothing I could think of to mention. A lot of ideas, ways to express things, come to me when I'm on the move, on the way to the office or even early in the morning before I get up. Even in the 'hard writing phase'. So I should be ready to take notes at any time. But I'm not always.

 ## How I work as an 'extrovert'

Lilian Kura alias @textzicke, advertising copywriter, editor, blogger

When I get into the office of a morning, I check all the accumulated emails and log on to Twitter etc., while chatting to my colleague and eating porridge. I start work 20 minutes later: copywriting, discussing, drafting, editing, proof reading.

In all these activities, I find myself in a state of permanent sharing and getting feedback both on-line and off-line – preferably on Twitter and texttreff, my 'network of female wordsmiths'. If I can't get my head round an idea, if I have a question (or an answer) or have to get a thought off my chest, my followers and network partners are sparring partners, knowledge base and agony aunts all in one. The topics I'm working on, some of them pretty specific, are widely known as a result.

Anyone who discovers my writing through Twitter and so on also gets an unvarnished look at the woman behind it. Anyone who can't deal with my, err ... um, forthright tone is hardly likely to give me work. So clients who end up with me by these channels fit like the proverbial lock with the proverbial key ... but enough of that. Could there possibly be a better positioning tool?

By the way, we nearly always cook together at lunchtime in our office. I regularly chuck the photographed results under the noses of my poor, drooling horde of followers to whet their appetites at hashtag #Gourmetbüro. And what happened? A best-selling cookbook author who's also on Twitter noticed me and we are now working out ideas for a collaboration.

Yes, but ... How in heaven's name do you get any work done in between all this communication?

Well. You probably need to be me to thrive on it that much. The constant, very frank and sometimes pretty cheeky communication with so many people mainly gives me a sense of security: there are people there who can stand me. Someone will always be able to give the right advice, there will be somewhere for me to get friction and test myself, I'm never alone. Of course that takes a certain amount of time and makes me highly transparent in the social web. You can think what you like about it. In my case, however, it mainly seems to fuel the synapses; I simply couldn't imagine working without my virtual open plan office any more. I'm much more creative, significantly more effective as a creature who's '360° open' – and in an even better mood than I generally am in any case.

(Oh dear. I've just realized the conclusion readers are bound to draw here: *'What a terrible! stressful! person!'* So I'd like to state here that I'm also very good at sitting still and listening. And at reading. And at having serious discussions. Honestly! ☺)

You can see very clearly from the contrast between these two professionals where typical differences arise in the production of written material: the extrovert copywriter needs contact and stimulation while writing, she is in her 'open plan office' online and off-line, she enjoys cooking with colleagues in the break. She has also chosen a writing profession where she is engaged in a variety of projects.

The introvert author, on the other hand, withdraws more and more in the course of his large-scale book project and reduces the proportion of his oral communication to concentrate entirely on writing and thinking. To produce quality work, he needs an environment that offers as little stimulation as possible, while his extrovert colleague gets her ideas from interaction and activity.

Here is a summary of the factors that help extroverts to write – I have added a few things that extrovert writers have told me help them to use their intrinsic characteristics and do alien things.

 Writing for extroverts: survival tips

- Be with people: in a shared office, in a cafe – this will energize extroverts and stimulate ideas.
- If that isn't possible, have the radio or television on.
- Make you get remote interaction: in social media, by phone.
- Incorporate new ideas, activities and impressions into the daily grind: eat with others, meet friends, go to an exhibition or event.
- Don't work for too long a stretch; it's better to take a break for some exercise or a bit of shopping.
- Even at times of high pressure it's a good idea to switch between several texts or sections of a bigger text.
- Remember how/important/exciting/influential/new the end product of the writing will be (this is the same as the final tip for scientists above – and it's just as valid here).

The introvert in 'extrovert territory'

Typical extrovert territories go 'from the outside to the inside' and therefore have a lot to do with turning towards the outside world and with having an impact within it: with pragmatic action and enthusiastic, hands-on intervention, with action under pressure and risk, with the search for new territories even where a great deal of effort is required and with swift reactions.

Such areas can also be attractive to introverts under certain circumstances. If, for example, shaping the world around you according to your own ideas is of interest, if what you like best is contact with people, if you have a special reason for wanting to change the world with a special case, even as an introvert you may decide on fields where you would mostly expect to find extroverts.

Just two examples are given here – for two reasons: First, I explored the work of introverts in extrovert territories in depth in Loehken (2014). Secondly, you will find a separate chapter (Chapter 7) on a major 'classic' extrovert territory, namely selling, including tips for introvert sales people.

Extrovert territory 1: politics

I WALK SLOWLY, BUT I NEVER WALK BACKWARD.

ABRAHAM LINCOLN, INTROVERT; US PRESIDENT 1861–1865

Politicians' personalities play a crucial role in their electability. If you want to be successful at municipal, regional or national level you will be subject to particular scrutiny as a person. Every election demonstrates this afresh, regardless of whether it's for parliament or the local town council. That makes it all the more important to be in harmony with yourself if you want to pursue this calling; it's hard enough work to start with.

Political roles in particular are often associated with extrovert characteristics: assertiveness, the striving for power, constant public presence and many, many speeches, not to mention strategic networking and constantly shaking hands with innumerable people who edge up to you frequently and up close: it reeks of extroversion. However, it isn't quite like that (there are parallels with successful managers, see above). Quite a number of extremely successful people in the political limelight are introverts. Even in the USA, a country with highly extrovert political (and other) communication, introverts such as Hillary Rodham Clinton, Al Gore and Barack Obama have risen to top offices. In Germany, there is currently have an introvert head of government in Angela Merkel, while the Green opposition elected Katrin Göring-Eckardt as its lead candidate for the Federal government elections in 2013; she is Vice-President of the Bundestag and another introvert.

Anyone who goes into politics becomes more and more of a public persona as his or her career progresses: people get close to office-holders and also use them as projection screens, figures to demonize or idealize. It takes something for an introvert to be able to put up with that all the time.

 Key idea

Anyone who goes into politics becomes more and more of a public persona as his or her career progresses.

Likewise, however, a political personality also needs to have the desire to help shape society in accordance with their own ideas, persistently and with a high frustration threshold. Important skills are facilitation, discussion and negotiating, all of which introverts do very well. Furthermore, they convey an impression of confidence, particularly in difficult times, with characteristics such as caution, analytical thinking and calm. Greece and Italy are two countries that placed introverts – Lukas Papademos and Mario Monti – at the heads of their governments during the great crisis at the end of 2011; that's clearly no coincidence.

I developed the tips below at a time when I was particularly involved in working with municipal executives. If you're an introvert and want to work in politics I hope one or two of these ideas will help you.

Here, too, the focus is on communication – in other words, I'm not talking about the craft of politics. You'll have that at your fingertips if it's your vocation.

 The introvert in politics: use intrinsics – do alien things

Use intrinsics:

- Think about how you want to organize your work in the light of your personality and the way you carry out your role. You want to be credible in the true sense of the word.

- Use introvert strengths such as calm, solidity, concentration, analytical thinking – they will create valuable trust and enable you to communicate authentically.

- Use the strengths of listening and empathy to find out what drives the people around you.

- Create and keep a small group of people you trust among your family, friends and colleagues, people you can depend on who will keep their mouths shut about your personal life.

- Exchange views with individuals and cultivate the art of personal conversation. Keep the people you want to be in touch with clearly in your mind – particularly when a lot of other people and appointments are making claims on your time.

- Perseverance and inner independence are important strengths in politics. Find allies and supporters for projects dear to your heart.

- It's fine to be a person of few words. But do say enough and be as clear as possible in your words. Otherwise, your calmness will easily give the impression of unpredictability or lack of transparency – which doesn't inspire confidence.

- Find your personal style for public appearances. Work on it. If Barack Obama were to act in the same backslapping, downhome way as his Democratic predecessor Bill Clinton, people would find that quite amusing and fake.

- Use your caution to protect yourself against attacks, manoeuvring and unnecessary conflicts.

Do alien things:

- For the sake of your energy levels, make sure you get regular rest periods – particularly when you think you've no time for them. Sometimes it may be just a few stolen minutes in the cloakroom.

- Make yourself a personal life that compensates for the enormous energy you use in your profession and gives you a dependable base with human warmth. Look after it and take enough time for it.

- Get the support of an experienced coach as an external sparring partner. Some experience in political life and absolute trustworthiness are more important in the selection of this person than certificates.

- Find at least one sport and/or relaxation technique that suits you (Chapter 5 may help you here). Occasional distance is inestimably important and is rarely created by the mind alone (sport will also help you to stay healthy and cope effectively with all those meals on public occasions).

- Learn the signals of status communication (on this point, see Chapter 7). There are status signals that are ideally suited to authentic quiet communication. Most experienced introvert politicians know them and use them.

- Avoid such situations by shopping elsewhere – but don't get annoyed. It's part of the job.

- Don't take it personally when people constantly pass comments on your actions and words. In public office, you are a projection screen. Many people will think about you and transfer characteristics and sympathies (or antipathies) to you. Quite a few will even try to penetrate your private life: one of the senior municipal administrators I worked with told me that he couldn't even go shopping without total strangers commenting on the brand of yoghurt he selected.

- Learn in good time how to handle media representatives (including difficult ones) and in particular principles of crisis communication so that you're prepared if an incident arises.

- In taxing times always remember why you are in politics and what you want to change.

- Keep and cultivate your sense of humour. It will stand you in good stead when the going gets tough.

Extrovert territory 2: education

A TEACHER AFFECTS ETERNITY; HE CAN NEVER TELL WHERE HIS INFLUENCE STOPS.

HENRY ADAMS

In the next chapter you will find out how to communicate with introvert and extrovert learners. This is both an important and a challenging task for teachers, trainers and other educators. But what if you yourself are introverted and you want to do a job that's important to you as effectively as possible? Teaching is intensive work at schools, universities and institutes, in seminars and training courses – and it can become a strain even if you love contact with people. Constantly dealing actively with groups, being accessible most of the time for very different people (students, parents, colleagues, customers), constantly switching from one thing to the next and rarely having the opportunity to be alone can take its toll.

Grammar school teacher and author[29] Sabine Grotehusmann tells us how to practise 'quiet' elements in everyday school life.

 ## Conflict with expectations: safeguarding quality and health!

Sabine Grotehusmann, Grammar school teacher, trainer and author

To be in a school means to be constantly responding: in lessons to contributions from pupils or disruptions of the lesson, in breaks to questions from colleagues, pupils or the school management team, and to parents who send e-mails or who turn up at the school unannounced. There is an expectation from all quarters that a teacher has to react immediately, which makes it a particular strain for those parts of me that are highly introvert.

So even as a centrovert I need quiet times to get myself together and handle my school day as calmly as possible. Over the years, I've acquired strategies in three different areas:

1. **Protect your voice:** Talking all the time is exhausting and takes a lot of energy. I end periods of quiet work, pair work and group work with a sound signal (e.g. a bell on the table). I chalk up the names of disruptive pupils on the blackboard when they misbehave in class. If they do it a second time they automatically get a written exercise to do which I note down on the board right at the start of the class.

   I often let pupils take on parts of the teacher's role. For example, I work a lot with tandem forms, where the pupils ask each other questions and check and correct the answers.

2. **Move out of the attentiveness zone during classes:** I schedule a quiet working period in every lesson in which I can do my admin work (e.g. make entries in the register) or sit at the back of the class for a short while and recuperate.

   I use extrovert pupils in particular as assistants. My assistant is responsible for the technology (OHP, CD player, possibly a projector), distributes worksheets, asks pupils to answer. The longer I know a class, the more tasks I delegate to my assistant (this method works best with ten to twelve-year-olds).

   In all my classes, every pupil gives one presentation a year. The pupils learn strict feedback rules for these. The presentations and subsequent discussions need a bit of support from me at first, but it gets less with everyone. I can primarily take the role of the observer.

3. **During breaks:** Most so-called breaks are filled with discussions with colleagues, photocopying, talking to pupils or supervising. The word 'break' is a misnomer. I regularly treat myself to a real break by staying in the classroom, closing the door and enjoying the quiet there.

4. **Avoid time pressure:** I don't communicate with parents by e-mail and talk to them on the phone by appointment only. There are several reasons for that. Firstly, a lot of parents fire off an e-mail straight away if something annoys them. They would neither write a letter nor make an appointment with me at the school about the issue. A quick e-mail is often just letting off steam. It's up to me whether I accept being burdened by these emotions all the time and whether I react to them.

   I don't allow myself to worry about emotional e-mails or to be pressured into a quick reaction. Naturally, I'm available to talk to parents, but only by prior appointment. Then I talk to them at school (for example at a surgery hour) or on the phone, but only with the phone number withheld.

Experience has shown that these discussions are much more focused and have a much more satisfactory outcome for all parties than a hasty exchange of e-mails.

Energy management in particular can prove slightly problematic for quiet educators. As a person with a high level of introversion I made it a policy to learn how to travel for speaking and training engagements in a way that allows me not to run my batteries too flat while I do the work I love. Here are my tips for training combined with travel.[30]

 ## Tips for combining introvert training and travel

- Complete your preparations before you travel, with a decent time buffer and with a guide to the place and the agenda for the venue to save yourself time pressure and uncertainties. You will demonstrate reliability and respect for your clients if you don't arrive at the last minute not knowing what has to be done when. If you can, choose the means of transport you like best.

- Be at the venue in good time. That, too, will spare the energies of both yourself and your client – and you'll have time to deal with technical and organizational problems or difficulties with the room. Things can happen that are beyond your wildest imaginings ...

- Be sparing with extra commitments during an assignment. Meet up with contacts on training days either at lunchtime or in the evening – but at both times only in emergencies. If necessary, add on half a day or a whole day; that way you'll be able to explore the town or the area a little bit after the presentation or the training session.

- You can build good relationships with your participants even if you don't eat with them at lunchtime or go out with them in the evening. Although I do that occasionally, I don't make a habit of it.

- If possible, use hotel accommodation even if you could stay with friends. A room where you don't feel obliged to communicate will do you good. So make sure you have opportunities to withdraw.

- Always have earplugs and/or noise-suppressing headphones in your luggage. That way, you will be safer from over-stimulation and insomnia.

- Take exercise to clear your head. Go for a walk around the area, or do strength training exercises or yoga in the hotel. Don't be under pressure to perform – your teaching role is your performance.

- Concentrate if possible on your training role – it takes a lot out of you to write book chapters or academic articles in the evening on top. Not a word of what you will read between the two covers of this book was written in a hotel room.

- Find out the frequency of events that allows you to work well and also regenerate. You owe that to yourself and also to your clients. What you can 'carry' differs from person to person and also depends on the type of assignment. I myself, for example, follow a rule of thumb of one trip per week and am flexible about the odd exception.

You've seen in this section how people fill very different areas with 'their own thing' and as a result achieve a very special performance with their own personality and voice. It is a good thing that introverts and extroverts keep turning up in areas that actually don't appear perfect for their personality type. Introversion and extroversion mould our characters, but they're not a straitjacket. Projects shared between introverts and extroverts and a certain amount of mixing can be very productive. The differences may give us a particular perspective on certain aspects – and thereby reveal particular ways to solve problems and create innovations.

That brings us to the most important part of this section: the question of how you yourself live to the full in those areas of your life that are important to you personally. If you answer only one question in the entire book, it should be this one. It indicates a way to start creating your own 'third level'.

How do you live your life?

First of all, go back to Chapter 1 where you looked at your own personality type in detail. What was your answer to question 4 in your initial assessment? Note it down again here:

Overview of my priorities – beyond my personality (key question: what is important to me – so important that I even do things which don't necessarily go with my introversion or extroversion?)

And now the real question: How can you live up to these priorities in such a way as to use your strengths and capabilities while at the same time coping as effectively as possible with the 'unnatural' aspects?

If you have problems answering this, there are several ways for you to 'track yourself down'. One possibility is a Reiss motivation profile.[31] I myself work with this method often, and I like it: firstly, it is scientifically based and is evidently particularly effective in helping my clients to get closer to their individual personal idea of meaning. If you prefer to read, I recommend you to use the books by Beck (2004) and Scheuermann (2013a).

 Key points in brief

1. The search for your highly individual sense of meaning in life can take you to areas that are well suited to your own personality type – but also to areas that are more tailored to others.

2. That's no problem, because flexibility is a human characteristic and people can do very well even in environments and jobs that are 'not natural' to them if they find it important.

3. Extroverts can perform brilliantly in introvert territories and vice versa, provided they use their own strengths and identify strategies for compensating effectively with aspects of their work that prove a strain. Clever energy management is particularly important here.

4. Typical 'introvert territories', for instance, are science, engineering and professional writing. Examples of typical extrovert territories are politics, education and also sales, which is dealt with separately in Chapter 7.

5. Introversion and extroversion mould our characters, but they're not a straitjacket. They may well give us a particular perspective on certain things – and therefore particular approaches to thinking and problem-solving.

4.
A chapter just for centroverts (finally!)

THEY KNOW WHEN TO SPEAK UP AND WHEN TO SHUT UP, WHEN TO INSPECT
AND WHEN TO RESPOND, WHEN TO PUSH AND WHEN TO HOLDBACK.

DANIEL PINK (2013B)

Have you noticed the gaping hole right in the middle between the distinctions we have been making between introverts and extroverts? One personality type has not yet come up for discussion. Centroverts (often called ambiverts by psychologists) deserve our attention. (The term 'centrovert' was coined in Zack (2012).)

People are described as centroverts (or ambiverts) if they have roughly the same ratio of introvert and extrovert characteristics. In the introvert/extrovert test (see Appendix) a centrovert would score equally on introvert/extrovert traits, with a maximum of two statements more on either side. Personalities are also considered to be centrovert if they have only a few pronounced characteristics.

Oddly enough, centroverts are almost always mentioned in any discussion of introversion and extroversion because they illustrate how the extremes are not poles apart but two ends of a continuous scale. However, centroverts get little attention in their own right and are rarely discussed. As in other areas of life, the middle seems to be unspectacular. Well, there's nothing to talk about. Or is this true?

Neglect of centroverts is unjustified on several grounds. Most people are moderate introverts, moderate extroverts – or even centroverts. Moreover, centroverts have much to offer from their balanced position.

Although centroverts are not the focus of the book, this chapter is nevertheless dedicated to them. You will also find a special section on centroverts in Chapter 6 on selling as this is a field in which they excel, but where they have until now never attracted much attention. Luckily, that is changing!

However, we won't explore individual strengths and hurdles for the centroverts in this chapter. Their natural position is in the middle – and this unassuming, less prominent position on the introvert–extrovert spectrum is anything but a disadvantage. On the contrary, it provides for agilityand stability in equal measure.

Centroverts also have an advantage compared to introverts: where introvert personalities battle with overstimulation, centroverts can process more impressions without becoming irritable or tired – although not as many as extroverts. However, they need less withdrawal time and are basically less sensitive to external stimuli than introverts. (I will leave out here the characteristic of hypersensitivity which can also lead to mild overstimulation. In my view, the best book on this topic is Aron (2005).)

Grant (2013a) describes the advantages of the centrovert position over extroverts: 'There may be a psychophysical basis for the greater flexibility seen in the behaviour of ambiverts compared to extroverts.' In terms of neocortical arousal, centroverts tend to operate near the optimal level, whereas extroverts tend to be chronically understimulated (Eysenck 1971, Little and Joseph 2007). To avoid boredom and maintain engagement, extroverts regularly seek out stimulation and social attention. Centroverts by contrast can devote greater time to listening without facing the risk of understimulation.

! Key idea

Compared to extroverts, centroverts are less easily understimulated. Compared to introverts they are less easily overstimulated.

There is more variability and flexibility in the middle of the scale: a centrovert might sometimes behave like an introvert and sometimes like an extrovert, and feels most comfortable when life includes both 'loud' and 'quiet' phases, i.e. time alone and time in company.

The art of centrovert living therefore has to do with variety, compromise and balance. Centroverts tend less to the recklessness, distraction or impatience seen in extroverts when they are bored or forced to be inactive. On the other hand, they also have less of a battle with passivity, flight and contact avoidance, which become hurdles for introverts because of too much external stimulation. Above all, however, centroverts usually get on very well with both the other personality types. As they do not themselves tend towards any particular direction, they find it easier to get on with both introverts and extroverts who are either side of them on the spectrum: from the middle, the differences can be approached in a relatively relaxed manner. They find their pronounced introvert or extrovert fellows less 'strange' than extroverts or introverts find each other sitting as they do at each end of the spectrum.

! Key idea

The centrovert position in the middle of the scale is a good place for understanding both introverts and extroverts.

Sitting as they do in the middle of the scale, centroverts are well equipped to understand many people and are in an ideal starting position for all forms of communication, such as diplomacy, mediation and negotiation.

However, the central position isn't always predictable. If you are a centrovert and you find yourself torn between your need for being alone and your need for being in company, if you sometimes draw energy from being together with others and sometimes from being in quiet contemplation, it is important for you to think about this a bit more. The following task will help you to get closer to undertstanding your own needs, which might be more easily identified in introverts and extroverts because of their biological differences.

 ## Overview: your centrovert position

1. **a.** Which situations provide you with energy?

b. What do you conclude from this in terms of your everyday life?

2. When do you tend to be more overstimulated and when more understimulated?

More overstimulated	More understimulated	Conclusions

3. When is safety or security particularly important for you?

4. When are incentives and reward particularly important for you?

5. What conclusion do you draw from this in terms of your everyday life?

If you are a centrovert, you should enjoy the changes brought by different activities and phases. Make sure that the introvert and extrovert phases form a ratio appropriate to you. And take pleasure in your gift of having a heart and mind capable of a good understanding of both introverts and extroverts. Enjoy discovering your personal middle position!

Key points in brief

1. There are prejudices and stereotypes which characterise the image we have of introvert and extrovert personalities. The true picture is much more complicated – and surprising. The differences between 'introverts' and 'extroverts' may be manifested in different ways to what you would normally expect.

2. Neither extroversion nor introversion is good or bad, better or worse. Both personality types are a mixture of advantages and disadvantages, strengths and weaknesses.

3. As personalities in the middle of the introvert–extrovert spectrum, centroverts have some advantages which allow them both flexibility and stability simultaneously.

4. Nevertheless, in this middle and less specific position they are still faced with the task of spelling out their own individual and social needs for themselves.

PART II

Differences between introverts and extroverts in practice

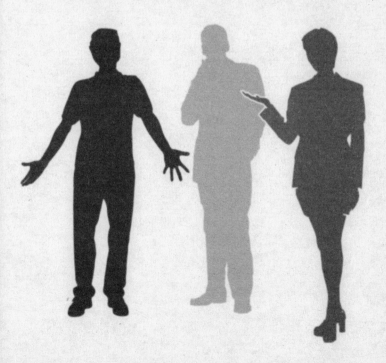

5.
Same results – different methods

The second part of this book focuses on the practical side. Typical areas of everyday life are showcased here to illustrate how introverts and extroverts handle themselves and deal with each other, how they benefit mutually and do their 'own thing' while understanding the different ways of the other personality type. I deliberately chose highly diverse areas in order to demonstrate that the *petit différence* makes its presence felt everywhere.

This section addresses first of all how you can do certain things in a way that suits your individual personality and translate them into action and impact.

That woman drives me mad!

Ellie has made it her New Year's resolution to get more exercise. Partly so that she can get into her jeans again, but also to improve her quality of life – reduce stress, breathe better, calm down.

Yoga looks ideal. A lot of her friends do it, Ellie wants to book a course and practise regularly on her own at home. Maybe she can even add a bit of meditation. Be more aware of what she eats. Attain inner peace.

Two weeks later, Ellie gives up. 'Attain inner peace? The peace of the grave more like!' she cries. 'Wisdom comes with a price tag of absolute boredom!'

She can tolerate the course because she goes there with two friends and looks forward to seeing them (and in particular to a nice cup of coffee together afterwards). But the yoga instructor gets on her nerves ever so slightly. Ellie says: 'Phenomenally agile, and she knows her stuff – but a voice like a sat-nav. Soooo gentle and monotonous ... sometimes

I'd like to give her a shake just to see if it puts a bit more energy into the sing-song. Somehow that woman drives me wild. I'm discovering my worst side. Inner peace is a long way off ...'

However, it's practising on her own at home that finally seals yoga's fate. I quote Ellie verbatim: 'It's the most boring sport I've ever encountered. Breeeathe. Streeeetch – I may as well be buried alive. I'd rather stay excitable, then at least I'll know I'm still alive!'

You've probably had experiences like Ellie's yourself. You want to do yourself some good, improve, pursue a new goal – and after a while the main thing you notice is the effort it takes. It's as if you were wearing a poorly-fitting, uncomfortable, one-size garment that doesn't fit you. Choosing clothing is a good metaphor here: we should pursue goals in the same way as we choose our clothing, to suit our type and activities, and should achieve them in a way that matches our personalities. Made-to-measure, not one-size-fits-all!

 Key idea

The great skill is to pursue goals in a way that suits your own personality.

Your character traits as an introvert or extrovert personality, your strengths and needs have very tangible effects on how you live your life. All these things have a major influence on what costs you a lot of energy and what you find easy, what does you good and what you do reluctantly – if you actually do it at all. Look at Ellie.

In this chapter we will look at how you can lead your everyday life as either an introvert or extrovert in the way that's best suited to you. The two main areas we will look at are what physical exercise is best for you, and how you learn best – understanding this will help you, whether you are introvert or extrovert, be successful in your own way. Both sport and learning are important aspects of life, irrespective of whether you are introvert or extrovert. These two examples are intended to encourage you to do something that's supposed to be good for you in *your own way* as an introvert or extrovert, and to make it accessible to both extroverts and introverts. The rewards will be a better quality of life for less effort – and a tailored approach to achieving goals in your very own, individual (introvert or extrovert) way.

Goal 1: Physical exercise

We all agree that exercise does us good – introvert or extrovert, sick or healthy, young or old. Physical activity ensures a good supply of oxygen and stimulates the metabolism, gives us working muscles, flexible tendons and strong bones. It makes us recover from illness faster and slows down the aging process. A leaner, stronger, more agile, healthier body beckons at the end (this is the reward aspect for extroverts!). So far, so good. Let's exercise!

However, Ellie's frustrating experience at the beginning of the chapter shows that we can make a good decision in principle and still fall down on its implementation. Not necessarily because we lack the willpower, but because our approach to reaching our goals is inappropriate for us. Ellie wants to reduce stress and become more balanced – but as an extrovert she needs to do something different from an introvert if she is to be successful. If she finds a sport that suits her she'll find it much easier to stick to, for two reasons: firstly, Ellie will no longer have to summon up an inordinate amount of willpower in order to make herself do something she doesn't actually enjoy. Secondly, a sport like yoga (or at least the very calm type with little external stimulation) will not energize Ellie in the long run but will drain her energy, because it takes her out of the comfort zone where she can charge her batteries. Instead, she's investing in an unsuitable activity that is costing her energy, which will prove frustrating in the long run.

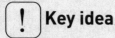

! Key idea

Sport can serve very different purposes: physically, it improves endurance or strength, socially it makes us part of a team. It can also be a way to find a balance between body and spirit.

So let's ask ourselves what it is about sport that is beneficial to extroverts and introverts. To begin with, in terms of personal fitness the goals are the same. I will use a very simple overview here of the criteria that are central to most people's interest in sport. From the physical point of view, sport is aimed at improving *endurance* by making the body perform over a longer period of time. A second physical aspect is the increase in physical *strength* (and sometimes muscle mass) which is achieved by exerting muscles in a targeted way. (Note, agility and flexibility are excluded here.)

Then, sport has a *social* function: we meet friends and belong to teams when we do it. Finally, sport influences the *interaction of body and spirit*. This element includes stress reduction, for example, which was one of the goals Ellie had in mind.

The following sections reveal how introverts and extroverts achieve these four goals in their own ways, with what types of sport and by what methods.

Sport for extroverts

Extroverts draw energy from interaction with their environment and from stimulation by various interesting sensory impressions. By taking yoga, an extrovert like Ellie is cutting herself off from these sources of energy. What should she do?

The following overview is based on the four described goals that sport may have and shows extroverts what kind of exercise matches their needs best in the different categories.

1. Endurance

Many extroverts have problems with the fact that endurance sport requires you to repeat the same action over a long period – often with no visible result (reward). The consequences are under-stimulation, boredom and frustration.

Strategies:

- Courses (join a club, go to a gym) where you can train along with other people, adding a social dimension.Outdoor activities with friends or in a club: running, walking, rambling, Alpine skiing, cycling tours. I don't recommend long-distance swimming as it's a pretty lonely activity. However, there is a small group of extroverts who swear by it. Maybe because it's a step up from meditation?

- Sports with a fun factor and variety: for example, in-line skating, boxing, circuit training or spinning.

- Competitive sports at a suitable level: races, tournaments, charity events, occasionally organizing a sports day with friends, children or colleagues, including prizes.

- Set goals that challenge you more than the sport itself – that provide stimulation and rewards. For example, time your running to measure progress, or enter a competition after a while in training.

2. Strength

With muscle training, too, extroverts soon run the risk of monotony with the attendant frustration and boredom.

Strategies:

- Train a few times a week just for a short time, around 15 to 20 minutes, and focus on one muscle group – bodyweight exercise programmes are available for home use or when travelling. If you know little or nothing about muscle training, your best bet is to start with a course or a period with a fitness trainer (yes, safety is sometimes important even for extroverts!).

- Attend strength-building courses – that gives you a regular routine and people to talk to.

- If possible, go to the gym with others or arrange to meet people there. Look for a gym with a lively atmosphere and music and people to your own taste. It's a good idea to pick a fairly large complex offering a lot of training options.

- Set concrete goals to allow you a reward effect. For example, track the size of certain body parts such as your arms or your stomach, increase the repetitions of certain exercises in a targeted way, etc.

- Make sure you get variety, seek challenges and try out new things – you've guessed it: swinging dumbbells every week probably won't work for you. So get a personal trainer to really push you. Or start a strength team together with friends and take turns from week to week at being responsible for the strength building programme.

3. Teams

Extroverts love meeting different people and doing sport together with them. They're absolutely in their element in team sports, which are often competitive and naturally only work when people do them together.

Strategies:

- Just choose whatever you prefer: football, handball, basketball, American football, volleyball, hockey or ice hockey, baseball – they're all fine. Or go bowling with friends and colleagues or at a club, etc.

- Come dancing! You can do it alone as part of a crowd, as a couple, in larger groups, and it almost always takes place in a communal setting. In other words, there are other people around – and that gives your exercise a stage. What's more, there's a huge choice of styles from the rumba to the Harlem Shake. And last but not least: the music is an ideal extrovert stimulus to accompany exercise.

4. The relationship between body and spirit

Regular strength and endurance exercise is enough to keep many extroverts on track. There's a risk of under-stimulation with very calm, contemplative sports that are aimed at achieving a balance of body and spirit. An extrovert normally achieves his own balance by raising his energy level a little and does so together with other people.

Strategies:

- In this case as well, give preference to courses and activities involving other people, for example tai chi or Pilates.
- If it has to be yoga, pick an energetic, dynamic type among the various schools, for example Ashtanga or Kundalini yoga.

Try out martial arts such as karate, judo, aikido, tae-kwon-do or kick-boxing: these involve a high level of mental training and also teach self-control and how to regulate your use of energy – perfect! Now you as an extrovert should be able to find your own personal smorgasbord of incentives to exercise at the end of this chapter – and make a choice that you enjoy and makes it possible for you to stick to it. Ellie managed to do it:

 ## That wakes the tiger in me!

Ellie now knows that classic Hatha yoga, which she had happened on by chance, was a crazy idea for her. 'I had picked something that absolutely wasn't for me – neither the exercise nor the people were my type,' she says.

Ellie has now found another way to acquire the knowledge of Eastern gurus and keep fit: for several months now she's been going to karate twice a week with her best friend.

'It's dynamic! I'm learning to react fast. I'm getting to know my body and my inner strength together. And now I can fight! That gives me a sense of power generally: I radiate the fact that I can defend myself. So instead of being driven wild, I've discovered the wild animal in myself: a strong, fast tiger!'

Sport for introverts

 Football? Never!

Imre is ten years old. Almost all his classmates are members of the football club in the little town where he lives with his parents. But Imre can't be bothered with football. He doesn't like falling over, doesn't like to fight for the ball and is half-hearted in attacking to get it.

As a youngster, Imre's father loved playing soccer and wants his son to discover the sport for himself.

He sometimes wonders if there's something wrong with Imre.

But football is pretty stressful for a young introvert like Imre. Consciously or unconsciously, boys in particular are often expected to pursue competitive team sports. The other lads are there, you learn to assert yourself and still be a team player – and a successful footballer is considered cool. There's some consolation for all parents whose kids won't play along: I found out in the case of my own son that there are always other options if, despite Dad's full support, football training is not a fun, relaxing activity but a real strain.

Introverts draw their energy from a quiet environment without a lot of stimulation, and they love safety and predictability – including in sports. Football delivers exactly the opposite: it's noisy, unpredictable and full of physical harassment (at least from the introvert's point of view). Although there are very successful introvert footballers (Cacau, Michael Ballack), many introverts prefer other sports for that reason.

As for the section for extroverts, the following overview is based on the four described goals that sport may have. It shows introverts how they can incorporate physical exercise 'naturally' into their lives in a way they will enjoy.

1. Endurance

Like team sports for extroverts, endurance sport is a natural biotope for introverts. Endurance training is an excellent opportunity for introverts to enjoy time alone. That way, exercise serves not only the purpose of training for the heart and circulatory system, but also of regrouping after a challenge.

Strategies:

- Enjoy outdoor activities, with one other person or with good friends: rambling, walking, running, cycling, cross-country skiing, swimming, rowing or in-line skating (on unfamiliar paths take your mobile phone (with GPS?) with you for a sense of safety).

- Indoor endurance sports are suitable, either at home – home trainers and steppers work well for many introverts – or in the gym. Opt for small gyms with a quiet atmosphere if you have the choice. If not, use earplugs or headphones as required. Most endurance equipment also allows you to read quite easily (treadmills are the explicit exception here).

- At stressful times, use the endurance training deliberately to relax and don't build up additional pressure to perform. Your pulse doesn't have to race for you to benefit from exercise.

2. Strength

Strength training can also take the form of quiet time out. Of particular interest to introverts is the fact that you can feel efficient muscles supplying energy and a sense of well-being. And here's a message for senior-citizen introverts with a high need for safety: muscle training is an excellent way of preventing osteoporosis and broken bones – providing an assurance of good mobility until an advanced age, among other things.

Strategies:

- Strength training can also be practised very easily on your own at home or in the gym – the same applies for introverts as for the extroverts: get information and start if possible with a course or one or two hours with a fitness trainer before you go it alone. There are plenty of programmes and good books.

- Against this background, there are many opportunities for training on your own: for example Pilates, bodyweight exercises, dumbbell and theraband training. An added possibility, particularly at the gym, is to use the equipment room. Strength training – again if necessary with earplugs or headphones – can also become valuable time alone there.

3. Teams

Introverts also like doing sports together with other people – but often in a different way from the extroverts among their friends. In most cases they don't enjoy large teams, particularly in the case of contact sports like basketball, handball or football. However, they do enjoy smaller groups where friendships or good conversations can develop through the sporting activity.

Strategies:

- Swimming and athletics can be done in teams – and you do the sport itself on your own. That works for a lot of introverts.
- There are team sports that don't get so up close and personal and involve fairly small groups. Many introverts feel comfortable with those. Examples: volleyball, cricket and baseball.
- Another good exercise for introverts is dancing. You can do it on your own or as a couple. By the way, dancing doesn't just make physical demands on you, but also develops cognitive thinking – that can suit introverts well. Besides, dancing is an activity that extrovert partners generally also enjoy. You just have to agree on the music and the style!

4. The relationship between body and spirit

Like endurance sports, this kind of physical exercise is as attractive to introverts as team sports are to extroverts. When you focus your mind on a series of exercises, your highly active inner life takes you to a good place.

Strategies:

- Consider tai chi, Pilates, aikido and so on. Pilates strengthens the muscles at the same time.

- Nature lovers among the introverts can also benefit from the inner peace that arises from such activities as a quiet walk, sailing, rowing, hill-walking or golf.

- Yoga suits many introverts well, particularly styles with a lot of breathing exercises and an emphasis on inner reflection, e.g. Hatha yoga.

- Last but not least, a little nap from time to time is also a good option for introverts to regenerate and refresh. I practise this 'sport' whenever I can and can warmly recommend it to introverts. There's no better way to recharge your batteries!

 Team? Fine!

Imre now plays table tennis. He already has several friends in the club. He enjoys the presence of a table between him and his opponent in this sport, and he absolutely loves the game.

His father has promised to take him and his four friends from the club to a tournament in the nearest big town next month. He sometimes practises with Imre on the new table tennis table in their garden.

Small steps

Often, the search for the right kind of exercise can take a long time and will also be adjusted to changing needs. Enjoy the freedom to try out different sporting activities and adapt them to your circumstances. Take note of whether the sport is doing you good and giving you energy. As you now know, that's by no means always the case and depends on what energizes you personally. And there are times in your life when gaining energy simply means getting more sleep and maybe doing a bit more exercise. Be good to yourself!

I've just put two and a half years of going to the gym behind me and handed in my notice because it's too far away for me, the background music is too loud and too irritating, and it's too tiring for me to be in a room with a lot of people. At the same time, I have learned so much about strength and endurance in those 30 months that I can now easily go on by myself: I can train every muscle group with a few small pieces of equipment and my bodyweight, and running along the banks of the Rhine is pleasanter than the stepper in any case. I will no doubt have revised my strength and endurance training practices several times by the time I'm 70.

[?] Overview: the right sport for you

Select your key goal (or goals) in pursuing sports. Bearing in mind the information in this chapter, what types of sport do you think are a good fit with your personality and needs?

I want to improve my endurance.   ☐

In this area, these are the sports that appeal to me most:

I want to have more strength and strengthen my muscles.   ☐

I prefer team sports, such as:

I want to take more exercise to achieve a better balance of body and spirit and/or to reduce stress.   ☐

So far, so good. And now down to brass tacks:

Exactly when are you going to start?

Exactly how are you going to start?

Goal 2: Learning

The same applies to learning as to sport: the subject is relevant to us throughout our lives. This chapter adopts a different perspective: it is addressed primarily to those who support others in their learning, such as lecturers and teachers, speakers, trainers and parents.[32] Educators, too, are introverts or extroverts. Although they always have both introverts and extroverts to deal with, they're inclined to see the students themselves and also methods of acquiring knowledge through the lens of their own personalities. An extrovert educator will tend all too readily to communicate for extroverts. This can be a problem ranging from obstructive to irritating for the introvert or extrovert learners in the group (depending on the educator's personality type).

Learning – a privilege and a duty

Introverts and extroverts have a lot in common when they're learning. Studies of language acquisition reveal an important unifying principle: even in digital times, we learn best from people – from real people, not from videos or websites. Ideally, these people are also enthusiastic about the topic they are teaching and understand their subject. Enthusiasm is infectious – and once a learner has caught the bug, acquiring knowledge is easy. Also, the process in itself is valuable for the brain: 'Enthusiasm is the most important fuel for the development of the brain.' says brain researcher Gerald Hüther.[33] If you inspire learners with enthusiasm for a subject you also put a stamp on the way they perceive the world and learn other things (see Brooks, 2011, p. 135). That's why it is a good thing for a teacher or lecturer to know how to use the capabilities of his or her own introvert or extrovert personality to ignite the spark. If you are an educator, you will have already have gained some idea of this in Chapter 1. Enthusiasm itself is an extrovert strength, along with the associated ability to inspire others. However, introverts can also teach in a way that makes students eager to work hard. They are often wonderful at encouraging people.

 Key idea

We only learn something if it's relevant to us.

We find it particularly easy to learn if an educator or a subject touches us, interests us, is fun, surprises us or appears useful in an attractive way – briefly, we process information especially well if someone or something reaches us emotionally. Psychologist Kenneth Dodge sees an important reason for this: emotions provide the energy needed for thinking, structuring and learning (see Dodge, 1991, for further reading on this).

But even if we have a lot in common when learning, introverts and extroverts learn more easily and enjoy it more if the road to knowledge takes their needs and preferences into account. It is therefore an important as well as demanding task for educators to incorporate the *petit différence* into their work so that they reach 100 per cent of the students effectively and not just a maximum of 50 per cent …

It sometimes appears as if extroverts have the edge in learning institutions: they like to speak up and to do so often, make their presence felt in group work and demonstrate a high level of activity overall – all these things please educators. However, these appearances merely show that extroverts are simply more visible and audible than introverts. Closer scrutiny will lead you to entirely different conclusions.

Susan Cain (2011, p. 260) cites a study that shows that extrovert primary school pupils in the USA really are more successful on average than their introvert fellows. Interestingly, however, the scenario switches around at high school and college: introversion is then an advantage and a good indicator of learners' academic prowess. According to the study, introverts receive more scholarships in the USA, have deeper subject knowledge, are better at intelligent problem-solving and are also more frequently to be found among the highly gifted.

It has nothing to do with intelligence – introverts and extroverts don't differ in that respect. However, the described academic success of American introverts has a very great deal to do with their personality traits. Extrovert problem-solvers tend to apply a practical, quick approach and act fast. They are very good at gaining insights and implementing them in practice (Cain, 2011, p. 260). The more abstract and 'academic' the material is intrinsically and in the way it is taught, the less extrovert learners benefit from these strengths. Introverts, on the other hand, also have strengths on their side in the acquisition of complex subject matter. You've already been introduced to these: persistence, conscientiousness, analytical thinking, calmness and concentration are helpful in processing complex matters, sticking to the task when unsatisfactory results are produced and developing unusual approaches.

So how can educators help introverts and extroverts to use their personal traits as effectively as possible to acquire knowledge and develop solutions? That's what the next two sections are all about.

Learning for introverts

Let's use the three key differences from Chapter 1 as our starting point and guide: introverts are turned more inwards, are relatively sensitive to sensory stimulation and are safety-oriented.

1. From the inside outwards

The ideal way for introverts to learn is from the inside outwards, in line with their personality structure: you should feed their minds first, then provide an opportunity to apply the results. Many introverts like to become acquainted with the theory first and the practical aspects afterwards, to watch and listen first before acting themselves.

So if a participant or interviewee doesn't say anything, it isn't an indication of passivity. Just remember that with introverts, more things happen on the inside – as the name suggests.

When faced with difficult tasks and learning materials that require reflection, many – very many – introverts prefer to put something in writing before they talk about solutions and attitudes. They also often score in the academic context in individual, introspective written work, including exams.

So incorporate writing periods systematically if you want to support introverts' learning processes as effectively as possible. For example, writing trainer Ulrike Scheuermann recommends 'thinking by writing' to activate introverted learners (for more about this method see Scheuermann, 2012).

2. Sensitivity to stimuli

Less is more. That's the rule with stimulus-sensitive introverts. When you are in the educator's role, you should avoid over-stimulating your learners. If an introvert has to absorb too much information too quickly he shuts down, so do not provide densely-packed information in quick succession. Change the subject with structured transitions, not abruptly. Also make sure of an introvert-friendly pace. Remember what we said in Chapter 1: introverts have longer neural pathways and therefore longer processing paths in the brain. They sometimes need a little longer to produce a result or a statement, but they mostly deliver solid and well-considered results.

Rituals and regularity are good ways to create space for new knowledge: if people who are easily overstimulated don't have to worry about the time, place, organization and agenda of a learning unit, enough room is available for the learning excursion into the unknown.

If you want to make learners work in groups, it's wiser not to burden stimulus-sensitive introverts with too many social coordination tasks on top of the subject-related work. Individual work or work in pairs (tandems, including consultation before having to make a statement to the whole group) are methods that suit most introverts better than group work with several people. They benefit if they have to deal with no more than one partner in shared learning. Lectures are also an ideal method for most introverts: they can concentrate on the lecturer and the material without having to talk to other people or switch back and forth between processing and implementation.

 Key idea

Methods for introverts: lecture, individual work, pair work.

Help your introvert learners to deal with an excess of information and filter out the important things – that's crucial particularly when learning with on-line resources.

When working in a large group make sure there are some quiet moments in between times, both during lectures and in plenary discussions. Introverts are often hopelessly overstimulated and therefore at a disadvantage in such situations – brainstorming is a perfect example. So create listening rituals and make it clear during the process that listening is just as important as talking. That's also excellent training for the extroverts in your group, by the way. So allow pauses. When you yourself are lecturing, speak slowly enough and not too loud.[34] Don't bombard your audience during every second of your talk. Plan moments where you stop speaking. With this kind of learning-friendly training you will ensure that the material is retained better – including by extroverts. It also benefits your presence as an educator: if you insert pauses and never go off at a gallop you come across as immensely self-assured. Your words will have more weight.

Make sure there are times when the listeners do something on their own, even in plenary sessions – jot down an insight, make a decision, remember a situation. Always make sure that all results are listened to and appreciated, not just those from the hastiest tongues. You'll be amazed at what the quiet ones will produce by way of substantive contributions when they have enough peace to work carefully.

Always make sure that learning is as undisrupted as possible. Noisy discussions, abrupt interruptions of a work phase or an aggressive tone among the learners add up to a disturbing nuisance. Create space for quiet, meticulous work.

3. Safety orientation

Some orientation about the learning environment gives introverts security. Take care to provide the following information in the initial learning phase – for example, at the beginning of a workshop: where can people meet during breaks? Where will lunch be served? When will the papers be available?

Introverts in particular only learn well when they feel protected. That means you should ensure predictable procedures. Don't take anyone unawares by addressing them personally when working with the whole group. Put your foot down on unfair remarks or peer group pressure and ensure an atmosphere of trust. Highlight the fact that errors are not only unavoidable but actually desirable: they are a particularly effective way of learning.

Also offer security in the form of structure and orientation in your communication. Introverts benefit particularly both in lectures and during the process of a learning unit if you structure your material clearly and ensure that the knowledge to be acquired is available in well-organized form. A good guideline is effective because it gives an overview of the whole of the material and at the same time prevents over-stimulation. And it is also an ideal way for analytical thinkers to process the information.

Many introverts need to know exactly what's what with new material and will want much more detail than the average extrovert. They like dealing with complex material and may want more depth. Provide background material and details – but make sure the guideline remains visible and the time frame reasonable. After all, you also have extroverted learners who lose patience easily. If you don't have enough time or knowledge or the other participants' attention is wandering, move the additional information into the break or send it by e-mail. But remember that 'safety and security' applies here too: be reliable and keep your word.

Teaching introverts: a brief overview

1. From the inside outwards

- The sequence: first enable an understanding, then let them apply the knowledge
- Don't misunderstand: quietness also often implies a high level of cerebral activity
- The medium: build writing periods into the learning process

2. Sensitivity to stimuli

- Don't work too fast: leave space and time for assimilation of the material, questions and transitions
- Reduce changes in the environmental stimuli: create rituals and regularity, provide information filters
- Use introvert-friendly formats: lectures, individual work or tandems
- Make sure of pauses, peace and mutual listening

3. Safety orientation

- Take care to provide orientation and establish predictable procedures in the learning environment
- Ensure fairness and an atmosphere of trust, grant licence to make mistakes

- Provide plenty of structure and orientation within the material
- Support complex problem-solving: make allowance for more in-depth explanations within certain limits and if necessary supply additional knowledge later
- Keep your promises

There are already some educators who accommodate the different needs of introverts and extroverts in their groups. As an example, the following report by grammar school teacher Corinna Lammert (an introvert) describes her teaching and methods.

 Developing introverts (and extroverts) in schools: this works!

Corinna Lammert, teacher and motivation trainer

Once I knew about the 'quiet' ones I could no longer continue teaching as I had done before. I now talk to the pupils about the different qualities and needs of introverts and extroverts. After an initial self-assessment, they also gain experience in separate work groups.

And I see clear differences: while every introvert group interacts in its own language (in other words without being exposed to permanent pressure to talk), in the extrovert groups discussions are conducted by many voices. I'm seeing how important it is to offer introvert pupils a variety of possibilities to contribute visibly so that they can discover their specific strengths.

The new learning under the conditions enabled by digital technology makes it possible to incorporate qualities like listening or reflecting actively into the learning process. For example, pupils quietly prepare portfolios or blog posts, work together on texts at a distance on iPads or quietly take part in the class discussion through back channelling.

Learning for extroverts

As you will recall from Chapter 1, extroverts are more turned outwards, they are receptive to sensory stimuli and they love rewards and incentives. Let's look at this more closely: what does that mean for the learning process?

1. From the outside in wards

The ideal road to learning for extroverts is not through the head as for introverts. In line with their personality type, it leads through the senses – from tangible impressions to general insights. Therefore, you should start by providing experiences through the sensory channels and allow extrovert learners to try something out, puzzle over things, improvise a scene, touch something or experiment with something new. New insights can then be deduced from what they have experienced. By using application-orientated access you both channel your extrovert learners' higher level of external activity and use it for the learning process.

 Key idea

Good learning methods for extroverts include group discussion, problem-solving, practical application.

Unlike introverts, extroverts often arrive at structured trains of thought by talking and are also more active in plenary discussions. Talking during the learning process supports their thinking and ensures that the knowledge is anchored in their memories. Although that's often true for introverts as well, it needs to be particularly highlighted for the extroverts.

In addition to the writing periods for introverts, you should therefore always ensure that there is an opportunity for a verbal exchange as well, either with the whole group or in smaller ones, since this is particularly beneficial for the extroverts. There's no harm in occasionally letting the 'quiet' group write and the extrovert group talk if they are doing different exercises.

2. Receptivity to stimuli

You can give extroverts more stimuli when they learn, because they love a variety of impressions. Offer the extroverts in your group a variety of learning formats and periods when there's something going on so that they don't get bored and switch off or seek stimulation by other means (distraction). That doesn't mean offering extroverts more information than introverts. Rather, the art lies in the variation of methods and the selection of channels for accessing knowledge, switching around between listening, watching (pictures, overviews), testing, comparing and discussing. The use of videos and podcasts also arouses interest and therefore stimulates the brains of extrovert learners. If feasible, you can also give introverts and extroverts different exercises here and expose them to different intensities of stimuli.

Another reason for separating introverts and extroverts from time to time is the speed of communication: just as introverts generally dislike an excessively fast pace, many extroverts find a rapid speed pleasant. For example, in a workshop about banking law you could give the extroverts in your group three practical cases to work on (with concrete solutions required), while asking the introverts to summarize the basic legal assumptions as concisely as possible (requiring a high density of processing and meticulous finishing).

Extroverts enjoy working in plenary sessions (where everyone's impressions can be expressed) or in groups. Four to five people is a good size for shared learning in this case. This number is just about small enough to allow the team members to consult on something in the presence of the whole group before presenting it. The best thing about this format, however, is that it enables stimulation-loving extroverts to enjoy social contact in addition to working on the subject matter and to structure their thought processes better by talking.

Extroverts can easily be distracted and led astray from the material when learning with online resources. Like the introverts sitting next to them, they therefore benefit from clear rules and instructions, but for different reasons.

When you work in a large group it's mostly the extroverts who like to speak up. Facilitation is required from you here. After all, you know that listening is as important as talking. And you'll make sure that both introverts and extroverts are heard out of fairness. This creates more stimulation than if only the fast and the bold have their say. And aside from all the introvert-friendly measures such as organized procedures and writing periods, leave time for spontaneity: shared laughter and unexpected outcomes often result. And you will save the extroverts from a lot of boredom in the learning process …

3. Reward orientation

It has now been proved that extroverts learn much better with rewards and incentives, which makes them particularly important to an effective learning process (see the study by Depue and Fue, 2013). If the learner is interested in the subject, working on the material is attractive per se. However, 'dry' and complex subjects (for which many introverts show a higher tolerance) can also be made fascinating by a variety of means.

The most direct way of introducing reward and excitement into the learning group is competition: make teams compete against each other in solving problems. Or drop a hint that a command of the new material will give the learners clear advantages over external competitors: these outsiders may be another project group in the company or a market rival in the case of service providers. In some learning periods, allow people to make discoveries independently and give the group space to develop their own problem-solving approaches. This is also a motivating factor, and is particularly attractive to the extroverts who have no taste for being 'nannied' by rules and structures.

However, the most important thing is to be able to answer the question: what is the value of what I'm learning? In other words, how can I use it in practice, and why is that a good thing? A reference to this 'reward' in tougher, more complex or quieter learning phases helps impatient, extrovert learners to pursue subjects that they find quite difficult to get their heads round.

Teaching extroverts: a brief overview

1. From the outside inwards

- The sequence: first enable experiences through sensory impressions, then make the learners process them
- Divert a high level of external activity into the learning process
- The medium: enable a verbal exchange, possibly in parallel to writing periods for introverts

2. Receptivity to stimuli

- Prevent boredom: take care to use a variety of learning formats and methods, appeal to as many sensory channels as possible
- A dynamic pace is possible
- Place the emphasis on active problem-solving
- Plenary sessions or group work (four to five people)
- Keep distraction within limits with clear rules and instructions, allow spontaneity

3. Reward orientation

- Make the learning process exciting and incorporate competitive elements
- Enable independent discoveries and solutions
- Highlight the value of the material

The educator's problem lies in striking a healthy balance, because a learning group normally consists of introvert *and* extrovert personalities, with whose preferences you are now familiar. You therefore need to combine methods so as to suit both personality types.

In my own seminars, I often separate introverts and extroverts – partly to allow them a pleasant working atmosphere, which will develop more easily among people with similar preferences. Mainly, however, the separation and training helps introverts and extroverts to be able to give each other feedback and thereby flag up a number of blind spots: the introvert group tells the extrovert that she barely let her introvert peer get a word in edgeways in a negotiation. The extrovert group hands the introvert the insight that a problem analysis doesn't equate to a solution and that he's barricaded himself in behind the details. In this manner, the needs of the other personality type become wonderfully transparent and actionable.

 Key idea

Combine teaching methods so that they suit introverts and extroverts equally.

Nevertheless, mixed teams in which introverts and extroverts combine their strengths can be enormously productive. You've seen that in the first part of this book. They can support and enrich one another through their different approaches and preferences in acquiring knowledge as well: diversity live! Try teaching based on introvert–extrovert pairs, which produces an interplay of the reflective and go-getting, persistent and spontaneous approaches – the results are often impressive.

Have the courage to experiment (even if you're an introvert!). The best thing that can happen to an introvert or extrovert learner is to have a committed, open educator – in addition to the freedom to be allowed to make mistakes during the learning process.

A question for educators

How will you develop introverts and extroverts in your groups in a way that works with their personal strengths and preferences? (Go back to the three basic differences described in Chapter 1 for more details if necessary).

1. Which kind of exercises can you use to help introverts (remember, thinking first) in the classroom? And to help extroverts, who in general prefer external activities?

2. What should you consider regarding stimuli, or the lack thereof, for introverts and extroverts?

3. How do orientation and structure benefit introverts? What roles do rewards and competitions play for extroverts?

Key points in brief

Many everyday activities can be mastered more easily and performed more successfully if they are organized in line with the needs and preferences of introverts and extroverts.

1. **Goal 1: Exercise.** Both introverts and extroverts should make sure they get enough exercise. This is best done with sports and routines that match their personality type and take account of the related differences in energy sources and habitual preferences.

2. **Goal 2: Learning.** Extroverts and introverts have different preferences and strengths when learning. Educators can improve and accelerate the acquisition of knowledge if they take these differences into account in their teaching and methods.

6.
Management

 This place is going nowhere fast!

Edward is the managing director of an IT business consultancy. He is particularly successful in his field: Edward is a strong salesman, has excellent industry contacts and has made some bold business decisions that are now paying off. He attaches a lot of importance to intelligent marketing and innovative products and listens closely to his clients. The company is successful.

Nevertheless, there are increasing problems with interpersonal relationships. Edward outlines the situation:

> WE DO HAVE VERY ABLE PEOPLE HERE. BUT SOME OF THEM ARE YOUR STEREOTYPICAL NERDS. VERY CLUED UP – EXCEPT ABOUT PEOPLE. A LOT OF THEM TAKE TOO LONG TO RESPOND TO CUSTOMER ENQUIRIES. AND THEY ARE FOREVER HAVING DOUBTS AND STONEWALLING. THEY SEE PROBLEMS EVERYWHERE INSTEAD OF OPPORTUNITIES.

Edward has recently been having problems with one of his best developers, Russian-born Igor. Igor is a man of few words and clients see him as a reliable problem-solver. However, Edward doesn't take him along to pitches. Edward feels that Igor lets him down in front of other people and presents over-technical material.

What would you do in this situation if you were the boss?

Managers nowadays have it tougher than ever. After long years of economic (and political) stability, the situation in most industrialized countries has changed. Maren Lehky describes the challenges – short and temporary contracts, the low-wage sector and work for temporary employment agencies, globalization and the digital age (Lehky, 2011). And pressure on another front is already looming large: a shortage of skilled workers because of demographic changes. According to estimates by the management consultancy firm McKinsey, the number of workers in Germany is likely to fall short of demand by two million in the year 2020. This situation applies to practically all Western countries. One in ten jobs could be vacant as a result.[35] In the face of such conditions, management skills could become a crucial competitive factor. It's getting ever easier for well trained people who work hard at their jobs to find other options – and they also move on more quickly if they don't get on with the boss, rather than bearing the frustration patiently. They also take conscious note of the people they will be working with, whether teams or superior managers. This is a stressful situation for managers – particularly middle managers, sandwiched between the pressures of expectations from 'above' and 'below' alike. The way you use personality-related communication is all the more important: it has to suit your counterpart's personality and your own.

This chapter answers two questions. First, how should you as a manager communicate so as to connect with both the introverts and the extroverts on your team and develop their skills? Secondly, what characteristics and strengths can you use as an extrovert or introvert manager in cases like our introductory example?

Management communication can soon get complicated, as we see when we add the other perspective to the picture – that of Igor, Edward's introvert specialist:

 Full of hot air! Igor's view of things

'It doesn't matter what I do, it doesn't matter how many successes I chalk up in projects: Edward always knows better. He interferes in everything I do. It takes away all my breathing space. And he takes all the credit anyway; that seems important to him not only as the boss but in other ways as well.

'I'm good – so why doesn't he let me take more decisions myself? My results are top-notch and so are my client satisfaction levels. All my projects are completed on time and on budget. And what does Edward do? He finds fault. And gives me instructions – and often enough he'll say one thing today and exactly the opposite tomorrow. He thinks that's all right.

'I get the impression that my performance isn't appreciated as I deserve. All the hours I spend online with colleagues on a development are invisible to Edward – somehow or other they don't count as work. My promotion to Senior Consultant is long overdue, but I haven't had any indications. I also believe that the "bluffers" are more successful in the corporate hierarchy – maybe because they're like the boss. He calls them "men of action". I call them masters of bluff. They talk plenty but they don't have much of a clue.'

How would you handle this star developer if you were his manager? You will be able to answer this question by the time you get to the end of this chapter, which, however, is not intended as a substitute for any management manuals. But it does add a fresh perspective: what have introversion and extroversion got to do with management? And what is their importance for communication?

 Key idea

Successful managers help the people around them to use their potential to the full in their work. And they also use their own potential to the full.

As a manager, you have a dual responsibility: on the one hand, you are faced with the task of supporting the people who work with you on something important. They should be able to carry out their duties with as little disruption as possible and use all their talents and experience – and should feel motivated while they do so. On the other hand, you also have the same responsibility for yourself. As much as possible of what you've got in you should go into your work – particularly when you encounter obstacles, difficulties and bottlenecks.

Introvert and extrovert executives

Introvert and extrovert managers have different ways of approaching tasks. Both can be equally successful with their own approaches. Bill Gates led Microsoft differently from the way Steve Jobs led Apple.

Good managers are not distinguished by how loud they are or by the energy they radiate (or otherwise). They aren't always extrovert, though they may be.[36]

Whether the better manager is extrovert or introvert depends on the environment. Scientists Steven Kaplan, Mark Klebanov and Morten Sorensen published the results of an impressive study (Kaplan, Klebanov, & Sorensen, 2008): they took 316 candidates for management positions and studied a total of 30 personality traits to identify the ones that are most likely to make an individual a successful top manager. Although the results couldn't be pinned down to one single feature, the authors identified certain characteristics that were particularly important to the executives' success. The surprising discovery was that (in addition to a willingness to work overtime) they are ones which many introverts have – tenacity, analytical powers, discipline, attention to detail and thoroughness in organization and planning.

 Key idea

Depending on the environment, extroverts or introverts may be the better managers.

David Brooks (2011, p. 214ff) cites from an earlier study 'that extroversion, agreeableness and openness to new experience did not correlate well with CEO success. Instead, what mattered was emotional stability and conscientiousness – being dependable, making plans and following through'.[37] Introvert strengths right across the board.

Adam Grant, too, showed interesting personality-based differences between managers in a study he conducted together with his colleagues Francesca Gino and David Hofman.[38] They found that introvert bosses may produce better results than extroverts with employees who like free scope and autonomy. Extrovert bosses, in contrast, are more successful in environments where instructions are implemented directly and a more hierarchical style is maintained. It can be concluded from this study that the head chef of a restaurant or the senior officer of a special task force in Iraq will ideally be extrovert while the CEO of a management consultancy or a Google executive is more likely to do well with introvert characteristics.

However, many of the success factors that make up a good manager have nothing to do with introversion or extroversion. Goal orientation, ambition, striving for power or status, the need for acceptance by a team – all these things may be features of either introverts or extroverts. It is definitely true, however, that extrovert factors such as a charismatic personality or enthusiasm have evidently been overestimated for years.

 Key idea

Successful managers help the people around them to use their potential to the full in their work. And they also use their own potential to the full.

Both introvert and extrovert managers are dealing with major tasks. They are supposed to achieve success by reaching corporate goals – and to achieve an innovative impact by challenging the existing goals. They are supposed to motivate their teams – and if possible motivate other employees, customers and their bosses as well. They are supposed to be able to create a 'we' feeling – and at the same time assert themselves when called for. They are supposed to be popular – and be strong enough to make themselves unpopular.

An introvert executive can be just as successful, become just as much of a role model and also come to grief just as easily as an extrovert.

The same thing applies here as before: we are talking about frequently recurring characteristics resulting from the strengths of introverts and extroverts (see Chapter 1). Extroverts, too, can promote independent initiative, and introverts can also give clear instructions.

Introvert leadership quality	Extrovert leadership quality
Is reliable and predictable	**Is dynamic and enthusiastic**
Ensures trust and security	Ensures stimulation and agility
Remains calm under stress	Takes decisions quickly
Acts in a considered, cautious, predictable and calculated manner	Likes fast answers
Makes sure people have backup	Can win over a team for a vision
Develops independent initiative	**Lets people know where they stand**
Enables responsibility	Takes responsibility
Doesn't feel threatened when employees act independently	Motivates insecure employees to act by using clear statements
Is easily capable of disregarding his own ego	Likes to pass on his own ideas
Encourages people to think of ideas	Likes loyal people in his team
Likes independently motivated people in his team	
Is empathetic	**Actively addresses conflicts**
Listens	Clears the air
Can understand other people	

Develops this understanding in others	Ensures that the team can function
Is not solely concerned with himself	Sets clear boundaries
Concentrates and is focused	**Is flexible**
Ensures effectiveness	Responds quickly to new information
Results-oriented	Revises decisions if necessary, can handle a fast pace well
Takes time to think	
Formulates complex ideas	**Has drive**
Makes analyses and includes all facts if possible	Changes strategies if necessary
Ensures orientation	Takes action where necessary
Prefers to develop ideas in writing and in peace	Prefers to develop ideas orally and in an exchange with others
Sticks tenaciously to the job in hand	

But here, too, there are typical downsides to each personality type, because introvert and extrovert hurdles (see Chapter 1) often lead to certain failings.

Introvert leadership failing	Extrovert leadership failing
Is too accommodating	**Is too tough**
Fails to clarify game rules and doesn't insist they are adhered to	Wants to keep hold of the reins himself,
Allows work and decisions to be pushed onto him	Doesn't really like independent initiative

(Continued)

Introvert leadership failing	Extrovert leadership failing
Does not always take leadership role when necessary and lets things run	Wants to appear powerful and is fixated on external high status (see Chapter 7)
Is too withdrawn	**Is present too much**
Doesn't spend enough time with the team	Withdraws too rarely from the team
Withdraws too much	Is easily distracted from important things for the sake of being with the team
Gives too little feedback	
Team feels abandoned	Team feels controlled
Avoids conflicts	**Leaves no space**
Shies away from addressing awkward subjects	Doesn't listen enough
Seeks too little clarification and resolution in difficult situations	Doesn't give others enough of a say
	Makes his own estimation the central point
Is too fixated on facts	Is too impulsive
Puts figures and results before relationships	Acts emotionally out of 'gut feel', especially if impatience is one of his hurdles
	May tend to lash out
	Has problems absorbing information without making a quick judgement

? What kind of leader are you

What leadership strengths do you perceive in yourself?

What leadership failings do you perceive in yourself?

Four communication tasks for managers

Of all the tasks that managers have to shoulder on a daily basis, appropriate communication is probably the most diffuse area. 'Appropriate' here means an exchange with the environment that fits the people, the situation and the manager's own personality.

But what's the best way to do this in the real world of management today? I've taken a look at the current literature.[39] Four different areas of communication stand out particularly.

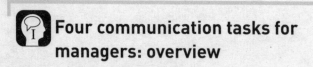

Four communication tasks for managers: overview

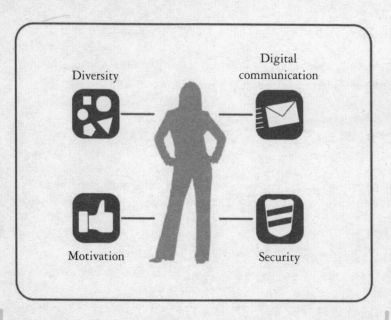

Diversity

Digital communication

Motivation

Security

Your perspective as an introvert or extrovert executive is naturally involved here. But this perspective takes second place. In each of the four sections, the first part of my advice is devoted to the employees, who are also introverts and extroverts.

Particular mention is made of things that are likely to be a 'blind spot' for you depending on whether you're an introvert or extrovert, in other words things that may easily be neglected. You are familiar with the term 'self-hugging' from Chapter 2. This tendency can have highly negative effects in the long term, particularly for managers. Managers who 'hug themselves' unconsciously assume that their personal characteristics are the epitome of a normal person. Accordingly, they give preference to people whose values and communication habits are similar to their own. It takes conscious reflection on their own characteristics and their differences from other people to achieve distance here (people are different – not better or worse.

Task 1: Dealing with diversity

Mixed teams are part of everyday working life these days. Men and women, baby boomers and members of Generation Y, people from different cultures, people with or without disabilities and with divergent traditions work in one and the same group.

And there's something else: the same teams often include employees with temporary contracts, people hired from temporary employment agencies and interns, i.e. people who are there for training. Compared to the permanent workforce, these people have little security (they're temporary), lower salaries (they're agency workers) and less status and skill (interns). Then there are people filling in for parental leave and sabbaticals, people filling project-specific jobs, specialists and consultants from external companies who are assigned to the team for a while – in short, personnel turnover keeps changing the composition of the team.

This trend is likely to increase. The German Federal Employment Agency's Institute for Employment Research (IAB) reported a new high in 2011, with 2.7 million people working on temporary contracts. That's one million more than in 2001. 45 percent of all new contracts concluded today are temporary.

Mixed teams can be very successful if they are operating under three conditions (explained in Chapter 2): you should be aware of and respect differences between the team members, you should help them to deal with hurdles and you should remember that strengths in combination lead to the best results. This can achieved by an intelligent communication strategy.

 Key idea

Turn diversity into versatility: know and respect differences, smooth out hurdles, combine strengths.

In your everyday management work you will be dealing with differences relating to status gaps, gender, age, health and culture. You know that a team is successful when people with different characteristics and different needs get along well. You need to enable this and make it easy.[40]

Have you noticed one difference that doesn't come up in this list, one with which you're now very familiar? That's right – as a manager, you're also wise to take the clear differences between introverts and extroverts into account – all the more so if you often have to deal with your opposite personality type.

Astonishingly, the difference between introverts and extroverts virtually never occurs as a criterion for diversity. If it does, it's from the point of view of the introverts and their needs. That's why it is the central focus in this chapter, by considering both personality types. And high time, too.

The following pointers for introverts and extroverts are intended to be clearly organized and easily accessible. I have used a standard format for all four communication tasks. This will enable you to go directly to the parts that interest you personally instead of having to work through different sections of the chapter. (It's a useful approach, and not just for impatient extroverts …!)

Let's start with what you should look out for in communication with teams that include both introverts and extroverts.

Important for both introvert *and* extrovert employees

- **Plan.** Think before you fill a new position: what personality traits and communication skills should the right person have? Should they be a doer or thinker? Introvert or extrovert? Power- or cooperation-oriented? Avoid appointments that could lead to tensions with members of the team (please note that this does not apply to the factor of performance; performance-based competition is an incentive and in the best case sets standards).

- **Integrate.** Make sure that the team shares experiences that facilitate personal encounters and relationship-building: a lunch together once a month, little birthday rituals, croissants before the weekly meeting, etc. This also helps new team members to get acquainted and prevents alienation due to too much digital communication (see below).

- **Ensure respect.** Lines of reporting and hierarchies are one thing. However, also make sure that your employees treat each other – treat everyone – with respect. Promote mutual understanding by treating everyone with the same respect and giving everyone the same opportunity to speak. Avoid any generalizations about specific groups, young or old, women or men, locals or foreigners, even if they are meant positively.

- **Ensure orientation.** Make sure that everyone knows what they are doing and why. Strike a good balance between a secure base (see also the section on security later in this chapter and necessary change. Handle resistance actively and consciously.[41]

- **Give feedback.** It doesn't do either introverts or extroverts any good to be left alone to deal with hurdles. Encourage both personality types to change their behaviour if you notice that something isn't going smoothly and communication, relationships or results are suffering because of it. And please note that this is not a matter of distorting or ignoring the respective needs of introverts and extroverts. Your leadership goal here is to help your employees. They should be able to adapt their communication in such a way that they contribute as effectively as possible to the team's results and are as successful as possible themselves in doing so, in terms of both sociability and substantive goal achievement. Even small changes in communication can have a major effect. You will find suggestions for introverts and extroverts below.

Particularly important for introverts	Particularly important for extroverts
Make solo work possible.	**Promote a sense of belonging.**
It may be useful particularly for introvert team members to have peaceful individual work periods (possibly even at home) that are as free as possible from disturbance and interruptions and for them not to have to be present in the group at all times. As a rule of thumb, knotty problems are best tackled alone.	It is important to extrovert team members in particular to be able to identify with the group as individuals and enjoy belonging to it. Make it easy to develop this kind of 'we' feeling.
Use empathy.	**Enable competition.**
Be glad of the empathy that many introverts possess. Encourage introverts with this strength, for example, to mentor younger team members. The 'Generation Y' members in particular demand feedback, learning and support[42] – an empathetic older team member may be the perfect person to take on this task.	Many extroverts love the stimulation of a sporting competition, both within the team and with other units in the organization. This can strengthen the sense of community and increase their pleasure in their work – provided that success in the competition and esteem are independent of one another so that the collegial atmosphere is preserved (see also the section on motivation).

Ask for contributions.

Many introverts feel uncomfortable in large groups. In meetings, find a way that will allow the introverts to make their contributions: maybe by asking for input to be given briefly in writing in large sessions and announcing the points to be discussed in advance so that they can prepare. You can also catch the person in question on his or her own before the meeting and ask explicitly for a contribution – that not only gives him or her time to prepare but also provides encouragement. Don't be afraid to mention that you appreciate the employee's in-depth contributions and that they benefit everyone.

Encourage the perfectionists among the introverts to contribute ideas even if they have not yet been worked out to the last detail. Make sure that they are not interrupted when they speak.

Slow people down and encourage them.

Talkative people and self-presenters can get into just as much trouble as introvert colleagues who are too quiet. Mention it to extroverts in your team if you have the impression that they do more than their share of the talking in meetings.

Demonstrate possible consequences, in terms of how they are perceived by others ('full of hot air') and of their professional reputation as high performers. This means you should encourage extroverts to deliver substance in their words as well as in their results. It's important for them not just to be skilled presenters, but also to deliver good performance.

If necessary, slow down the pace of discussions that are dominated by extroverts and bring these people back to the point if they stray too far from the subject. That helps to ensure good results – and at the end of the day saves time for all concerned.

And now let's have a change of perspective. What should you yourself as an introvert or extrovert manager watch out for when you are dealing with mixed teams and want to avoid the above-mentioned self-hugging approach? This overview contains some suggestions.

Dealing with diversity: what to watch out for as a manager

If you're an introvert	If you're an extrovert
Use your gift of putting yourself in other people's shoes. Practise management by walking around and meet your employees at their workplaces, where you can talk to them individually or in small groups. On these occasions, give the people around you your full attention. By doing so you will find out a great deal and be totally in the picture about your team.	Communicate in a way that's suited to the team member addressed. Give the controller audited, individual data, offer the 'doer' active support, show the pioneer the attractiveness of new paths and the introverted, substance-oriented person the background to a measure.
Respect extrovert employees' wish for community and interaction. In contrast to yours, their ideas and approaches flourish best when they can develop them together with other people.	Respect introvert employees' wish for quiet reflection (instead of brainstorming in meetings) and an undisturbed working environment (rather than open-plan offices and permanent company of all kinds). A quiet room with a closed door will protect them from overstimulation and enable exceptional performance, particularly on complex tasks. Thinking quietly in solitude often produces better ideas than verbal ping-pong among the team.
Encourage your employees to pursue unusual ideas and paths – unusual points of view resulting from several perspectives make diversity an advantage. Use the	Make it your task to assess the individual performance of each employee. 'Showmasters' who sell their performance to perfection are often achieving

introvert manager's strength of giving your employees space (see Grant et al. 2011). less than 'quiet sloggers' who sit in the background and deliver top results. And people who invest less 'social time' have more time to work. Close scrutiny is worthwhile because it motivates people and ensures fairness.

Task 2: Communicating digitally

With the possibilities of digital communication, we are living in an age of unprecedented mobility. If we do 'brain work', we can essentially work anywhere with today's technology. Mobile phones, laptops, wireless LANs and tablet computers mean we can be reached anywhere and enable us to conceptualize, communicate and write anywhere. Presence at an office or other workplace is not a necessary condition for being productive on an employer's behalf. It's also possible to hold meetings across vast geographic expanses (and time zones) using video- and teleconferencing. First and foremost, that's wonderful. Honestly, would you want to be back in the days when grabbing the phone or sending a fax were the only alternatives to a letter or a personal meeting?

However, the new capabilities also entail risks and side-effects. They blur the lines between work and personal life. A lot of people are always online. It seems quite normal these days to check your work e-mails in your time off, or to have an evening appointment on Skype with a colleague in the USA. And this 'new normal' causes stress on a number of fronts.

 Key idea

It's not easy, but it's possible to use digital media in a way that suits both personalities.

There's the stress of always having to be available and not being allowed to miss anything. Added to this is the stress of always having to respond to tensions that arise from difficult or conflict-ridden processes – constantly arriving on your smart phone by e-mail, demanding reactions. And then there's the special kind of stress that arises when e-mails, SMS or social media posts are allowed to disturb the process of your work unfiltered: that also affects productivity. Not to mention creativity – particularly if you're an introvert.

The technology often turns direct human contact into indirect contact: instead of physical meetings, there are Skype calls, e-mails and conferences by webcam or phone. Particularly in transregional or international companies, some project teams or management committees only get together at long intervals.

How do you use the advantages offered by digital communication in a way that also suits your (introvert and extrovert) employees? How do you in your executive role handle digital communication in a way that suits you as an introvert or extrovert? As in the previous section, the answers to these questions are given here as overviews to enable quick access.

 Communicating digitally: what employees need

Important for both introvert *and* extrovert employees:

- **Rules.** Create and communicate rules for using digital media. What information should be distributed how and to whom? When do you expect a reaction to emails?
- What priorities should be set for dealing with floods of electronic mail? What times outside office hours are taboo? Ideally, you should develop these rules together with your employees.
- **Role model.** Live up to these rules yourself. Nothing is more effective than your visible example.
- **Competence.** Develop your own and your employees' skills in all digital media, systems and software that you rely on in your daily work. It is at least equally important to provide training, coaching or materials on time management and self-management to make clear which way round it is: the person controls the medium; the medium does not control the person.

Particularly important for introverts	Particularly important for extroverts
Presence.	**Digital tea station.**
Many introverts like digital communication because it reduces direct encounters and enables them to write during their everyday work (by e-mail) instead of talking on the phone or in person. Writing is more in line with their typical strengths profile. In addition, online contact enables them to communicate with others while they are alone and have more time to think before they answer.	Extroverts love their smart phones, social media and e-mails, which enable them to stay in touch with their team and network contacts. They may feel something's missing if they are cut off from the communication flow, particularly when they're travelling or spending lengthy, low-stimulation work periods on their own. And digital presence enables them to embody the strength of emotional warmth better.
Digital communication makes working away from the company premises possible in many professions. Might it be good for an introvert employee to do part of his work at home? This could significantly improve effectiveness, particularly for peace-loving thinkers and easily-overstimulated specialists. And it could definitely benefit quality of life.	Administer the right 'dose' here – and ensure that the extroverts in the team don't overload the introverts with spontaneous messages. Incorporate this factor when drawing up the rules (see above).
However, take introvert hurdles such as contact avoidance or passivity into account if appropriate.	

(Continued)

MANAGEMENT   173

Particularly important for introverts	Particularly important for extroverts
Time out.	**Accessibility.**
Think about the way your introvert employees regenerate – they need undisturbed, low-stimulus breaks. Make sure that these people in particular allow themselves offline periods with a clear conscience. It even pays off economically, in terms of productivity and creativity – remember the introvert strength of calm.	Don't begrudge your extrovert employees the digital accessibility that's important to them. At the same time, remember typical hurdles such as impatience (not every message needs to be answered straight away) and distraction (a lot of messages are written in order to put off having to write that long-due report). Counteract these tendencies cautiously and respectfully.
Take care to ensure that your introvert employees maintain a healthy level of personal presence and direct interaction. Incorporate this factor when drawing up the rules (see above).	

Some tasks in the overview above will come easily to you as an introvert or extrovert executive, and of course others will not. You will find below some key pointers for handling digital communication that may be of particular value to you, depending on your personality type.

Communicating digitally: what to watch out for as a manager

If you're an introvert	If you're an extrovert
You find it relatively easy to give employees independent responsibility. Make sure that this responsibility remains within predictable limits in digital communication. For example, your employees should not overdo accessibility outside working hours without authorization – but it should be possible to reach them in certain instances.	You find it relatively easy to give clear instructions. Make sure your employees have a certain amount of personal scope to use at their own discretion in digital communication. Don't define this scope too narrowly.
You yourself may be tempted to use digital media so that you can withdraw. Ensure that your employees get enough personal attention in the form of physical presence – including your own. This encourages bonding and will provide you with a lot of important information that you won't get from digital communication. By the way, 'presence' includes not only meetings but also informal occasions.Consciously ensure that you yourself are not using digital communication as an excuse for avoiding contact. Measure the 'doses' accordingly. Find appropriate opportunities to send positive signals when communicating by computer – even a smiley can work wonders!	You may be tempted to increase your direct contact with employees through digital communication. Ensure that your employees have quiet times for complex tasks. In such situations, you yourself should avoid spontaneous or impulsive communication even by e-mail. As an extrovert, you should exercise self-discipline and make sure that you yourself observe the rules on digital communication. Measure the 'doses' accordingly.

Task 3: Motivating the best – and the rest

One characteristic of today's world of employment is that we are constantly working on things that show very little in the way of visible results. The outcome of our work is often sketchily perceived. The carpenter with a finished desk in front of him or the farmer who has ploughed a field are better off in that respect. Modern-style work, in contrast, is more like a bottomless pit; its results are often delayed (e.g. the outcome of a draft paper) or remain invisible (e.g. a briefing for the Managing Board). Different incentives are therefore needed, such as recognition from others, and from managers in particular. Even more important is self-motivation, the will to do something that is important to you (see Chapter 3). This kind of attitude helps people to keep going even during lean periods in which, to all appearances, nothing much is happening (this may of course be more difficult for reward-oriented extroverts than for tenacious introverts).

However, self-motivation is not evident in everyone. The public opinion research institute Gallup produces an annual Engagement Index which shows corporate employees' level of motivation, using surveys based on twelve statements. The 2012 results are best described by a quote from the press release:

THE BULK OF EMPLOYEES WORLDWIDE (63%) ARE NOT 'ENGAGED', MEANING THEY LACK MOTIVATION AND ARE LESS LIKELY TO INVEST DISCRETIONARY EFFORT IN ORGANISATIONAL GOALS OR OUTCOMES. AND 24% ARE 'ACTIVELY DISENGAGED, INDICATING THEY ARE UNHAPPY AND UNPRODUCTIVE AT WORK AND LIABLE TO SPREAD NEGATIVITY TO CO-WORKERS (...) ACROSS 19 WESTERN EUROPEAN COUNTRIES, 14% ARE 'ENGAGED'.[43]

The things that motivate a person vary widely. I consider psychologist Stephen Reiss's personality-oriented approach to be the one of the best. According to Reiss, human behaviour is a consequence of needs. Needs arise so that personal (intrinsic) values and goals can be embodied and expressed (see Reiss, 2010, p. 43). These values are basic desires that cannot be influenced because the form they take is part of the personality. They influence how we choose an activity that suits us, beyond the needs of introversion and extroversion (see Chapter 3). And the question of whether the basic desires can be sufficiently embodied in our working routine has a strong influence on our attitude to work.

In concrete terms, this means that we cannot motivate others to pursue an activity with pleasure and success if their own basic desires don't perceive a value in it. If what you like to do best after work is to relax on your own and above all have a bit of peace and quiet, the prospect of an evening out bowling with the project team is unlikely to float your boat. If you have a strong desire for status, on the other hand, the prospect of a bigger company car or an office with a window will thrill you much more than it would a colleague with a low need for status who considers the pursuit of bigger company cars and offices to be a stupid carry-on. Money, too, has only a limited motivating effect from the middle salary brackets upwards – and that effect is derived from the fact that the cash serves other motives.[44] For example, a salary increase or a bonus may raise status, provide security or extend a lead over rivals. All the factors that have a greater motivating effect than money lie in the realm of communication. A collegial atmosphere at the workplace, sufficient free scope in carrying out your work and terms of employment that suit your own personality are all important. Which brings us back to the core topic of this book: personality-based communication.

 Key idea

What motivates people is a highly individual question.

Introverts and extroverts differ in their motivation – but not just because they're introverts or extroverts, but because their personal motives mean that they have individual 'drivers', as all people do. I make the assumption that clusters of motivation types will be observable, because of the differences in biological make-up. For example, it's likely that security or safety will be more important to an introvert than to an extrovert, while on average an extrovert will more frequently be driven by such motives as risk and competition. However, this has not yet been proved.

In studies of motivation, one element repeatedly stands out that is popular with everyone – introverts and extroverts, new managers, senior specialists and interns all find that respect for both person and performance provides a stimulus for enthusiasm.[45]

People who know that they are perceived and appreciated as individuals work with much more motivation than those who feel that they are treated as replaceable cogs in the machine. That sounds like a truism, but it isn't. There are evidently many managers who fail to communicate respect to their employees.

 Key idea

Managers need to reconcile their own style with the need to show respect in a manner suitable for each individual. This sounds like an important communication task, doesn't it? There are several levels of difficulty involved. First of all, you should know how to communicate respectfully – in a way that suits you and doesn't come over as artificial. Secondly, there is no such thing as off-the-peg respect. Respect only works if the person you are talking to feels they are being addressed, well, personally. Uniquely.

It is dangerous to make one person liable for the whole team. It's quite understandable that no individual team member would want to be responsible for the results of the whole group and will 'hide' when blame for delays, problems or crises is being dished out. Conversely, it is important to make an individual's performance visible. Receiving a reaction to a personal success is a basic human need and a great motivator. Moreover, the individual team member's performance declines as the size of the group increases.

! Key idea

Management tasks in the area of motivation are to make performance visible and responsibility clear.

Two management tasks can be deduced from these facts: both the *performance* and the *responsibility* of the individuals in the team should be clearly recognisable. Define the individual responsibility of the team members – and make sure they take it. That's a challenge, particularly for extroverts.

Motivating: what your employees need

Important for both introvert *and* extrovert employees

- **Attention.** Pay attention to your employees. Be accessible to your team members. In direct exchanges, concentrate solely on the person in front of you. Develop a perception of what they need to feel in order to feel comfortable at the workplace. If you can contribute to solving a problem, do so. Remember that managers may be more strongly motivated by different factors (e.g. individual responsibility) from those driving team members with no leadership responsibility (e.g. job security) or employees with low incomes (e.g. bonuses). Address your employees in a way that suits their personal characteristics and needs.

- **Respect.** Respect what your team members achieve and attribute performance to the performers or to small groups. Make outstanding performance and special efforts visible in a positive way, naming the individual concerned. Be specific and say exactly what the outstanding performance consists of. Offer opportunities for further training in order to develop team members particularly or help them to acquire skills that they need. Get team members who make a direct contribution to your department's results to present them. Take account of your employees' personal interests and motives (e.g. work-life balance, personal responsibility, increased status or power, recognition within the team). If a team member is given respect above and beyond his status and official duties for his achievements, that is an excellent prerequisite for motivated work.

- **Recognition by exceptional means.** Generally speaking, of course, you cannot distribute promotions and permanent jobs, buy company cars or raise salaries at will. However, you can make recognition visible. Be inventive, taking the things that are important to the person as your starting point (see above: motives). Examples:

  - Give your power-oriented intern a task involving responsibility.

  - If a temp is a high performer, single him or her out for mention to the temporary employment agency.

  - Praise the recognition-hungry assistant in front of everyone when she has performed especially well.

  - Support the family-oriented employee in his care sabbatical and make it possible for him to work from home part of the time thereafter.

- **Communication about meaning.** A sense of doing something meaningful is one of the strongest drivers there is (see Chapter 3). Communicate the point of a task or a project if at all possible: where does the benefit lie? What will have been improved once it is completed? Whom will it help?

Particlarly important for introverts	Particularly important for extroverts
Positive feedback.	**Positive feedback.**
Give it! Be specific. And give it in front of other people as well. That's not always particularly important to introverts, but it does raise the person's status in front of the other team members and also shows your respect.	That's the soil in which extroverts flourish best: recognition from outside. It's good if as many people as possible know about it, as well. This is a classic external incentive which is valuable to many extroverts.

Demand results.	Demand results.
Many introverts tend to pay too much attention to detail and spend a lot of time on cases that are already good enough to pass on. Motivate your introvert employees to submit their work within a reasonable time and communicate the timing as an important part of their performance.	For many extroverts, 'agreed and discussed' is far from meaning 'delivered'. Motivate your extrovert employees to implement and deliver high-quality work as per your discussions. Make clear to them that the actual work is an important part of their performance.
Deepen the meaning.	**Celebrate successes.**
Introverts are more motivated by inner processes than external incentives. Introverts who consider their work to be meaningful, important and necessary have no problem at all in motivating themselves.[46] So help introverts in particular to plumb this deeper dimension.	External rewards and incentives are more important for extroverts than for introverts, as is conviviality. So create occasions for extroverts to celebrate their successes. A party with the team after a project is successfully completed or when a major order is won may fit the bill, but such occasions may also include personal distinctions in the case of high performers.

Once again let's change perspective: as an introvert or extrovert manager, what is your individual approach to motivating people? Here's an overview for you.

Motivating: what to watch out for as a manager ...

If you're an introvert	If you're an extrovert
You find it relatively easy to understand your employees and their motives, because you look and listen attentively. This gives you a good basis for motivational communication.	Use your capacity for enthusiasm and your capability of emotional warmth.

(Continued)

If you're an introvert	If you're an extrovert
You can create trust and attachment in employees effectively with your 'quiet' characteristics. Make sure that you communicate enough and make transparent decisions so that you don't leave your team members in a state of uncertainty: that is demotivating.	Keep an overview. Who achieves what? Who needs what? It's great that the 'joint is jumping' and the last high-pressure project was a success. But who made that happen? And what can you do so that the person concerned will be happy to give a repeat performance the next time?
As an executive, you have the scope to take decisions and make things happen. So don't just let them run. Take decisions. Make things happen. Show a direct interest in the people around you. That will motivate your team. Be there with them.	Give employees personal responsibility if they want it. This includes employees with career ambitions, people with a high need for independence and many younger team members from 'Generation Y'. Take care to speak to them on terms of equality and avoid communication that may be perceived as authoritarian. Instead, use persuasion.
Be approachable. Can your employees talk to you without having the feeling that they're disturbing you? Do your team members have a positive emotional attachment to their work? Do you address your employees in line with their individual communication needs?	If you encourage competition among your team members, make sure that the collegial atmosphere is maintained. It's one of the key motivators.

Motivation is a complex subject. You have discovered in this section how you can enrich your team by including the differences between the introverts and extroverts and using your own characteristics as an introvert or extrovert. At the same time, you have been given some suggestions that may not have been right at the top of your list because of your personality type. You will find further ideas in the excellent literature on the subject of motivation. For the big picture, I recommend in particular Pink (2011) and Reiss (2010). You will find more concrete pointers about employee motivation and the effects of certain management actions in Leffers (2012).

Task 4: Providing security

Security is a relative term. The days of life-long employment and predictable career opportunities are long gone. In purely statistical terms, anyone embarking on their career today will have a very much higher number of jobs before taking retirement than previously. In addition, people may have a succession of periods of employment and self-employment, or sometimes the two may run in parallel. Corporate acquisitions and major structural changes in companies may even lead to what appear to be rock-solid jobs in an apparently secure employment situation becoming redundant.

As you're aware from Chapter 1, safety is particularly important for introverts. However, when it comes to preserving their own livelihood, it is also very important to extroverts. Who would want to be left in uncertainty as to whether their job will still be there tomorrow? Is there anyone who feels comfortable not knowing how the boss will react to a proposal for change? When we lack a secure base, it is easy to be distracted from the real purpose of our work, which is to deliver products or services to an employer or client. Fear impedes good work and leads to depression and burnout, whereas a level of security boosts performance.

Of course, you're a manager and not a magician. You can't transform a temporary project contract into a secure job. You have no influence on who your direct line manager is or on that person's priorities for your department. And you most certainly can't decide which of your company's sites will remain open.

Communication in the team can provide a sense of security in uncertain times and therefore keep stress under control.

But when the situation is unstable and unpredictable, communication in the immediate work context is all the more important. The herd instinct in all of us, the way team members behave towards each other and, above all, the behaviour of the managers are then particularly important. You can provide a sense of security, a kind of 'inner home', that can keep stress under control during change processes.

So in fact you do have an influence: it lies in the way you handle your team in uncertain times – in short, how you communicate in tense situations brought on by insecurity.[47]

Advanced skills are needed here: conflict resolution, dealing with confrontations and tensions, giving and taking critical feedback, conveying unpleasant news, handling critical opinions and enduring unpredictability together with others.

In a word, be dependable as a person. That lends psychological stability even in times when nothing can be relied on.

Providing security: what your employees need

Important for both introvert *and* extrovert employees

- **Explore opportunities for control.** It has been proved that in stressful and uncertain periods people suffer more if they feel they have no influence on the situation. They are more inclined to feel helpless, they become passive and their performance deteriorates (see Maehrlein, 2012, p. 94ff.) for more detail). Counter this spiral by getting together with your staff to explore the opportunities to take action and make something out of the situation. Take a realistic view of chances and risks. Even if this process doesn't produce anything earth-shattering in many cases, shared communication about options for action dispels a fair amount of helplessness.

- **Embed fairness:**

  - Establish feedback rules and ensure fairness in communication. Every team member should feel safe about saying something in front of others – even if it is critical or unpleasant.

  - Ensure a fair balance of interests, particularly in oppressive times. This, too, is within your powers and will have a stabilizing effect on your employees. So take care to ensure that work is fairly distributed and that the key performers' contribution is respected. Communicate rules that apply across the board. Communicate and act transparently, i.e. clearly and with no hidden agenda.

  - Protect your team from being overburdened, particularly the very high performers. They suffer on two counts. Not only are they more at risk of burnout than their colleagues, they are also often frustrated rather than motivated: they see themselves as the 'departmental mugs' and feel that work is offloaded on them that others have managed to avoid.

  - Less performance-oriented people settle comfortably into their roles, moan about their workload as a precautionary measure when new tasks are being handed out, and see it as a win if they can avoid being very busy. This kind of (frequently unconscious) laziness in teams is known as 'social loafing'. You can reduce these risks as a manager if you protect your high performers from a permanent heavy workload and make sure that very busy times are balanced out. Express appreciation of exceptional performance explicitly.

  - Deliberately push mediocre and below-average team members. Part of this task involves having a realistic idea of their actual workload. Communication (moaning, frantic activity) is not always a sound indicator here. Train yourself to spot the difference between show and real stress. That's a good way to ensure fairness and therefore more emotional security in the team.

- **Ensure information and communication.** Announce the fact when turbulent times are approaching for you and your team, whether it's due to changes in the environment within your company or an unusual situation regarding incoming orders.

- Ensure there is no knowledge reserved to a select few in the team for the sake of power politics – this leads to insecurity. Let information and communication flow freely as far as possible. In times of high employee turnover, turn your attention to know-how transfer. You can not only secure important knowledge for the team, but also save the time and resources that would be needed if you had to keep starting from scratch. Use IT tools, but also put systematic communication in place: ensure structured handovers, make employees specifically accountable and ask about their experience during final reviews.

- Plan meetings carefully and bring the players in the team together into a direct exchange in a systematic, targeted manner. Intranet resources or Web 2.0 are also useful for sharing contents (see above, Communicating digitally).

- **Build trust.** Loyalty is an inestimable asset in times of high uncertainty – even if you have no influence whatsoever on the decisions that will decide the future. You know from the section about social connections that functioning networks and genuine relationships lend perspective and therefore a particular kind of security. Above all, be a loyal, reliable and discreet contact yourself – for everyone. Because you don't just want to have trust-based relationships in your team, you also want other people in key positions to have confidence in your capabilities. An inestimable asset in uncertain times – almost an insurance policy!

- **Provide a 'home'.** Make sure all your employees feel they belong to the team. After all, you know that people are gregarious creatures. They can endure uncertain times better if they can identify with a group and know their place in it. Don't make this sense of belonging dependent on performance. Be accessible to team members, celebrate minor rituals at meetings or after the end of projects, show respect for all employees.

Particularly important for introverts	Particularly important for extroverts
Maintain relationships. Hurdles such as passivity or contact avoidance come into particular prominence when people are under stress. Therefore, you should consciously communicate to introvert employees how important it is to build and maintain contacts right at this moment. If an employee is a good performer, offer to give them a reference or recommend them actively elsewhere. This is important particularly for those team members who are working with you in temporary positions or for training.	**Make changes.** For extroverts in particular, striving for security should never become a straitjacket. Support the initiatives of hands-on extroverts, direct them into specific channels if necessary and check that the new ideas and proposals on changes are not just frantic actionism as an outlet for stress. Basically, though, are new ideas ever more valuable than in uncertain times?
Create predictability. Introverted team members in particular like it if you make processes predictable in tense situations and allow sufficient lead time in the event of upcoming changes. Offer support as required. Allow your introvert the lowest-stimulation environments possible when uncertainty is providing stimulation in abundance on its own (see Loehken, 2012, for more detail).	**Keep ploughing on no matter what.** Encourage the extroverts in the team to be tenacious and keep going in difficult times – even in the face of resistance and incalculable factors. Particularly where employees suffer from extrovert hurdles such as impatience and impulsiveness, that isn't easy.[48] Your goal is to be able to rely on the performance and communication skills of all team members.

(Continued)

Particularly important for introverts	Particularly important for extroverts

Endure the tricky parts.

1. Express criticism the right way. Introverts often find it hard to deal with criticism though they don't wear the fact on their sleeves. Therefore, be careful with critical comments, only make them when the two of you are alone and always close on a positive note about the performance of the person concerned. Ask for suggestions about how to deal with the critical area, thereby encouraging inner processing. Show that you yourself can take criticism.

2. Integrate sceptics. Particularly in periods of change, many introverts (especially those with the hurdles of fear and passivity) tend to have a sceptical, disapproving attitude towards forthcoming innovations. Bear in mind that although sceptical people are inconvenient, they may also perform an important warning function. Early warners may under certain circumstances avert major financial and other damage from the company when an innovation is pending.[49] So do listen to critical feedback – and

Endure the tricky parts.

1. Express criticism the right way. Extroverts often feel that doubt is being cast on them socially when they receive criticism – although they need feedback, they want it to be positive wherever possible.

Here, too, only express criticism when the two of you are alone. Suggest that the extrovert employee take concrete actions – discuss initial thoughts orally.

2. Cushion sweeping attacks. In periods of change, extroverts, particularly those with the hurdles of aggressiveness and impulsiveness, may have a tendency towards sweeping aspersions and emotional outbursts (see Grant, 2013b).

This can lead to significant career disadvantages. If this problem arises, help the extrovert employee to manage trouble when they make suggestions and give feedback. Help the extrovert to use intelligent strategic timing when suggesting improvements or making critical comments.

then move on to the constructive part, i.e. problem-solving: 'I understand your concerns. What are the possible negative consequences – and how can we avoid them?' Your goal is not to dwell on the scepticism, but to bring about improvements with the help of this alert introvert. Above all, however, you should encourage introverts to voice sceptical feedback as well as ideas and suggestions for improvements. This will pay off in the long run for the company, the team and also for the prospects of the introvert employee.[50']

The best approach is to address the boss or team members individually in a positive emotional situation, not just when the extrovert – possibly an impulsive or impatient individual – happens to take it into his head.

Make clear rules for feedback and conflict management, don't tolerate killer phrases and make sure that an atmosphere of fairness prevails. If at all possible, bring communication back to the impartial level: 'I see you don't agree. From your point of view, what other sensible options do we have?' Always intervene if attacks are made on other team members. But the same applies in handling extroverts as for the introverts in the opposite column: encourage an atmosphere in which dissatisfaction and scepticism can be voiced without fear.

Just as with the previous communication tasks, when managers communicate a sense of security they should pay attention to certain aspects that can easily be pushed to the back of introverts' or extroverts' minds or that they are actually unaware of. Here is an overview.

Providing security: what to watch out for as a manager ...

If you're an introvert	If you're an extrovert
You find it relatively easy to remain outwardly calm when things are hectic or uncertain. Use this strength to build trust and create the above-mentioned 'inner security'.	You can be a courageous role model in turbulent times: strengths such as drive, emotional warmth, courage and conflict management skills will support you here. Use these strengths to keep your team together even in stormy times.
As a quiet person, you need to be particularly clear in your behaviour and in your words. Make sure your employees know where they stand with you and what you stand for.	However impulsive, impatient or spontaneous you are, be predictable in what you do. It's quite enough for the times to be uncertain. So stick to the rules yourself.
Conflicts are more likely in stressful times and may cause a sharp deterioration in your team's performance and internal relationships. If you're a conflict-avoider, learn to deal with tricky situations quickly.	Pay attention to your employees' need for harmony, predictability and balance.Keep the level of disagreement as low as possible. It's better if you show your employees how to deal with conflicts.

A good manager understands the need for security properly. It's not about ensuring as much routine and lack of disruption as possible and 'stone-walling' in the face of changes. It's more a matter of not just tolerating diversity, unrest and change, whether with gritted teeth or a relaxed attitude, but seeing the good in them, in a similar vein to cultivating a garden: plants change as they grow. And growth is exhausting. Security means creating good conditions for growth: sound, fertile soil as well as internal and external encouragement.[51]

Good managers are experts in growth. That means not only integrating change and innovation, but also introducing it into routines. Michael Zerr, former CEO of the 'yellow electricity' company Yello GmbH, once said: 'Today's managers have to disrupt intelligently' (Jánsky and Jenzowsky, 2010, p. 87). And he's right. Nevertheless, like captains on the high seas, managers are steering their vessels into the unknown. Their duties include occasionally breaking rules in order to accommodate new situations to which the old regime no longer applies. Providing security under such circumstances is a hard task: it consists of ensuring, in the midst of change, a basic stability that is founded not only on the immediate circumstances but also the human relationships within the team and in the company.

 Application: extrovert manages introvert

Do you remember the points of view of the extrovert manager Edward and the introvert developer Igor at the beginning of the chapter? If you need to, read through it again and then answer these questions with the help of the pointers above.

1. **Helicopter view:** Edward as an extrovert is barely aware of some of Igor's personality traits at the moment. To which ones should he be alerted?

2. **Diversity:** how can Edward do Igor more justice?

3. **Motivation:** what may motivate Igor?

4. **Security:** what kind of security does Igor need?

Key points in brief

1. Successful management communication is nowadays no longer just nice to have, it is a pressing need. This calls for managers to have an eye for the differences between introverts and extroverts, an area which has previously been neglected.

2. Successful managers help their employees to use their potential to the full in their work. And they also use their own potential to the full.

3. Managers have four major communication tasks here: they have to handle diversity, master digital communication, motivate employees and provide security.

4. Introvert and extrovert managers have different approaches to this matter. In addition, they should pay attention to certain aspects which they easily overlook or neglect because of their personality types.

7.
Selling

In contrast to the last chapter, this section is not about communication between opposite sides, but about people being together in a sales situation. The importance of the personality and social relationships can be studied in its pure form better here than anywhere.

In our networked world, more and more products can be purchased on the Internet. However, the web isn't the only source. And even when we go to a shop, we are generally well prepared if the purchase is important. Nowadays, everything we need to know about a product is just a click away on the World Wide Web, including reviews, comments on customer service and the cheapest price available. If you want to make a major purchase – or a small one, for that matter – you can obtain better information than ever before entirely on your own. The kind of strategy in the introductory quotation above is becoming ever less feasible. There are customers who know more about the product than the person who is supposed to be selling it to them.

A salesman's real task nowadays is to forge a contact with the customer that does justice to the meaning of the word: the literal meaning of contact is 'with touch'. Sellers and customers touch one another both in real life and on the Web's social platforms. Management thought leader Anne M. Schüller has already shown how customers can optimize contacts at touch points internally and in external communication (Schüller, 2012, 2014).[52]

If there is one professional field in which personality is the crucial factor today, it is selling. That's because we make very deliberate decisions as to whether and how we allow ourselves to be 'touched' – and particularly by whom. Let's take a closer look.

Selling takes personality

 No thanks!

Ernie is a salesman in an electrical goods hypermarket. He has just approached Ingrid – a somewhat reserved customer who is looking for headphones. She's holding a set in her hand and appears to be thinking.

Ernie: 'These headphones are the very latest thing, we've just had them in after the trade show. Any music sounds great with this audio transparency. You won't really hear any outside noise. Our customers are thrilled with it. I've just bought one myself!'

Ingrid: 'Thanks. I'll think about it.

'Here, a reserved introvert just blocks an enthusiastic extrovert salesman. Neither of the people involved enjoys the experience: Ingrid knows all about headphones already from visiting various portals, and doesn't exactly feel that Ernie has understood her. Ernie really wanted to help her (well, yes, and also to sell the headphones, which don't exactly come cheap). He's just got the brush-off – one of the many situations in sales that get people frustrated.

After this brief exchange of words there is no discussion between him and Ingrid on the factual level. And no positive encounter at all on the relationship level.

 Yeah, yeah, okay!

Isabel works in IT Support at a medium-sized company with just under 250 employees. They're about to have a change of e-mail server. She has therefore asked all staff members via the intranet and by e-mail to change some settings on their e-mail accounts within two weeks. Emma from Purchasing is one of the ones who haven't done it.

Isabel calls her.

> Isabel: 'Right, so we're going to migrate the server the day after tomorrow. It'll be a huge amount of work. And the e-mail accounts will all have to be changed by then. Can you just take a second to do that for yours? That would be great!'
>
> Emma: 'Yeah, yeah, okay.'
>
> Isabel: "Great. See you!'

To Emma, this technical stuff is a nuisance, and she's trying to steer well clear of the process as far as possible. Isabel puts forward her own point of view – but she doesn't manage to convince her colleague and get her to act. A selling attempt made in vain.

Selling is by no means always about products or services. The situation between Isabel and Emma illustrates that selling can also relate to completely different things. If you set aside the notion of generating revenue, Isabel suddenly becomes a saleswoman: she wants Emma to 'buy' something by doing something that's important from Isabel's point of view – i.e. changing her e-mail settings.

 Key idea

Selling is a matter of persuasion.

Against this background, selling means persuading more than anything else. The person who wants to sell something is trying to motivate another person to do something. For example, you can persuade your boss to give you a pay rise. Or to think something: in that case, the object of the transaction is an idea or a conviction. Whether you want to get a friend to join a political party or persuade your adolescent son to come home on time at night, or whether you're drumming up support among your colleagues for a charity campaign – all these things are selling. In other words, selling is ultimately a form of motivation. (For more on the subject of motivation, see Chapter 6.)

Key idea

Selling is ultimately successful motivation.

There is also a very direct parallel with the acquisition of knowledge – i.e. learning, which you looked at in detail in Chapter 5. The same principle applies to selling as to learning: we only acquire something if it is relevant to us and motivates us to take action.

Key idea

Learning and selling have this in common: we only acquire something if it is relevant to us.

If the core of selling is persuasion and motivation, then the core of sales *communication* is dialogue. Ingrid will only accept Ernie's offer of a discussion if she feels it will help her make her purchase decision. Isabel is faced with the task of persuading Emma that it is in her own interest to reset her account.

Key idea

Selling only works through a dialogue between the vendor and the purchaser. A dialogue requires contact – and therefore a response to the personality of the other party.

Ultimately, a sale only takes place if at least two participants agree on at least one point: the product or service is a good choice for the person buying it. The facts are easy to sort out as there's plenty of reliable information available on the Internet, including comparisons and reviews. You've guessed it: the crucial point in a purchase is something else. And you're not wrong. When you talk to a salesman you're seeking a person-to-person connection that will support your purchase decision. That always has something to do with feelings. Feelings, in turn, always have something to do with personality. And that's how making a purchase works: safety or reward will come to the fore depending on whether a person is safety-oriented or reward-oriented.

The sense of satisfaction a person gets when making a purchase also depends on what aspects satisfy that individual – for example when buying a car, is it the luxury saloon's quality or its status? Is it loyalty to a brand or innovative design that draws the buyer's attention? What's enticing: the nice feeling of getting value for money or the unrepeatable bargain in the shop window? And not least, how much do I like the person in front of me whose job it is to help me make my purchase? And is he interested in giving me his professional support in my purchase decision?

It is equally important for the seller to be aware of his own strengths, preferences and hurdles – you can only be authentic in dialogue with others if you know yourself and consider your own needs.

 ## Selling is like chemistry

Claudia Kimich, negotiation expert.kimich.de

For buying and selling to be fun and make people want more, the chemistry has to be right. It is therefore important in a sales situation to pay attention to both your own personality and that of the other person. The principle can be summed up in one sentence: consider your opposite number but still think about how comfortable you feel yourself.

Selling is about successful communication, in other words about sociability, feelings and relationships – and you can probably see now why selling is a perfect showcase to describe the things that may go on between different personality types.

The best emotion that can develop between a seller and the customer is the customer's trust. There is wide agreement on this in the literature. A positive experience such as particularly attentive service, a humorous remark or a surprising twist in the sales pitch can also lead to a positive experience for both parties. In the best case, the customer will reward the trust that has developed with loyalty and will recommend the article purchased or the good service – that's at least equally important.[53]

 ## How positive emotions influence sales performance

Lars Schäfer, author and expert in emotional selling

Since the biggest motive for purchasing nowadays and the hardest currency in selling is trust, a core question arises: how do trust and security actually come about?

When your brain perceives a new situation or a previously unknown person, it automatically searches your subconscious for comparable people or situations, or some similar experience. It searches for strong and trustworthy links in your past (similarly to Google). The more of such connections your brain finds, the stronger will be your trust. That is the reason why we tell some people our entire life story in the first conversation and are more wary of others: some detail that we are not really conscious of gives us a positive feeling – or otherwise.

When selling, you can give the customer's subconscious a nudge by communicating in such a way as to generate positive emotions which then make him feel good and secure about making a purchase.

There are a few rules of successful communication which you should follow: ask open and activating questions, don't be afraid to be curious, take an interest in the person behind the customer. That's the only thing that will enable you to offer him the right product and the only way to find out what he really wants.

Listen more than you talk yourself. It is said that across all industries the salesperson's share of the talking in a successful sales pitch is around

30 per cent. But the exact figure doesn't matter: the more you ask questions and ask them well, the more you listen and listen attentively, the less you will overwhelm the customer with things that are of no interest to him. The times of the classic chatty person are long gone.

However, the customer doesn't always know that there is a different and better product that he is unaware of and that would suit his needs better: in that case, don't hesitate to give him the benefit of your expert advice. That's why he comes to you, after all – otherwise he could have ordered the product online. But please don't fall into the 'expert trap' here and tell him 'I know exactly what you need'. If the customer doesn't respond to your advice then that's the way it is. In that case just sell him what he feels is right. Provided you're not doing him any harm, that's perfectly fine.

Lars Schäfer demonstrates the importance of the relationship level in sales communication in his book *Emotionales Verkaufen* [*Emotional Selling*] (Schäfer, 2012) on the basis of actual selling situations. In his opinion, three factors are crucial for a successful relationship between the seller and the customer: attentiveness, authenticity and adaptability. Personality is the alpha and omega of the last two – we can only be authentic if we know ourselves. And we can only adapt if we have at least some idea of what the other person needs.

Let's look now at the influence of personality on communication during a sales dialogue. Selling appears come naturally to extroverts – people who are brilliant at making contacts, flexible decision-makers and smooth-talking limelight-seekers, with energy, enthusiasm, drive and ease when approaching other people. However, this impression can be refuted on three counts. First, it has been scientifically proven for more than a decade that there is no correlation between extroversion and sales quality or sales volume.[54] Secondly, half the population are introverts – and this half does not always appreciate all the typical behaviours of extrovert sales personnel. Thirdly, there are very successful 'quiet' sales professionals who can beat their extrovert colleagues hands down. However, the introverts fare no better in sales than the extroverts. In a new study, Adam Grant (2013a) shows who the really successful ones are: the centroverts (or ambiverts). I will talk more about that later on in this chapter.

So we'll now take a look at the differences between introvert and
extrovert salespeople. What strengths do introvert and extrovert
salespeople have when interacting with their customers? Where could
there be possible improvement opportunities? And what kind of
communication do introvert and extrovert purchasers need in order to
feel comfortable?

Let me say again at this point, we are all a *mixture* of introvert and
extrovert (and most of all the centrovert)! The differences discussed
below are trends – they are not intended as rigid boxes. So you may
recognize yourself in the points made across all the personality types.

The extrovert salesperson: inspires enthusiasm

Some of the extrovert strengths you were introduced to in the first
chapter would seem ideal for persuasive selling.

 Five strengths of extrovert salespeople

- **Enthusiasm.** Many purchases are not necessities like typical
  supermarket or DIY store goods – they are also, or even solely,
  intended to give an emotionally pleasant experience. These may
  include a high-end car, a fine meal for a special occasion or your
  offspring's first mobile phone.

  Extroverts with their enthusiasm are good at putting such
  purchases across as experiences. An experience-oriented purchase

is particularly attractive to buyers geared towards incentives and rewards (i.e. extroverts who see the purchased product or service as a reward). They enjoy the idea of the positive experiences the purchase will bring: awestruck colleagues, a pleasant memory, shared family experiences enhance the probability that the customer will be happy to come back another time.

- **Flexibility.** Extrovert salespeoples' skills in responding nimbly to the signals their customers send help them in the selling process. They aren't reliant on a guideline but are able to shape every discussion actively, even when it takes a surprising turn. They can make inferences easily and – particularly if they also have the strength of courage – deliver surprising and humorous twists.

- **Drive.** The connection between sales negotiations and drive is easy to make: for extroverts with this strength, a sales pitch is only successful if it ends in a purchase. This thinking is often too short-sighted, but it does ensure a clear goal orientation on the seller's part. In the best case, the customer should make a purchase. And the communication is focused on precisely this goal.

- **Emotional warmth.** Extrovert sales people with this strength love talking to their customers. This exchange with a lot of different people is probably one of the drivers that make them choose a career in sales. Emotionally warm people like to invest attention and energy in their communication, incorporate small talk quite naturally into the exchange and thereby build relationships. They are also glad to receive emotional warmth from others. This accessibility and openness is very pleasant for many (particularly extrovert) customers and ensures an emotionally positive purchasing experience.

- **Speaking.** Speaking, as direct contact, is very much more important in the sales process than writing and is an important element in implementing the above-mentioned strength of emotional warmth. A skilled talker can take an interesting and clever approach to presenting the object to be sold, and himself as well. What's more, without the spoken word the customer would ultimately be just as well to make his or her purchase online.

These extrovert strengths are major assets in sales communication. However, the hurdles that many extroverts have to cope with also emerge in the work of informing and persuading.

For example, Ernie in our example displays *self-centredness* and *self-dramatization*: he makes his own view of the headphones the central focus and presents himself as competent and well informed. His concentration on himself takes away his eye for Ingrid's needs. Ingrid probably also feels that there has been a touch of *aggression* in his approach to her – not everyone appreciates being deluged with words. The extrovert tendency to build up too much pressure and communicate too frequently or forcefully is generally speaking one of the main obstacles to extrovert sales people's success,[55] the more so because 'pushing' the customer is not so crucial in our world of informed purchasers. The point is more to enter into a joint discussion about a purchase decision in which the other party has equal rights. Don't forget, there's a chance that Ingrid may have known just as much about the headphones in her hand as Ernie at the beginning of the exchange. And Ernie needs to discover which points his customer needs to discuss.

The introvert salesperson: listens and holds back

Of the ten introvert strengths discussed in the first chapter, five are particularly useful in dealing with customers.

 Five strengths of introvert salespeople

- **Listening.** Just as extrovert sales people tend to talk well and talk a lot, many introverts score with the strength of genuine listening. An introvert listener gives his opposite number his full attention – which, by the way, is a wonderful form of emotional warmth. During this stage he will take in the customer's words and filter out the essentials. He will therefore also register where and under what conditions the customer would make a purchase. And in our example, Isabel will definitely hear that re-setting her account isn't at the top of Emma's to-do list.

- **Calm.** Calm is the polar opposite of aggression. Those who have this strength can give the customer space in the sales pitch. They don't feel under pressure to fill every pause with their own contributions. Introverts in particular appreciate sales personnel who give them room to consider and make decisions in this way.

- **Analytical thinking.** Together with listening, analytical thinking makes the introvert salesperson a first-class information processor. He pieces together what the customer says (or doesn't say) into an overall picture which enables statements to be made about her actual needs. This is the starting point for what he offers or communicates, concisely and in a structured form. It's also easy for the analyst to draw comparisons between different offers. The customer not only feels that she has been understood, but also that she has received first-class advice.

- **Tenacity.** Some customers take their time in reaching a purchase decision. Some customers want to be persuaded. Some customers need to be approached several times. Tenacious introvert sales people have a clear advantage here: they don't give up easily and remain quietly and patiently in touch.

- **Empathy.** People who can empathize with others in a sales situation can perform a service function in the best and truest sense of the word. Daniel Pink (2013a, p. 219) names empathy as a key factor in being able to identify and solve the customer's problems. Those who are able to put themselves in the customer's shoes find it very much easier to perceive and take account of his interests.

Introverts have advantages that are quite different from those of their extrovert colleagues, but which are just as important. However, like extroverts, introverts also have their weaknesses in certain areas of sales communication. In our example, Isabel struggles with the hurdle of *conflict avoidance*: she keeps describing her own project but doesn't say anything about the neglect of duty that Emma is guilty of and is satisfied with her somewhat 'airy' agreement. That gets in the way of clarity and a binding deal. A conflict avoider also tends to suffer under the inevitable 'No' responses that salespeople constantly encounter. Let's face it, not every customer makes a purchase and not every prospect can be persuaded. So when a 'Yes' meets a 'No' it creates tension, which is easily perceived as rejection.

Maybe Isabel was even dealing with *contact avoidance* and first had to summon up her resolve before she picked up the phone. After all, Isabel would rather work away quietly on the technical migration. In the worst case, *fear* enters the discussion: in this case, fear of making Emma commit herself and bringing a binding element into the discussion. By when exactly does Emma have to take action? When it comes to selling a product or service, fear may prevent the introvert saleswoman from finding a clear closing signal – even if she thinks that the customer is ready to buy.

Centrovert salespeople: unobtrusive stars

You are already acquainted from the first chapter with the characteristics of the people in the middle. You are meeting the centroverts again here for a particular reason. The position in the middle of the introvert/extrovert continuum ensures a certain balance: centroverts have the same strengths and face the same hurdles as introverts *and* extroverts in pretty even proportions. At the same time, they have an advantage in communication: in their centre position they have good access in discussions to introverts and extroverts alike, in other words they are closer emotionally to both sides and can understand them better than introverts and extroverts can understand each other.

 Key idea

Most centrovert salespeople can handle introvert and extrovert customers well, because the distance isn't as great as that between introverts and extroverts.

American management scientist Adam Grant demonstrates an interesting and very concrete approach to the centroverts' advantages in recent research (Grant, 2013a). For this study, Grant observed sales employees at a software company. He first determined their level of introversion or extroversion. He then tracked the sales performance of the individual employees for three months. To enable a direct, quantifiable comparison of their success he calculated their average earnings per hour in the sales department. It turned out that introvert sales people (US$120) earned somewhat less than extrovert ones (US$125). However, the victors were in the middle: centroverts, at US$155, earned more than a quarter more than their extrovert colleagues.

Four strengths of centrovert sales people

- **Versatility.** Centroverts are less defined by their own needs than introverts and extroverts. They sometimes feel at home in one environment, sometimes in another. They aren't tied to any great extent in terms of customers, either – they like a mixture and also have few problems with purchaser groups like couples or families. They don't see it as a great leap to move from thought to action and can link the facts and fascination of a product with ease.

- **Adaptability.** The ability to place the personality and needs of the customer in the centre is another typical centrovert strength that stands them in good stead in the sales process. They find it easy to adapt to very different people without getting the feeling that they have to make a big effort or even put on a pretence in order to do so. If the next customer marches to a completely different drum they aren't that fussed.

- **Mediation.** In their moderate position, centroverts are the heroes and heroines of diplomacy, (price) negotiation and conflict resolution. This strength makes them ideal partners when a complaint is made or in volatile situations. Centroverts can then pour oil on troubled waters, balance interests and make customers happy because the latter feel they are noticed and respected – and centroverts don't lose sight of their employers' interests in the process.

- **Level-headedness.** In the middle of the introvert/extrovert continuum, centroverts find it comparatively easy to handle highly introverted or extroverted people. Negative emotions and intuitive assessments don't get in their way so much because they have less of a tendency towards self-hugging (see Chapter 2) than the other two personality types. They are therefore able to respond to customers whom introverts or extroverts would find 'difficult' without a major expenditure of energy.

- Level-headedness and goal orientation are an ideal combination. Pink (2013a, b) conjectures that centroverts actually close sales deals with relative ease for this reason.

The balance between introversion and extroversion therefore seems to be a real strength in the sales field. In centroverts, the golden mean predominates rather than marked strengths and hurdles or specific needs. Centroverts can probably respond more easily to the person facing them for this reason and avoid disadvantages typical of extroverts ('too pushy') or introverts ('too hesitant'). Long live the centre!

Introvert and extrovert customers: what the differences mean when selling

By now you know what strengths introverts, extroverts and centroverts have in sales situations. If you think back to the beginning of this chapter, however, you will notice one striking feature: neither the extrovert Ernie nor the introvert Isabel was particularly successful in their attempts to persuade the other person.

It takes two (as a minimum) to make a successful dialogue in a sales situation, so it isn't just the seller's strengths that are important. How introvert and extrovert customers feel about the way their different needs are addressed is at least equally crucial. In purely mathematical terms, anyone in the seller's role who goes on auto-pilot on the basis of his own needs will be fairly much off course in half of all cases. Ernie just talks to Ingrid in a way that suits himself. What Ingrid needs is off his radar. And although Isabel describes how important the server migration is, she doesn't focus on Emma herself. And she doesn't really have the confidence to ask her straight out to cooperate.

But how do you spot whether the customer facing you is an introvert or an extrovert? The difference isn't always evident. It is easier, of course, if you already know the person. When you meet for the first time, an initial observation is helpful. Introvert and extrovert customers differ particularly in three areas with which you are now familiar, and from which certain typical preferences follow.

Introverts ...	Extroverts ...
... work 'from the inside outwards' and therefore appreciate inner space.	... work 'from the outside inwards' and therefore appreciate external stimuli.
... are easily overstimulated, i.e. easily overwhelmed by a lot of impressions. They therefore like things to be clearly organized and calculable.	... like an interesting mix of stimulation via the different sensory channels. For this reason they appreciate different impressions – and also switching between a variety of information and media.
... love safety.	... love incentives and rewards.

These differences affect what's perceived as pleasant in a sales pitch – and also what influences a purchase decision.

The following overview will help you when dealing with an introvert or extrovert customer.

Introvert and extrovert customers: five tips for communication

Introvert customers	Extrovert customers
Leave your customer time to process information. Introverts want to consider, evaluate, compare. Pauses aren't embarrassing, they're important thinking time. Maintain eye contact. Signal openness. And keep quiet.	Make your product or service attractive to your customer. Is it new? Especially innovative? A limited edition? Listen to what your customer finds interesting. Select your information accordingly.
Too much choice can be overwhelming. Find out what's important to your customer. Present the selection resulting from the answers.	Offer your customer an attractive range of options. This may include extras, combined packages or discounts. Extroverts mostly regard choice as positive.
Introverts easily get lost in details. So keep the main thrust of the argument in mind. Summarize and recap on essentials: 'You mentioned a moment ago that you travel a lot. What's the largest size of earphones that you can pack conveniently?'	A lot of extroverts like exciting, playful, entertaining or surprising stimuli. If it suits you, play along. What detail is completely out of the ordinary? What can the customer try out? What can you stage as a 'mini-show'?
Be careful with small talk. What extroverts consider to be a pleasant exchange will destroy introverts' trust and get on their nerves. Talk to the point, not too loudly and not too fast.	Many extroverts like small talk, the actual aim of which is the relationship. Feel free to use this preference in the sales situation. It makes it possible to create a personal base.

Take the lead cautiously when closing. Being cautious goes like this, for example: 'It sounds as if these earphones meet your requirements best. Is there anything more you would like to know about them?' Here, too, wait, maintain eye contact, allow pauses. Then you can lead into the sale. And, for example, refer to the guarantee or return terms. After all, you know that safety is king.

Extroverts are more spontaneous than introverts. And they also tolerate more pushiness in the close.Give your customer reinforcement with the fact that she has made a clever choice – but don't use empty words, tailor it to the situation. After all, you know that in the best case, the product has the character of a reward.

With centrovert customers, the situation is a bit trickier: quite apart from the fact that they're harder to spot, their needs are not as clear as those of highly introverted or extroverted people.

However, Ernie could re-jig his encounter with Ingrid relatively easily if he knew about introverts' needs.

 ## I want peace to work!

Ernie (sees Ingrid at the headphones): 'Hello. I see you're looking at our headphones. What would you be wanting to do with a new model?'

Ingrid: 'What I mainly need is good noise reduction. I want peace to work when I'm travelling.'

Ernie (quietly, friendly tone): 'I see. Have you already got a short list that you would consider?'

Ingrid: 'Basically, yes I have. At the moment I would just like to try out how the models feel. I don't like it when the ear-pads are too tight.'

Ernie: 'Well, let's see – which ones do you want to try out? I'll bring them to you.'

Ingrid: (names three models)

Ernie: 'One moment – I'll be right back.' (fetches four models) 'Here are those three models. And I've got another set of headphones here. It wasn't on your list, but it does have particularly soft ear-pads. And it's also way above average in filtering outside noise.'

Ingrid: 'Oh, that's great – I'll try those as well.'

And Isabel can also choose a better, more extrovert-friendly way of persuading Emma to reset her e-mail account.

 Of course I'll do it!

Isabel (on the phone): 'Hi Emma. Is the enforcer at your door yet?'

Emma: ???

Isabel: 'The server migration is the day after tomorrow. You're the only person in the whole place who hasn't reset her account yet. If you don't do it the boss will kill me. So the last resort that remains to me is my enforcer .'

Emma: 'Oh come on, chill. Take a deep breath.'

Isabel: 'Yeah, yeah, yeah. You've got one last chance. I'm sending you the details again. Now. Straight away. The reset will take you three minutes. Will you do it by lunchtime?'

Emma: 'Well, all right. Since it's you, of course I'll do it!'

Isabel: 'Great. I'll call off the enforcer. See you!'

A word in conclusion: paying heed to the customer is a wonderful thing – but do be alert to your own authenticity. Always sell in a way that suits *you* as well. Your contact with the customer will go best if you don't pretend to be someone you're not. And it will also make you happier if you put your own personality into selling, as you do into every form of communication. So always give attention to your own style and your own needs.

Selling convincingly

Think of a person you want to persuade about something in the near future.

1. Remember the introvert, centrovert or extrovert strengths and hurdles described in this chapter and write down the ones that relate to you personally.

2. Is the person you want to persuade more of an introvert or an extrovert? Read through the needs and write down what you feel you need to consider.

3. On this basis, develop a strategy that will help you with your plan.

Key points in brief

1. Above all else, selling is about persuasion. This requires a genuine dialogue – and this dialogue works best if it suits the seller's and the customer's personalities.

2. Extroverts may frequently score as sales people with the strengths of enthusiasm, flexibility, drive and emotional warmth. On the other hand, the hurdles of self-centredness, self-dramatization and aggression may have a negative effect.

3. Many introverts may use the strengths of listening, calm, analytical thinking, tenacity and empathy in sales situations. However, they can be blocked more easily than extroverts by conflict avoidance and contact avoidance.

4. Centrovert personalities are particularly well equipped to succeed as sales people with their mix of introvert and extrovert characteristics and the fact that they are relatively close to both personality types.

5. Introvert and extrovert customers often like different approaches. A sales person who takes this into account has clear advantages. The seller also has to bring in his or her own personality and remain authentic.

8.
Stressful encounters: status games

IF THE BOLD AND AGGRESSIVE GENERALLY PREVAIL, WHY WERE THE SENSITIVE NOT
SELECTED OUT OF THE HUMAN POPULATION THOUSANDS OF YEARS AGO, LIKE TREE
FROGS COLORED ORANGE?

SUSAN CAIN (2011, P. 226)

Status communication: the tools of power

 The meeting – a sliding tackle

Irene and Edgar are colleagues. They both hope that they have a chance
of the group leader position that will soon become free. At the moment
they are sitting in a departmental meeting. The topic is the expansion of
the sales network abroad.

Irene: 'I've done my research – the best option is expansion into the
EU markets of Eastern Europe. Poland and Bulgaria have locational
advantages (looks at her paper). We could also benefit from the
connections we already have in Hungary, and then there is still the
alliance that we have with the Czech company Ybos, which could
then ...'

Edgar: (interrupts) 'The suggestion is basically not at all bad – if we
watch out for a few details in the implementation, it could work. Here
are the risks: (...). If we can resolve these three things, I would say: Let's
do it!'

> *Head of department*: 'Hmm. I understand. Edgar, would you take on the matter and clear up the open issues?'
>
> *Edgar*: 'Right, I'll do that!'
>
> *Irene*: (looks bewildered)
>
> *Head of department*: 'Thanks! Splendid. Let's move on to the next point: (...) *Irene*: (rolls her eyes and folds her arms)

This sort of friction in everyday working life probably doesn't seem at all unusual to you. Irene and Edgar are competing for an attractive promotion. Both want to position themselves appropriately within their group and in front of their boss. Edgar gained a stage win in the meeting, launching a sliding tackle on Irene's contribution and carrying off a strategically important project – definite progress for his positioning and visibility. Irene was not able to get another word in and gave up when the head of department as chairman of the meeting moved to the next item.

Situations like these are about demarcation, hierarchy, confrontation and competition and belong in the special area of vertical or status communication.[56] Status communication is an important factor in human exchange. It demonstrates a claim on our social position in relation to our fellows – in speech, body language and behaviour (e.g. by interrupting or omitting to answer). It helps to organize our interaction within social structures and keep it easy to understand. It also makes a contribution to drawing up and securing boundaries, provides guidance about the members of a group and offers an interesting set of information on the partners in the dialogue. Who has power? Who is making a claim for leadership? Who cooperates with whom? Who stands where in the group hierarchy?

I left this area of social interaction out in the general section about our lives in the community as it quite clearly deserves its own chapter.

Key idea

Status communication is necessary in social interaction. It provides the group and individuals with important orientation signals.

Status communication in the form of friction as in our example has a special place in professional life as well. In extreme cases, the 'dog eat dog' mentality determines interaction to such an extent that a large part of communication revolves around who is right or who comes out on top and unfortunately not about how the best objective solution could look.

But demarcation of boundaries, trials of strength and hierarchical strata always play a part in an exchange. If you want to shape your career actively, you should understand this and be aware of the relevant rules (even if status wrangling often bears a strong resemblance to kindergarten). The next step is to play the game – in a way that matches your own personality. Because if you don't play, your career could easily suffer. But this field of communication is stressful – no wonder that many people prefer to steer clear of it.

Because, of course, dealing with confrontations and fights about status has its price. Even when a meeting is fairly relaxed and on a level playing field, experienced status seekers make sure the hierarchical distinctions between participants are defined, even though the messages are less clear than in the original example. Consciously or unconsciously, people want to know their place and the place of others in the pecking order.

In the relationship between two people there are basically only ever two positions in a given situation: a relatively high status or a relatively low status compared to the other (see Johnstone, 1989, for details on this). These positions are variable and can change from one situation to another, although there are certain tendencies depending on the personalities. As with everything, we tend towards preferred behaviours, i.e. to 'favourite status signals' which we send out especially frequently. In our example, therefore, Edgar very probably considers it completely appropriate to interrupt Irene publicly. He is embodying his own favourite status, and he also knows Irene's (including her usual behaviours) through working with her all the time.

 Key idea

Status communication is neither good nor bad in itself. It is part of how we interact with each other.

With some training and determination, however, Irene could have surprised Edgar with an unexpected riposte ('Just a minute, Edgar – *who's* speaking just now?'), causing the status game to take a surprising turn.

In other words, status confrontations usually proceed with a calculated risk – but just as in a game where the result is unknown, there are also many different possibilities for the course of the communication and no guarantee of the outcome.

Formal position within a hierarchy is often crucial when it comes to confrontation. If there has to be a decision as to who is to take on a task, for example, then the person with the power to give instructions has a clear advantage. But this is not always the case. There are status-conscious employees and indulgent bosses, aggressive assistants and hesitant chiefs. Power is not something we just 'have' even if it is assigned by right of a public position. Real power includes a willingness and preparedness to actively shape your own environment and send out appropriate status signals. These can run contrary to the expectations of a formal role, like the chief who 'submits' to his assistant.

Things really get interesting when the position of the two rivals is about the same, as with Irene and Edgar – then other factors decide who wins through in the end. And these factors almost always have something to do with personal characteristics. This, in its turn, makes the topic of status communication especially interesting for the interchange between extroverts and introverts.

Tom Schmitt and Michael Esser (2009, pp. 23–36) differentiate between 'inner' and 'outer' status. As the focus of this book is on personalities who are 'inward' or 'outward' looking, this approach particularly lends itself as a basis.

I use it as a basic starting point and use inner/outer status as one of the elements which help introverts and extroverts to select their status position. So here first of all are the basic tenets of Schmitt and Esser (2009):

The 'framework' of status communication

Example

The initial case: Irene and Edgar in the meeting

- **High status:** brings respect, costs liking
- **Underlying desire**: distance from others
- **Low status:** costs respect, brings liking
- **Underlying desire**: closeness to others
- **Inner status:** What do I feel? What do I want to achieve?
- **Outer status:** How do I represent that outwardly, i.e. how do I play it? – the 'façade' of status communication

This produces four configurations:

1. Inner high and outer low status

Strategy: Inner clarity about your own goals, combined with outer commitment, diplomacy, circumspection and courtesy

Consequence: Good opportunity for gaining respect and retaining liking

Example: *Irene* (continues speaking and looks at Edgar): 'Wait, Edgar, and let me get to the end ...'

2. Inner and outer high status

Strategy: Inner clarity about your own goals, combined with outward dominance; fixation on 'determining role'

Consequence: Brings high respect, often costs liking

Example: *Irene*: 'Wait! I'm speaking here. And I haven't yet finished. Thank you.'

3. Inner low and outer high status

Strategy: Inner sense of powerlessness, outwardly not authentic dominance because only feigned

Consequence: Brings neither respect nor liking, not very credible

Example: *Irene*: 'Well, that's incredible. Just interrupting me like that. Where do you think you are?'

4. Inner and outer low status

Strategy: Inner desire for harmony outweighs the desire for increased power, outward subordination of own interests to those of other people

Consequence: Gets liking but little or no respect

Example: *Irene*: (annoyed, bites her lip and looks right and left for help)

Depending on the situation, the very same person may decide on different configurations. But usually there is a preference for a specific configuration.

In competitive and confrontational situations, 'inner high' usually wins. The insight behind it is ancient: if you know what you want, you can often convince other people to support you in your aims. If you don't know what you yourself want to achieve, you will often help others to achieve their aims. Neither high nor low status is (un)pleasant or (un)friendly per se.

A power claim in high status can be expressed for example in a friendly ('May I just?') or unfriendly ('Make room here!') manner.

> ## ❗ Key idea
>
> The high status currency is respect. The low status currency is liking.

Basically however there are two key 'currencies'. In low status the currency is liking and in high status it is respect. Being liked and respected are therefore different areas and cannot always be reconciled. You often get one or the other. So Irene may have the liking of many meeting participants on her side – but her behaviour will gain her hardly any respect. The reverse is probably true of Edgar: respect yes, but probably not liking. Depending on what is important to you, it can be more difficult or easier to win through in the status stakes. If being liked is especially dear to your heart, you will be more easily prepared to remain reticent in confrontations. And if you demand respect above all else, you will find it easier to sacrifice liking than someone for whom respect is less attractive.

> ## ❗ Key idea
>
> In competitive situations 'inner high' wins.

Dominant personalities (inner high/outer high), who like to exercise power and therefore influence on others, have no problem with confrontations and competitive situations. They consciously use them more frequently than reticent people to assert their claim. Other people learn that status communication is just one of those things you have to accept and is a necessary evil for standing your ground in a group. They do not find confrontation and competition pleasant but do not suffer inordinately from occasional disputes, boundaries or withdrawal of liking.

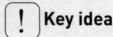

! Key idea

If you know what you want, you can often convince other people to support you in your aims. If you don't know what you want to achieve, you will often help others to achieve their aims.

There are others again for whom status communication causes anxiety – especially introverts who are less often on the offensive and have little appetite for conflict because of their hurdles. It is particularly difficult when classic female socialization is also present, where liking tends to be valued more highly than influence and assertiveness. In a framework where such norms prevail, low status behaviours are regarded as appropriate: always let others finish what they are saying, be nice, be as popular as possible and liked by everyone, don't rub anyone up the wrong way, play by the rules … You will have realized by now that what may work in school is not very helpful in dealing with the Edgars of this world![57]

Remaining authentic under stress

In confrontation, personality differences between introverts and extroverts are particularly prone to becoming a problem. There is basically no connection between introversion and extroversion on the one hand and the claim to status on the other. The tendency to strive for a high status is a quite different personality trait. Of course, both personality types can communicate both high and low status, both inside and out. But people tend towards 'self-hugging', as you now know (see Chapter 2).

Remember: we believe that the way we behave as a result of our personalities is natural, and we automatically expect others to behave the same way; these behaviours are difficult to change. On the other hand, our rational mind teaches us to know and (possibly) value character types and behaviours which differ from ours. We can also learn to behave differently from the way we would if we were on 'autopilot'. Nevertheless, such adjustment can only be done easily if we are relaxed (and of course motivated). In stressful and fraught situations – including the meeting in the initial example as well as most other confrontational situations – we tend to revert to behaviours which are closer to our personality types and suggested by our unconscious. This is easily explained: when we need our energy to deal with confrontation, our emotional unconscious claims priority and all too easily all the good intentions and strategies which we work out with conscious deliberation in quieter times are relegated to the background. There is simply no strength left for them.

(Which is why in phases of stress certain kinds of food find their way into our mouths when from a rational and purely theoretical point of view we would normally be inclined to avoid them for the sake of our waistline …)

 Key idea

Under stress the emotions easily take command. We then revert to behaviours which are closer to our natural tendencies than anything strategic, conscious or planned.

That is why the introvert Irene freezes in a passive attitude after Edgar's determined initiative, instead of saying something. She avoids open conflict – but it is easy to imagine what is going on in her head.

Luckily, this does not mean that in stressful situations we helplessly surrender to our unconscious 'autopilot'. But it does mean first of all that it is more difficult for introverts and extroverts in these cases to deal with each other because their differences are more likely to clash. Secondly, it means that we find it easier when we can create security for ourselves and others – without waiting until a burning need arises.

Included in this is that we become aware of our unconscious patterns of behaviour (and for the advanced: the unconscious behaviour patterns of others). If Irene knew a bit about her own typical reactions and observed them consciously when there are signs that they will arise, if she also knew exactly what she wanted, if she knew how Edgar as an extrovert tended to react and how she for her part could deal with him, then she would have been able to act more self-confidently and with a greater focus on her objective.

Key idea

Knowing yourself makes you stronger!

What's more, if you communicate authentically, you have especially good prospects for success in status disputes. In this context 'authentic' means 'in harmony with your own motives, values and characteristics'.

It is therefore a matter of pursuing your own aims with your own personality – and not acting the big shot or the little bunny because some role model seems to demand it. Perhaps what Edgar was doing in the meeting was consistent from this point of view.

Irene should act just as consistently if she wants to fight back. If you know your options, you can consciously use them beyond your 'official' position and in many cases convince others who are purely formally very much more powerful. According to Schmitt and Esser (2009, p. 165),' As long the status game is unconsciously being played, in the end the higher status will always use its power and exact punishment and vengeance, take the advantage and leave others standing in the rain …'. That's what it's about: using our own options and capabilities consciously as best we can – when we want to achieve something important enough for us to make the attempt.

! Key idea

Be aware of your own ways of communicating and know the differences between introvert and extrovert ways of behaving. These two factors provide authenticity and detachment. That is how negative emotions remain within sensible boundaries under stress – and personal self-assurance provides the basis for persuasiveness.

However stressful confrontations and rituals relating to trials of strength may be within a group and between groups, they show current power shifts or the capacity for preservation of power and are therefore necessary. Power positions (in humans just as in the animal kingdom) are repeatedly re-tested and re-negotiated. They will always be around and should generally do more good than harm. And we need to learn to consider this type of exchange through the lens of rationality and to scrutinize it more closely – even it is sometimes stressful.

The remainder of this chapter mainly revolves around the following questions:

1 How do humans actually organize their status communication?
2 What should extroverts and introverts particularly be aware of in their status communication?

Status communication: introverts and extroverts

Two things should be stated up front. First of all, this section is expressly *not* about manipulating or intimidating others or using some trick or other to put them at a disadvantage. Secondly, it is expressly *very much* about encountering others using the resources of your personality in such a way that they find it easy to respect you and to observe the limits you want to be observed. In the same way as you should respect others too …

The introvert perspective

Many introverts find status communication decidedly difficult. It is heavily geared towards an outward effect – and this is exactly what quiet inward-looking people often find stressful. Because of their need for security, they also feel threatened particularly easily. They tend to be somewhat overcautious about addressing conflicts or confrontations openly. Public criticism causes them stress. Introverts also tend to loathe unpredictable and violent reactions. A tackle like that which Edgar launched in the meeting creates a particularly threatening setting for anxious people. That is why introverts prefer to withdraw into their shells rather than face the situation and embrace the challenge of a trial of strength.

Involuntarily, introverts easily slip into low status by giving the relevant signals. They are quiet, they look away or they hunch their shoulders. The hurdle of attention to detail can also result in low status signals such as speaking quickly and quietly when listing details or making quick, undefined movements and touching the head and neck area. (Later in the chapter you will find a summary of status signals.)

Other hurdles which make it difficult for introverts to deal with aggressive or unfair discussion partners are flight, passivity, and contact and conflict avoidance. What these hurdles have in common is that introverts like Irene flinch or withdraw in a confrontation and, in order not to have to 'fight', even put up with it when someone unacceptably steps over the boundaries.

The introvert will then often shut down vis-à-vis the conflict partner, so that communication is deflected or even denied. This certainly saves stress and energy in the short term, but nevertheless entails high costs in the medium to long term because 'shutting down' is usually not a successful strategy and causes severe inner pressure (which cannot escape if everything is shut down). The consequences can even be detrimental to health – no one can keep on bottling up the things that don't agree with them with impunity. A life on which others are just allowed to trample is in the long term stressful and energy-sapping.

! Key idea

A life on which others are just allowed to trample is stressful and energy-sapping.

But there is a positive view as well. Introverts have certain strengths which make it easier for them to deal with status disputes and aggressive discussion partners. The main ones are calm and tenacity. These two strengths can ensure and even communicate inner high status in a way that remains outwardly socially acceptable and ensures a healthy measure of liking. Analytical thinking and close listening (and watching) supply the necessary input for reacting appropriately.

Empathy in particular is a part of the strength repertoire of the introvert which can become an important key to finding common ground in tense situations. Even when Edgar attacks, Irene's ability to empathize can be an important guide to distinguishing an appropriate answer ('I'd like to be part of that – I've found a fair bit of insider knowledge in my research!') from a less appropriate retort (publicly humiliating Edgar by aiming verbal poisoned arrows) and not putting the winning of the verbal skirmish above all else. That's another way to earn respect.

The extrovert perspective

Nor do extroverts always have it easy in confrontations and conflict situations – introverts are all too inclined to think they do from the other side of the fence. If you don't approach things quietly and cautiously you pay a different price for your communication in tense situations.

Introverts live inwardly, extroverts outwardly. In contrast to introverts, the main hurdle for extroverts is accordingly not in bottling everything up inside but in managing their energy – so that it is directed to where it benefits external impact. The hurdles of too much impatience, too much aggression, but especially impulsiveness and overpowering force build up pressure and communicate concentrated energy. In withdrawn people this pressure often arouses a defensive impulse or an urge to flee: 'He or she is out to get me, 'Steamroller!' or 'Oh dear – how do I get out of here?'

 Key idea

The two big tasks for extroverts in a confrontation are firstly energy management, and secondly dealing with lack of feedback.

Because extroverts are also more dependent than introverts on resonance from the outside world, they find it particularly difficult when this resonance is denied them. It can drive an extrovert to desperation when he or she has the feeling that talking to an introvert is like talking to a brick wall or are falling like water off a duck's back. Many extroverts have emphatically assured me that it is particularly bad if their opposite number says nothing. If you also tend towards self-dramatization, it is then very tempting to increase the pressure.

On the other hand, many extroverts have plenty of characteristics which make them strong in status disputes and conflicts. The courage to initiate or deal with a dispute is, like the strength of conflict management, especially advantageous in difficult communication situations. If these arise in oral dialogue, extroverts with speaking skills have the upper hand – especially if they also have flexibility and speed. With characteristics like these they are able to react like lightning to their discussion partner and to what's happening. What stresses introverts so often is the unpredictable, the high speed, the emotionality in a dispute: extroverts sometimes find that downright stimulating – and when a reward also presents itself, as for Edgar, then status communication becomes downright dazzlingly stimulating.

Introverts versus extroverts

Here for your guidance is a summary of the strengths and hurdles which are frequently found in introverts and extroverts in status disputes, confrontations and conflicts.

Status clarification – strengths and hurdles in introverts and extroverts

Introvert strengths and their effects	Extrovert strengths and their effects
Strength 4: listening Accurate perception of the situation	**Strength 1: courage** Readiness to actively structure confrontations
Strength 5: calm Good prerequisite for certain high status signals	**Strength 3: flexibility** Easy adjustment to opportunities and changes in situation
Strength 6: analytical thinking Precise planning of procedure in a dispute	**Strength 5: speed** Good prerequisite for certain high status signals
Strength 8: tenacity View of the bigger picture: long term gain is the priority	**Strength 9: speaking** Good prerequisite for convincing manner
Strength 10: empathy Good assessment of opposite number	**Strength 10: conflict management** Aggressive communication
Introvert hurdles and their effects	Extrovert hurdles and their effects
Hurdle 1: anxiety Low status as apparent safety	**Hurdle 3: impatience** Unconsidered attacks if momentum is lacking

(Continued)

Introvert hurdles and their effects	Extrovert hurdles and their effects
Hurdle 2: attention to detail Low status signal: too much talking	**Hurdle 4: self dramatization** Smoke and mirrors or disparagement of others instead of real persuasiveness
Hurdle 4: passivity Low status is accepted because effort appears too great	**Hurdle 5: aggression** Especially if annoyance is a factor: unnecessary or too strong an attack
Hurdle 5: flight Too quick to withdraw in awkward situations	**Hurdle 6: impulsiveness** Losing sight of rationality and allowing emotions the upper hand
Hurdle 9: contact avoidance Social isolation to avoid confrontation	*(The differences between introverts and extroverts are not always symmetrical, hence the empty box!)*
Hurdle 10: conflict avoidance Low status accepted because the risk appears too high	**Hurdle 10: overpowering force** Using a great deal of energy to exert too much pressure on the opposite number, accepting possible breaches of rules

From this list it is easy to identify certain difficulties which are produced when introverts and extroverts clash. If an introvert decides after much deliberation to engage actively in a confrontation, for example, it comes across as too quiet or innocuous, especially to extroverts, when combined with conflict avoidance or flight. That is why extroverts often do not take counter-confrontation or criticism from introverts seriously at first – or they may not even notice them if they are expressed only very guardedly or indirectly.

If you cast your mind back over the last few sections, it appears at first glance that extroverts have the advantage in confrontations:

strengths such as courage, presentation, speed and speaking well equip extroverts perfectly for awkward situations. Extroverts also find it easier to address conflicts and to lay things on the line because of their drive and their ability to manage conflict. These are precisely the kind of characteristics which many introverts would be all too happy to have more of. A sense of inferiority can easily arise here.

But it is not that simple. Extroverts are by no means always more successful than introverts in confrontations – even though they have the ability to appear domineering and forceful. As you can see from the above list, introverts have their own strengths to stand them in good stead in status communication. Put yourself in extrovert Evan's shoes in the following situation.

 ## He's leaving me to stew!

Evan is group leader in a medium-sized company. He is confident and jovial, also has an excellent network and is considered to be hands-on and flexible. He has had a younger boss for some months now. As head of department, Ian has a quiet management style and allows his staff a great deal of freedom in decision-making.

Shortly after Ian took up his new position, Evan lost a big contract by precipitate action. To cap it all, the rejection came from an important customer. The effects on his group's sales could very clearly be seen.

Ian has so far not mentioned this blunder to Evan, nor has he had much else to do with him. However, Evan senses his critical gaze and is stewing in his own juice – he himself is rather open, but does not know how best to handle the 'new guy' in this matter. In the meantime, he is steering clear of Ian. And at the same time, he knows it's wrong. In short, he feels very uncomfortable.

Here it is the extrovert who is feeling the effects of an introvert's typical status signals and finding them difficult to deal with. Introverts can let others run aground, ignore them, or play one off against the other … Ian isn't actually doing much. But it is clear who is quietly dominating the situation here.

Let us now take a look at what status signals there actually are – and how introverts and extroverts use their own natures especially frequently to flesh them out with their own manner of communication. The two personality types have different tasks to perform here because of their different orientation inwards or outwards.

 ## Status tasks for introverts and extroverts

Schmitt and Esser (2009) assume that inner high status and outer low status are the perfect combination because the player may gain both respect and liking. If introverts and extroverts strive for this combination, they have various options available.

- For introverts, who focus on their *inner life*, it is mostly about how to actively shape their *outer* status.
- For extroverts, who focus on their exchange with the *outer world,* it is mostly about actively shaping their *inner* status.

If an introvert like Ian knows what he wants, he is strong. The difficulty is to design outer status signals so that they are accommodating but cannot be interpreted as weak or too acquiescent.

If an extrovert like Evan is strong in communication and has plenty of positive connections, he has a different task. For him it is important to establish his inner high status so that if someone says nothing to him it does not knock him off balance and maybe cause overreaction.

The next section deals with actual status signals and the question of what you as an introvert or extrovert should particularly take into account.

The five status zones

So that you can proceed systematically when considering your own status signals, I have organized them here for you into distinct sections, but please keep in mind that people occupy status territories in a very wide range of contexts. Distinctions are normally made between verbal and non-verbal signals, but I have reorganized them in order to provide the most concrete personality-specific advice. The result is the five status areas you see here. They are logically structured so that after reading them you can very quickly and easily deduce for yourself the individual expressions of power. And that's what it's all about: you should be able to quickly recognize and deal with power signals in real-life situations.

The most obvious and literal area is probably 'space', which is top of the list. But status signals can also be associated with other 'currencies': time, energy, emotional warmth and self-presentation.[58]

I have added specific advice for introverts and extroverts for each of the five areas. The hurdles often present themselves very differently in the same area depending on the point of view and the on personality!

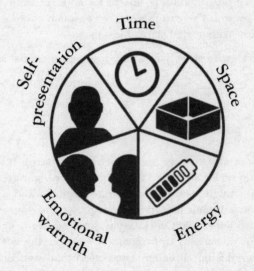

The explanations and overviews in the next few sections have two purposes: they should firstly provide you with reliable guidance – including when you are observing others. Secondly, the list should help to prevent you inadvertently sending out 'false' signals – especially in your body language but also with your voice.

Even if status signals have not seemed very important to you in the past, this will teach you the 'basic vocabulary', so to speak.

Status area 1: space

The space around us is our territory in a very concrete sense: it is where we and others are located and where we move about. In confrontations and competitive situations, high and low status are often determined purely spatially: who controls the space? Who is allowed to penetrate the other party's territory, i.e. to enter their work area or even their personal comfort zone? How big are the participating actors' movements?

But space as a status zone also has a less obvious side. Small, calm movements can be much more effective than flailing around with your arms: because (assuming they have a beginning and an end to define them) they signal purposefulness, an eye for appropriateness and an impression of control. There are therefore obviously other aspects to take into account with spatial status messages.

Here is an overview to show you where to look for spatial status signals in future.

Status signals relating to space

Space between people

- **Standing room and seating area (horizontal space):** If you place your feet a hip width apart and distribute your weight evenly, and also stand up straight, you have a definite 'stance' – and with it a claim to status. If your feet are close together and your weight maybe leans to left or right, it is easy to send out signals of low status: there is no stability or firmness. If you take the whole seating area of a chair, this has a higher status effect than someone who only takes up half the seat or sits on the edge.

- **Body size and vertical spatial relationship:** It is easy for tall people who physically take up more space to seem powerful. Nevertheless, this impression can be quickly dissipated by a lack of energy, or especially through poor posture (such as hunched or dropped shoulders or limp arms).

Sitting and standing can create an imbalance of status between people. As an example, are all the participants sitting down? You may stand up to welcome a visitor when they come in out of quite different motives: to prevent the person from sitting down (high status signal) or out of respect for him (low status signal). Standing can ensure distance, establish level terms, display respect or also signal a claim to power.[59]

- **Standing your ground:** If you don't alter your position, remain standing or sitting and possibly manage to keep calm eye contact if someone moves towards you (perhaps in confrontation or charged with energy), you show calm authority – assuming the rest of your body signals match. So no nervous fumbling about, please, no looking away or hunching your shoulders!

- **Entering someone else's space:** People have spatial comfort zones: they need a certain distance from others, a zone in which they feel safe. There are different gradations depending on the nature of the relationship: the closer a person is to us emotionally (e.g. partner or child) the more we allow this person access to our comfort zone. In professional interaction, however, a greater distance is usual and touching is rare. But the culture in which we grow up also leads to differences. In Japan or Finland the distance between people is greater than in India or Italy.

Stepping over the boundary and entering someone else's comfort zone demonstrates a claim for power. This happens, for example, if you make yourself at home in someone else's office or look over someone's shoulder while they are sitting down (example: PC display on the desk). Being too close when in conversation can also cause discomfort and stress.

Probably the most extreme form of (outer) high status in a space is to push someone away aggressively. The handling of such an intrusion also sends out status signals: does the communication partner allow the intruder to get his way (low status)? Does she move out of the way (ditto)? Does she find a way to get him to step back (high status)?

- **Going to someone:** Who goes to whom to resolve something? Normally the low-ranking person goes to the higher-ranking one – unless the latter wants to send out a definite signal of esteem.

With people of equal rank the least complicated place in conflict situations is a neutral meeting area away from their personal places of activity.

- **Placing of objects or arms and hands:** If you place objects in an environment you will send out a particular status message if they are placed in someone else's area. Sometimes something is put down to extend one's own 'territory' vis-à-vis someone else. For example, a colleague may put her handbag on your desk (a counter-measure with a corresponding signal effect is to remove the object from your own area without comment, e.g. put it on the floor!). But also, at the conference table, if you put your hands and arms visibly on the table top this can send a similar message: you can see I'm here! Particular claims to status are made by people who move their arms and/or hands emphatically and possibly even noisily.

In that case, the use of energy is added. Examples might be impatiently drumming your fingers on the table, fist on the table, elbows placed left and right. At the top of the dominance scale is banging your fist on the table.

Space as a personal status area

- **Office:** The room where a person works signals their status in many ways. The key points are size, position, number of windows, obstacles to access (e.g. outer office or hallway), restricted access (e.g. access only by appointment or restricted by an assistant in the outer office).

- **Conference room:** If you sit in the front row, i.e. right at the table, this indicates your active participation. You are then someone to be reckoned with in the discussion rather than someone who withdraws into the second row even if there are spaces free.[60]

- **Parking space:** Your parking space is also part of your spatial territory. How close is your reserved parking space to the main entrance of the company building? And what happens if someone makes use of your space without permission?

Different spatial strategies on the part of introverts and extroverts can frequently be observed and consequently differences in the status signals they send out. Introverts and extroverts also feel stress for different reasons. This is because an inward looking attitude (introverts) leads to different signals from an outwardly oriented attitude (extroverts). If hurdles such as caution or conflict avoidance are added in the case of introverts, or hurdles such as aggression or overpowering force in the case of extroverts, these can heighten the differences in behaviour and perception.

Here are a few tips to help you to use your personality to recognize and make use of status signals.

The status area of space: tips for introverts

Even if you prefer to deal inwardly with status encounters and outwardly prefer to avoid direct confrontation, you should very consciously shape your signals in the spatial area (which obviously is 'outward'). Experiment with various behaviours.

1. Use the strengths of analytical thinking and tenacity to be clear in your own mind about those situations in which you want to avoid a person or want to leave a place of communication because of fraught communication. Consciously practise not giving way. Instead, actively participate in shaping the communication. Stand up if someone positions themselves behind your chair. Approach anyone who unexpectedly enters your office and thereby limit their access to 'your' space.

2. Occupy the space with analytical power and your capacity for observation. Where is the best place in a meeting for you to be seen and heard by decision makers and important contacts? How should you sit to be perceived as confident? Start by placing your arms and hands visibly on the table top – you don't have to stretch them right out. It's a lot easier if you have your work material on the table.

3. If you are dealing with a 'space-filling' communication partner, take a deep breath. Remember that extroverts often have a particularly dynamic outward effect.

Practise your own behaviour particularly in situations where you feel under fire or under pressure – such as when someone comes too close to you or flails around with sweeping gestures and therefore appears aggressive. In such cases keep your eyes and body posture turned towards the aggressive other party. Avoid nervous movements, looking away or hunching your shoulders.

The status area of space: tips for extroverts

Extroverts prefer more than introverts to occupy the outer world. It is therefore probably easier for them to create a spatial presence. Their critical points in spatial status communication therefore lie in other areas.

1. Make sure (especially with people of higher formal status) that you do not invade their territory all too aggressively. Also consider that a fairly introverted person may be more sensitive than an extrovert. As examples, knock before entering an office *and* wait for an answer; place objects close to yourself.

2. Reticent people easily feel harassed if you get too close to them, touch them or wave your arms and hands at them. Keep your movements calm and keep your distance. The key phrase from earlier in the chapter is 'comfort zone'.

3. Be careful with your own movements if you are dealing with a communication partner who keeps his distance, moves away or appears nervous. That will prevent additional stress.

But watch out: although introverts frequently move in a smaller radius, that says nothing at all about their claim to power or their self-confidence. And the nervous conversation partner may be an extrovert ...

Status area 2: time

SOMEONE WITH POWER DOESN'T RUN. AND VICE VERSA: THE PERSON WHO RUNS DOES
NOT HAVE POWER.

PETER MODLER (2012, P. 129)

Time is a precious and limited resource. It is also a territory which
can be 'occupied' in status communication. Just observe in relevant
situations: who is allowed to waste someone else's time by making
them wait or interrupting them (as Edgar interrupted Irene in
the initial example)? Who allows himself time by waiting before
answering an e-mail or by speaking slowly or for a long time? In
short: who uses other people's time, and who yields time and allows
others to determine the duration and momentum of a meeting?

The speed at which we communicate also reveals something about
our status behaviour. As Peter Modler highlights, a quick pace
when moving or speaking expresses one thing above all others:
subservience.

Status signals relating to time

Speaking time

In Western cultures, the more powerful are usually allowed to talk for
longer and are usually not interrupted.

Speaking pace

If you talk quickly you appear less powerful than someone who takes
his time when speaking. Even though we often find it assumed in
American literature that (extroverted) fast talking comes over as lively,
competent and likeable, this does not apply at all if it leads to the
impression that the speaker is nervous, insecure or is just in a hurry.
Quietly and quickly in combination is almost always low status. So
take a deep breath and do not be rushed.

If you speak very slowly you also have a problem. The intonation is
important here: for slower high status speakers, the dynamic lies in

the melodiousness of the voice and in the skilful use of accentuation and pauses. If you belong to this group, it is better to keep it brief. That is generally better in conflicts and tense situations anyway.

Pace of movement

The same applies to movement as to speaking time and speaking pace: if you are high status, you can afford to move slowly. A prerequisite is that this slowness appears confident, defined and therefore powerful – and not just dreamy, obtuse, insecure or feeble: more a lion than a snail.

A frantic pace has the reverse effect. As with talking, haste is usually low status in movement as well. As quoted above, the person who runs does not have power.

Reaction timing

Reaction timing can be understood as the pace of movement in a metaphorical sense. It assumes that someone is turning to you, be it with a question, a task, a concern or even to tackle you. You send out high status signals if you take your time with the answer to an e-mail or look questioningly without comment at the person trying to tackle you. It looks quite cool if you turn to something completely different and let the attack come to nothing.

Punctuality

Punctuality, like politeness in general, signals respect (see status area 4) – here it is respect for another person's time and the wish not to waste it. Intentional lack of punctuality in meetings can be a status signal – few people will risk the others starting without them. Or it signals that the person is otherwise engaged and had to keep the meeting waiting.

For the status area of time, introverts and extroverts should focus on their personal strengths and hurdles.

The status area of time: tips for introverts

Introverts tend to value having time. The risks, but also the options, in time-related status communication are based above all on two points. First of all, introverts process a lot of information in a complex manner and therefore generally like to consider and think for longer. Secondly, introverts sometimes need more time before they can put thoughts into words to their satisfaction.

1. Introvert strength lies in calmness. Use the fifth introvert strength to give you confidence. Allow yourself time in moving and speaking (but not *too* much time!). Confidence is difficult to reconcile with frantic activity.

   If the hurdle of excessive attention to detail applies to you make sure that in a discussion you select your information according to the line of argument you are pursuing and do not supply too many details. It does not matter how confident you seem, if you recite miniscule points as if you had all the time in the world, you give the impression that you are not focusing on essentials. And it takes too much effort to listen to you. So you are not just losing the 'status currency' of respect but also attentiveness.

2. Your tenacity is a strength which is directly connected to time. Just as you can stand your ground in space you can also stand your ground in time. Do not therefore be rushed by frenzied, loud or energetic people. Even when you appear to come up against insuperable obstacles and rejection *en route* to an objective, accept a 'no!' only outwardly. Do not give up but do look for another way. This adds up to determination and ensures inner high status.

   Do not allow yourself to be interrupted either – tenacity will help you with this too. Continue speaking by saying something like, 'Just let me get to the end!' This is a possible strategy which Irene could have used in the meeting in our initial example. An exception would be if someone of formally higher status (e.g. your boss) interrupts you. In this case, persevering would be a very risky confrontation – especially if you are not on your own with the person.

3. On the other hand, give your communication partners stimuli which ensure their attention. Remember that extroverts in particular like messages which signal that there's something going on. Even if it is mulling things over – or the need to gain time. If a spontaneous suggestion comes from an extrovert, a statement such as 'Just a minute, I'm just taking out something about that!' can get this task done with minimal expense of time.

Even clever timing of the reaction (see the time status categories above) to such a suggestion can provide this stimulus: 'Let me think about it, then I'll get back to you right away.' By taking such an action you claim the confidence to think about something at your leisure instead of letting yourself be caught on the hop, reacting without thinking and making time, energy or work effort available to the other person.

When under attack, reaction timing may mean a premature interruption of the conversation: 'Let's talk about this again later. I'll get in touch with you in the morning.' Or you can be silent and go …

The status area of time: tips for extroverts

Extroverts like filling their time with different types of activities. They are more likely than introverts to cherish dynamism, variety and pace in communication.

1. A particular temptation for extroverts under stress is to speak faster (or louder). Carefully adjust your pace to that of your opposite number. You are usually successful if, first of all, the other person can follow you and, secondly, if he does not feel overwhelmed or driven into a corner by you. And you know of course that the hurdles of aggression and overpowering force are listed on the extrovert side …

If speed becomes frantic activity, what is originally a strength can easily tip over into weakness and become a risk to the way you project yourself on your environment. In heated moments, bear in mind that rushing has a *low* status effect!

2. Integrate systematic time planning into your life. Make sure that you can keep all your important appointments – and can in principle be punctual as well. You could benefit here from the caution typical of introverts to avoid being unintentionally rude and wasting time in your meeting.

3. You should usually let the person you are talking to finish speaking and only interrupt under very exceptional circumstances. An interruption can have a fatal effect if you break into the time territory of someone of higher rank – even if you don't do it at all intentionally. Many extroverts interrupt just because they think they know what their discussion partner wants to say. Attributes like energy, speaking and speed which are actually strengths can also become a risk here.

Status area 3: energy

'Energy' as a status area means the use of power. However, power is more than the physically measurable parameter, i.e. the physical application of power, for example. In this context we mean the inner and outer intensity that goes into communication.

In our example, Edgar uses energy to gain the attention of the meeting participants and direct them away from Irene. Such behaviour demands above all resolute courage and an ability to handle conflict – typical extrovert strengths. But introverts, too, can show their resolute spirit by using energy appropriately, taking up a position and if necessary defending it.

Status signals relating to energy

Assurance

This term does not at first sound as if it has anything at all to do with energy. But look a bit closer. People who communicate in high status move with greater assurance – as if they know precisely what they are doing and why. They appear to have the situation under control. An assured voice with fluent, clear intonation also sounds confident and has a kind of suspense which makes listening easy and often even enthralling. It is a specific use of energy which gives rise to the impression of assurance in these areas.

Emphasis

Emphasis in the voice lends an utterance intensity and urgency. The person speaking invests energy in intonation, volume or accentuation. This leads to a high status signal which shows that the person or what is said are important. Or both!

But beware: volume does not automatically win out in status disputes. A quiet voice can also convey great energy and may well signal high status. Many powerful people do not speak excessively loudly. They do speak coherently, articulately and with a well-judged use of energy, but not in a big, booming voice at all.[61] Here again, it is the assurance which conveys strength.

Movements

Energetic movements often express high status – provided that they are not jerky and uncontrolled but defined and smooth, i.e. flowing and inherently consistent. Sweeping gestures certainly come across as imposing, but small, controlled hand and arm movements can also seem very energetic, purposeful and decisive. Also make sure of tension in your body posture: keep your head held high and your spine and shoulders straight.

Powerless movements resulting in passivity (such as folding your hands or shrugging your shoulders) signal forbearance or helplessness, and therefore low status. However, this also applies to persistent or repetitive movements which as a result lack definition: these also appear weak and low status. Imagine someone who is forever nodding, waving his head to and fro, playing with his fingers or shifting from one foot to the other.

The status area of energy: tips for introverts

Introverts expend a large part of their energy on inner processes instead of outer ones. This can easily make them seem powerless and therefore low status.

1. Avoid the impression of powerlessness by using your own resources to strive for confidence in your expression and movements. What that actually means is that small, calm, defined movements signal control and intensity (that is energy too) while you feel secure at the same time. Because you don't in any way need to 'train yourself up' to send extrovert energy signals. You can use your own resources to send out the message: 'I know exactly what I am doing. And I will also stand by my actions in tense situations.'

   On the other hand, avoid any non-verbal signals of powerlessness:

   • hands folded virtuously and passively in your lap;

   • hands dangling at the side of your body without any tension;

   • immobile facial expression signalling stress or inner absence. That will especially irritate extroverts who are not able to 'read' you and therefore do not get any stimulus from you.

2. The same applies to your intonation and volume while speaking: a high use of energy can be very effective (strong accentuation, loudness, fast pace) – but you can just as easily end up on the winning side with a calm, quiet, well-accentuated voice. If you are quite literally quiet you must keep eye contact, make sure the pace is moderate but not too slow, consciously add emphasis and include pauses. Be particularly careful to breathe deeply and slowly right down to your stomach so that your voice carries well and remains steady. It is also possible to speak powerfully and energetically as well as quietly in this manner. Simple, short, clear words will then be completely sufficient.

3. Also display your strength with your use of inner energy. You don't need to have a particularly outward-going personality. A reflective silence (see Ian's behaviour – and also the separate status area

of emotional warmth) combined with serene eye contact and a confident posture can appear very energetic and powerful. Strengths such as concentration and calm will be particular supportive here. But beware: if silence is supposed to be powerful and high status it should not be either an aggrieved or a helpless silence!

 ## The status area of energy: tips for extroverts

Extroverts often translate energy into movement with their drive, striving for reward and their enthusiasm. They might use lively gestures, a dynamic manner or loud, emphatic speech.

1. As already mentioned in the status area of time, frantic activity is also a risk when it comes to the use of energy. A high energy level combined with stress and an outward orientation can mean that the hurdle of impulsiveness gains the upper hand. Add to this the hurdle of impatience and the effect is increased. Then movements can become erratic or jerky – or undefined because the energy turns into wobbling and swaying and the definition of the body language is lost. The effect to an outsider is that you have lost control of your ability to communicate. Low status par excellence!

   So do move about and release your energy – but make sure that your movements are smooth and not jerky and have a beginning *and* an end. Then you will combine your outward energy with high status signals and still appear confident even with expansive gestures.

2. For all the energy you have available as an extrovert and your strength of speaking, you are *not* responsible for keeping the conversation going! Too much energy in such a situation may shift you into low status. So learn from introverts like Ian the strength of being silent and waiting – best achieved by taking a deep breath ...

3. If you are battling with the hurdle of aggression try never to suppress, ignore or break your discussion partner's will. Even if you can afford to expend the high level of energy, the results are usually bad on the relationship level – and even on the substantive level your

own interests are all the more likely to be sabotaged (you can read more about the effects in Etrillard, 2013).

Another negative consequence of this behaviour is an escalation of tension to the extent of fully fledged conflict.

Keep breathing deeply in such cases, then, when it's already on the tip of your tongue an open question. For example: 'I see we have different ideas here. Where do you think we should go from here?'

Status area 4: attention to others

The fourth and fifth status areas deal with attention both to yourself and to others. This fourth status area is about the signals we send to other people and by doing so give them attention. This type of attention is not to be confused with the extrovert strength of emotional warmth (see Chapter 1).

Attention and emotional warmth initially sound positive – and indeed they are in many cases, as people generally react positively when you take notice of them. Attention is described as a motivator in the section on management (see Chapter 6).

Attention can however also express something else: if you are forever on someone's case you become controlling. It can accordingly become a challenge if for example a line manager is always keeping an eye on an employee so that he can criticize him and find fault with him. In an even more extreme case, the level of attention can turn into confrontation: 'You're already 35 minutes late again today. Where were you?' In such cases the status positions are obvious: if you criticize or confront, you are high status.[62]

Something similar applies if the opposite happens: consciously withholding attention is also a high status signal.

Status signals relating to attention

Politeness

Politeness is ritualized attention within a culture and it signals respect – i.e. the key currency of status communication. There can be great differences in ways of behaving which may be perceived as polite or the opposite. In the (generally extrovert) USA for example it is considered impolite not to say anything to your counterpart, while in predominantly introverted Japan it is more likely to be considered impolite if you ramble on in communications with your discussion partner. However, one thing always applies: we lend people high status when we are truly polite towards them (without irony or exaggeration) and take the submissive position ourselves.

So if you as a person of higher formal status go towards a visitor to the office or take them to the lift when they leave, you are demonstrating politeness – simultaneously honouring your visitor with a behaviour not required by your status. This also applies to a warm welcome at a reception or before a meeting.

Showing attention is making a statement. On the other hand, impoliteness is a way of demonstrating 'I don't think much of you and I am of a higher rank than you.' So if you do not knock before entering an office, if you interrupt your conversation partner or yawn and look at your watch, you are also sending out a statement. But a very different one!

Giving: gifts and benefits

Giving is an important part of social interaction everywhere. I am referring here to all status-oriented forms of giving in vertical communication, i.e. *not* friendly sharing among group members in horizontal communication. If for example you give a (possibly expensive) gift to an office holder you outwardly lower your status. This is perfectly compatible with inner high status when the giver wants something from the recipient and wants to get his own way. Inner high status also protects the giver from being exploited in this role.

In ethically questionable cases a gift can be a bribe; in more innocuous situations the giver wants the receiver to see him positively.

In terms of status communication, if you offer benefits you may also be giving the beneficiary something by deliberately placing him at an advantage. This may take the form of a recommendation (for a contract or a job), an introduction to a new contact (who could become important for at least one participant) or giving them a knowledge-based edge by passing on exclusive information (about an upcoming vacancy, for example).

If you cultivate giving in inner high status and outer low status, you help others – via the gift – as much as yourself – by creating a congenial impression which in turn generates positive attention.[63]

Gathering information

In conversation, attention can mean listening with concentration and making use of the information gathered, perhaps by making suggestions or asking pointed questions. The crucial status signal here is the manner in which this happens. Are you attentive and interested, for example calmly nodding your head from time to time? Or condescending, judgmental or even derisive – for example pulling a face?

You can also pick up information by remaining silent – perhaps while concentrating particularly hard. It is important, especially for extroverts, not to confuse silence with passivity.

Withholding attention

If you turn your attention away from your counterpart (regardless of whether it is demonstratively or subtly) this usually sends out a high status signal.[64]

No matter how precious your conversation partner's time is, if he checks his e-mails during the exchange, looks at the computer screen or looks through files during a discussion, he is sending out a definite status message that says that the surroundings or the counterpart are not worth his undivided attention.

If you do not acknowledge your communication partner or deliberately delay acknowledging him, this also sends a high status signal.

Returning attention

What is meant here by 'returning' is how to handle attention which has been received. This is an interesting area of attention, because the question of status may be changed entirely by the manner in which attention is returned. For example if you confront your counterpart aggressively, you can easily slide into low status if the counterpart rewards your effort with a smile, a raised eyebrow or a friendly question ('What exactly do you mean by this?'). If the laws of politeness are not followed, this type of reaction is a good means of asserting your own status.

Head posture

Attentiveness can often be read from the posture of the head or a movement of the head.

Schmidt and Esser (2009, p. 118) point out that lifting the head when listening indicates high status – especially when associated with a corresponding eye expression: the listener is evaluating what you are saying.

Eye contact

The eyes deliver some of the most intense and expressive aspects of communication. Looking at another person lends probably the most direct form of attention apart from physical contact.

According to the prevailing opinion in the literature, if you lower your eyes when you meet someone or, alternatively, you are the first to look at the other person, you lower your status. If you look away and then back in the direction of your counterpart you may also be signalling (although not always) that you are a soft touch and therefore of low status.[65]

In meetings the participants usually look most frequently at the highest ranking participant. This is not always the facilitator nor is it always the boss sitting within the circle of the others: it is more likely the person to whom most of the participants attribute the most power and the most respect.

Physical contact

Touching a communication partner is in our classification an interesting mixture of attention and space. Physical distance is completely removed in at least one way and signals from both high and low status a quite immediate form of attention. If you put your arm around someone it signals familiarity or (in front of others) demonstrates support. If you tap someone on the shoulder, you are asking for immediate attention.

In confrontations physical contact from a high status person may express a very strong claim to power – especially if it is carried out very energetically. A hand shake can then become a vice, a pat on the shoulder a slap on the back and an arm placed around the shoulder becomes a bear hug …

Every culture has its own rules – types of contact that are acceptable in one country may be taboo elsewhere. Determining factors include the customary distance from each other, greeting rituals (bowing, shaking hands, kissing), gender relationships (are men and women generally permitted to touch each other?) and body parts which can be touched or are taboo (e.g. upper arm: yes; thigh: no).

Smiling

Smiling is a direct form of attention and is normally friendly above all else. But there are both high and low status types of smiling here as well. A condescending or pitying smile is a high status signal, like a political opponent 'smiling for victory' with overtones of confrontation. And if a conversation partner deliberately does not respond to a smile and keeps a straight face, this shows high status.

It is a different matter when a person has a permanent smile: this tends to signal anxiety, inoffensiveness and in the worst case unassertiveness, helplessness or even incompetence. A smile in reaction to aggression also shows low status.

The following are tips for both introverts and extroverts, who often see attention from very different viewpoints.

 ## Status area of attention: tips for introverts

The area of attention may prove a challenge for those introverts in particular who have to overcome the hurdle of contact avoidance. People to whom attention often seems stressful in any case may also find it difficult to handle the related status signals confidently. Added to this is the basic need for security that is part of most introverts.

If you actively display attention to others, you will often feel as if you are entering high-risk territory.

1. For that very reason, practise the range of active attention in your communication. Just experiment with sending certain attention signals with conversation partners you already trust (safety!): deliberately ask questions, send signals which show you are listening attentively (e.g. nodding your head, making eye contact; look at point 3 as well). Watch your counterpart's reactions. You can make a start by consciously including your body when gathering information – i.e. when listening with concentration.

    Also avoid offhand behaviour and verbally dismissing someone else's views ('Yes, but ...') . By all means keep it short, but do take enough time for a discussion when appropriate. If you are taken by surprise and do not have much time, don't risk stalling the conversation as the social cost may be too high. Defer it to another time – or ask specifically for the discussion to be brief.

2. Be aware that withheld attention can send out strong status signals which you perhaps do not want to communicate at all. If for example you keep a straight face, avoid eye contact and turn your body to the side when a boss talks to you, you are sending out messages like, 'I don't want to acknowledge you because you're not worth it!' (high status) or 'I don't feel confident with you!' (low status), depending on the exact combination of your signals.

    Usually, you probably consider what you say carefully. Watch your body language signals as well – introverts are often very 'quiet' in this area. Now and again during a conversation check your head and body posture and your eye contact. Smile when it is appropriate and you feel like it.[66]

3. Attention and emotional warmth are not one-way streets, they can be used to achieve so much – and that's what it's all about in status communication. Ask other participants about their opinions before a meeting where an important decision is on the agenda and listen to them carefully. If the decision is close to your heart you can champion your position in a one-to-one conversation and possibly win some support.

And get your own helping of attention!

Even if you have an infallible memory, don't act vindictively if an exchange has not gone too well or a conversation partner has disappointed you. Attention does not mean keeping tabs on failures or disappointments. As a cautious introvert you should be alert – but also take note of any opportunity to change the situation. Learn from the insouciance of some extroverts ('Better luck next time!').

If you don't get your way, avoid the temptation to sabotage any decisions by paying too much attention to detail, criticizing after the event or being passive. Even though these behaviours send out power signals, you will quickly damage your professional reputation.

 # Status area of attention: tips for extroverts

Extroverts usually find it easy to dispense attention. They have little difficulty finding a rapport even with people they don't know (a true extrovert strength!), are relaxed when doing so and tend to find attention pleasant – providing that it does not consist of the critical control mentioned above.

1. As an extrovert you especially value external feedback, so your need for attention may be particularly great. Conversely, withheld attention can mean stress – as with Evan from our example, who suffers as a result of Ian's silence. This may cause you to try to spread attention to gain outside appreciation. And that again means a risk of low status. Remember that although it is nice to be liked, it is no substitute for respect, which you don't get in return for liking. So don't be nice and kind and attentive if your counterpart is basically not nice and kind and attentive. In that case it is better if you are serious and focused, instead of nodding and smiling kindly.

2. You should also avoid overpowering others or demanding too much of them with attention signals. Refrain as far as possible from interrupting your communication partners or putting them on the

defensive with over-the-top signals (think about loudness, the radius of movement, physical contact) or very suddenly averting your attention and 'abandoning' your counterparts (that can happen especially easily if your hurdles include distraction or impatience). If anything like that were to happen to you, you wouldn't like it either.

If you're getting bored with a conversation, it's up to you to provide sufficient stimulation. Ask yourself, 'What do I find interesting about this exchange?' If you must, try a game like 'spot the meaningless phrases' (e.g. 'at the end of the day...', 'step up to the plate') – but do not just switch off.

3. Use the extrovert strength of emotional warmth to your advantage. Actually ask if something interests you or worries you (inner high status, outer low status is especially advantageous again here). Strengths such as drive and enthusiasm make you particularly convincing in this active form of control.

Do not confuse silence in your conversational partner with passivity. If you have an introvert before you their brain may be running in top gear as they listen quietly. If you want feedback from them, an open question is especially helpful (why, to what extent, how, what) – one which cannot be answered with a simple 'yes' or 'no'.

Status area 5: self-presentation (paying attention to yourself)

The fifth and last status area concerns the attention which people give to themselves. This can be observed in how they present themselves to the outside world and how they conduct themselves to get their communication partners to pay attention to them. If you attract admiring or respectful glances, you have achieved your goal in this category.

The message you are sending with self-presentation is: 'I lay claim to something special. I have earned it.' You therefore signal respect for yourself and at the same time raise a claim for respect from others.[67] This can have a significant effect especially in professional life: if you value yourself and communicate this with appropriate signals you can convince others to treat you accordingly.

Consider a salary negotiation: if you seem convinced of your own performance, you have more chance of success than an employee who sends out low status signals in terms of self-presentation.

Status signals in relation to self-presentation

Show status levers

Status levers are symbols of power and communicate high status. They can consist of quite different things depending on your environment, gender and position. Here are some examples – then you'll know the score: clothing and shoes, watch, jewellery, spectacles, company car, quality and design of business cards, stationery, fountain pen, office equipment, category of hotel for business trips, budget for literature and technical equipment (e.g. laptop, headphones) for personal use.

It's not necessarily about boasting. Simply taking luxury objects for granted sends out high status signals.

Distinctions can also be used to show high status. Everything that sets a person apart from others in a positive way belongs in this category: awards, ranking positions, lists of publications, medals, rotary club pins or badges …

Showing self-esteem

If your self-presentation signals show that you feel you are worth something, other people will be encouraged to accept this. These signals can be very different: making sure of particularly good quality in clothing, food or the home, surrounding yourself with interesting people, deliberately making sure you are equipped with status levers by the company – all these things can be associated with high status signals and indicate self-esteem. High self-esteem can also be signalled by making a deliberate choice of proposals, speaking positively and with conviction about yourself and moving about spaces (see above) in a confident manner.

You can also draw attention to yourself by causing deliberate disruption, for example loud telephone calls, disruptive paper-rustling or having other conversations while a colleague is speaking. However, a tendency to complain or to get irritated also demands attention and energy.

A particular way of demanding attention is the conscious and obvious transgression of social rules. The scope is enormous: putting your feet on the table, not saying hello, belching loudly during a business lunch, and of course significantly exceeding your allotted speaking time – all these are used to demonstrate high status. The message is 'I'm allowed!' And because it is to do with status communication, the currency is not liking (which rarely occurs here) but respect from outside which is a frequent effect of breaking the rules.

Being self-conscious or nervous

Signals such as filler words and spoken softeners (see below) as well as blushing, shrinking back or touching your upper body (head and neck, own hair and jewellery) show low status. Dacher Keltner (2009, p. 89) nevertheless points out that such signals of embarrassment also have a positive side: they show that the person feels bound by rules and is in a way approachable and human.

But strictly speaking, embarrassment ensures liking in horizontal communication, but unfortunately not respect in vertical status communication.

Be cool!

Signals of coolness provide protection because they all emit a certain unapproachability. For example, dark sunglasses prevent direct eye contact. But very low-reactive body language with little use of energy or apparent indifference may also signal coolness. Susan Cain (2011, p. 222f) speaks of a 'physiology of cool'. It provides protection by suggesting a lack of sensitivity which is not at all true of introverts in particular.

Humour

An inner form of coolness is humour – you might call it coolness with a warmth factor. If you don't always take yourself seriously and can laugh at yourself you make yourself approachable and usually appear exceptionally powerful as a result. You signal an ability to be objective about yourself, being comfortable with your own shortcomings and therefore show genuine self-confidence. Humour can be played many ways – it can be dry or it can be a hearty laugh.[68]

Here are some tips specially for introverts and extroverts regarding self-presentation.

 ## Status area of self-presentation: tips for introverts

Many introverts aren't really into self-presentation: they tend to be more concerned with the inner world rather than outward signs and compared to extroverts it takes them quite a lot of effort to present themselves and demand attention.

1. Show that you are important to yourself: otherwise other people will find it difficult to take you seriously. Do not worry that you might upset anyone – it will only upset your self-presentation. Quiet reserve is totally in order.

   But avoid low status signals such as touching your head, neck or hair or nervous movements such as rocking back and forth or fiddling absentmindedly with your fingers. If you have a tendency to blush, you can't just turn this off.

   It usually subsides faster, though, if you acknowledge it – quietly and without judging yourself.

2. The manner in which you make your point is also a form of self-presentation. You have probably thought things through sufficiently thoroughly – our key phrase: from the inside outwards – before uttering an opinion or making a suggestion. So stand up for what you want to say. Cautious people replace the important self-presentation words 'I' and 'you' with 'one' or passive constructions ('this and this should be done'). That appears ineffectual – it is better to say 'I' and name the person who should do something. For the same reason avoid softeners such as the subjunctive ('We could ...', 'It would also be possible ...'). And little words like 'perhaps' or 'possibly' which weaken the effect of what you are saying. Avoid fillers such as 'err', 'so', 'somehow or other' or 'oh well'. The reason is that all these expressions send the message: 'What I'm saying isn't that important. I'm not really convinced of it myself. And I'm not very good at expressing myself clearly.'

You can do better: say exactly which problem will be solved or which suggestion you are making, what work you have accomplished – and say it so that it signals your confidence and self-belief.

Keep it brief and to the point. This shows self-presentation in a good sense: in the sense of self-confidence.

3. Schmitt and Esser (2009, p. 186ff.) suggest a short emergency mantra for situations where you could easily slip from high to low status; you can bring it to mind and bring the situation mentally under control. For introverts I recommend an activating mantra such as 'I can do it!'

Status area of self-presentation: tips for extroverts

For many extroverts outward presentation comes naturally because of their basic orientation towards their environment, and it is normally not a hurdle. These tips therefore relate more to how much at a time and to strategy.

1. If you expend too much energy on your self-presentation (due to the hurdles of self-dramatization and self-centredness) this appears over the top and meets with neither liking nor respect. Judge the degree of your self-presentation signals skilfully – rather like adding a good spice.

2. Avoid attracting negative attention by breaking all kinds of rules to gain attention. You are no doubt already aware of that from your schooldays. For example, genuine annoyance accompanied by clear signals is always a problem – the only thing you really reveal is loss of control. If your hurdles include impatience, impulsiveness or aggression, breathe deeply and use your energy consciously instead of unleashing it without regard for the consequences.

3. Schmitt and Esser (2009, p. 186ff.) suggest a short emergency mantra for cases when you could easily slip from high to low status; you can bring it to mind and bring the situation mentally under control. For extroverts I recommend a focusing mantra such as 'Calm is power!'

When introverts and extroverts clash

Now that you know about the individual status areas you will already have guessed that power communication is a particular source of misunderstandings and stress between introverts and extroverts. The differences between the personality types can become particularly stressful if you don't succeed with your own strategies or if you suffer particularly under certain strategies practised by someone else.

In our examples Irene and Evan experience that from their respective introvert and extrovert perspectives. Irene particularly dislikes Edgar's interruption during the meeting because as an introvert she would be unlikely to choose this status signal herself. Edgar for his part possibly doesn't find interrupting all that bad: as a reward-oriented extrovert with a capacity for spontaneity, he takes a risk in publicly interrupting Irene. He takes the risk because a good outcome – such as being perceived by the boss as competent and dynamic – is an attractive enough reward. If the situation does not develop successfully for him, though, it will cost him. A public telling off by the boss ('Just let your colleague speak please!') or a confident counter by Irene ('Did I say I had finished?') would make Edgar look silly in public and lose him status advantages. Edgar has the added risk of appearing to other colleagues as a heedless steamroller, publicly flattening a colleague. Within the team that could cost him a lot of liking (especially if there are a number of introverts in it). Introverts know that it is sometimes cleverer not to make the venture if a risk exists, and to approach your objective with less audacious actions.

Key idea

Introverts and extroverts can make life especially difficult for each other in status communication.

Evan the salesman suffers under Ian's silence because as an extrovert it is particularly painful to him not to get outside feedback. He may easily be tempted to 'talk down' the silence to make the atmosphere more bearable. However, if Evan does not use his talking to clear matters up but just strives for dialogue *per se*, this would improve neither the situation nor Evan's status. For Ian on the other hand, the silence is energy-saving, puts him in a high status position as manager and suits his tendency to avoid contact in difficult situations. But he pays a price for his part too: if you avoid communication, i.e. 'shut down' and leave others in the dark, you don't just make an open exchange difficult, you create a bad atmosphere and will find it difficult as a manager to motivate your staff. A clear strategy, few words and clear messages would be the solution for an introvert and would make an enormous difference without costing Ian status points. Extroverts know that addressing and articulating tensions and conflicts represents a special opportunity.

Both confrontations between an introvert and an extrovert personality in this chapter have so far not offered you any satisfactory further development in communication. They do, however, offer pointers as to how you can best prepare for a tense and status-charged encounter with the opposite personality type. If you can answer the two following questions you will be able to look after yourself *and* improve your communication:

Guiding questions for personality-based status communication

1 What makes the introvert or extrovert personality that you are dealing with tick?

2 How should you, as an introvert or extrovert personality, act if you want to communicate on your terms – genuinely and in line with your personality?

Consideration of the first question will help you to develop an understanding of the behaviour of your counterpart, even though that person may be very different from you. It is worth analysing your counterpart's personality using the knowledge you have now gained about introverts and extroverts.

Dealing with the second question will help you to explore your own options and how to act while remaining true to yourself. If you have answered the questions in this book for yourself, you should now have little difficulty in doing so.

Be active as early as possible in status battles. Conflict research has shown that a tense situation otherwise easily escalates and in the end you will have to invest much more energy in clearing matters up or rectifying any harm to your status impact.

But back to our example. How can Irene and Evan as introvert and extrovert now send out appropriate status signals to show they are not just 'back in the game', but also to show those around them that they are acting confidently and responsibly (you know what I'm talking about: status 'inner high'!)? This, dear reader, is your final task in this chapter!

 ## Status training for introverts and extroverts

Work out solutions for the examples in this chapter and record your thoughts below.

If you are an introvert: Develop a strategy for Irene to handle the situation in the example *The meeting – a sliding tackle*. Name the type of status signals.

If you are an extrovert: Develop a strategy for Evan to handle the situation in the example *He's leaving me to stew*. Name the type of status signals.

For the ambitious: Develop different solutions with different status patterns: inner and outer high, inner and outer low, inner high/outer low and inner low/outer high.

1. My case:

2. Suggested solution:

3. (For the ambitious): Second solution with different status patterns:

4. Types of status signals in the suggested solution(s):

! Key points in brief

1. Confrontations, aggression and the testing of boundaries are part of status communication. Status signals are needed in social contact because they offer important guidance. People want to test out their relationship to each other and consciously or unconsciously strive to create rankings. They show who has more power in a group and who has less.

2. Basically we differentiate between inner and outer high or low status as expressed by speech, non-verbal signals and behaviour. They are not directly associated with formal positions of power.

3. A communication in high status aims to win respect, a communication in low status to win liking.

4. For both introverts and extroverts, status communication is often associated with stress and therefore with risks and hurdles – or even anxiety. This leads to typical reaction patterns under pressure. People who can be objective about themselves and those who can select from different strategies are at an advantage here.

5. The most stressful life is one where others can trample about with impunity.

6. The difficulties and strains produced in status communication are often different for introverts and extroverts. At the same time, however, both personality types can bring their own strengths and advantages to bear in status wrangling. This can be very clearly demonstrated using the five areas attributed to status signals: space, time, energy, attention and self-presentation.

7. When introverts and extroverts enter into status disputes they are at an advantage if they can, firstly, assess the point of view of the other personality type and, secondly, if they can communicate authentically and according to their own personality type.

9.
Being special together

There is a lot in this book. Which parts of what you have read will you use in your own life and your communication with others?

In this last section, I have summarized what I think are the key conclusions about the differences between extroverts and introverts in five points.

Just start with the first point – and then gradually, step by step, transform your life by taking that point on board more and more: discover what makes you special. Enjoy the journey.

1. Discover what makes you special

Work out from the statements you made when answering the questions in the test (see Appendix) what you do and don't like in your daily work. Investigate your strengths and hurdles (Chapter 1). Find out which situations energize you and which ones sap your energy. Then consider what your characteristics mean in concrete terms for your, your work and your fellow human beings.

The gentleness, quiet intelligence and caution of the introverts, their ability to listen – characteristics like these may be invaluable. The same applies to the enthusiasm, bold drive and cordial emotional warmth of extroverts. It's just that most people take their strengths for granted. So much that we constantly have available is of little value in our own estimation. The introverts' frequent modesty and the extroverts' need for external feedback add a further dimension: the things that make us strong don't really seem all that significant.

It's just that if you don't appreciate your strengths, you also make it difficult for others to respect you. So discover what makes you special. Use these insights by leading your life more and more in a way that suits you. It's no better or worse than any other life – but it's yours. Allow yourself to live it. And live it with all your special facets.

2. Live a meaningful life

Your personality type shapes you, but it isn't a straitjacket. No one forces you to keep looking out for new contacts because you're an extrovert. No one forces you to barricade yourself in behind a computer or a pile of books because you're an introvert. Develop impact – and yes, do use your introvert and extrovert strengths for that purpose. But also accept that you will sometimes display introvert characteristics as an extrovert and extrovert characteristics as an introvert. Our freedom lies in our agility!

What we consider significant, what counts for us as a reward, differs from individual to individual. One of the greatest tasks in your life is to find out what you feel is essential. What is the favourite thing that you want to do and will definitely do on this planet before you leave it again?

Extroverts, learn to apply your enormous energy to things that mean something to you. That will give your life a dimension of depth which an exciting, stimulating existence with money, fame and kicks alone cannot offer – even if you enjoy that kind of life. So consider the following question: what is truly important to me – even if it requires a lot of staying power? Implement the answer. Seek introverts in your environment who will help you to develop strategies.

Introverts, learn to take risks for the things that are important to you. Sometimes the greatest risk lies in refusing to budge. Changes have their price. But they are an important part of your development. So consider the following question: what do I really want to achieve – even if I have to put up with uncertainties to get it? Implement the answer. Seek extroverts in your environment who will give you a push at the crucial moment.

3. Enrich your team

Bring your strengths and special personality traits into the groups you live and work with: your family, your friends, your professional environment.

Let others benefit from what you want to do and can do, and in turn, benefit from what other people can do better and the things they want that are different from your own desires. Divide up tasks and responsibilities accordingly. Bear in mind that mixed teams in which the members combine their strengths may be particularly successful.

Think from time to time of the risks of self-hugging: if a team member marches to a different beat to you, he or she is not a worse person (or a better one, for that matter). Respect different outlooks on the world. And also demand this respect from others.

4. Communicate for others

What we communicate to others in our words, gestures and actions is particularly important when internally oriented and externally oriented personality types meet. These individuals are not very likely to reach an understanding without words. In these cases, communication may build important bridges.

Therefore, be prepared to say more as an introvert and less as an extrovert than you would do by nature. Be more generous with explanations of what's important to you. Observe how others react to you and adapt your communication in accordance with the conclusions you draw from their reactions. Consult people you trust if you are not sure.

Introverts, please, please speak up. Make sure that the substance in your thinking can be used by the outside world. If you need time for reflection, say so. Give the extroverts around you sufficient stimulation. Help to steer the discussion – as soon as you participate you are entitled to do that.

Extroverts, give yourself and others time. The introverts in your environment in particular will thank you if you take your time in speaking and above all listening. Adequate reflection before you act is at least equally important. And there is a reward: those who take their time come across as much more in control than those who are hasty.

5. Celebrate differences

We obviously need both introverts and extroverts in our societies – otherwise evolution would have gradually sorted out one personality type or at least shifted the balance of numbers between introverts, centroverts and extroverts. Attentiveness and reflection, quiet reflection and caution are needed – but so are drive, enthusiasm and the ability to manage conflicts.

Take pleasure in the differences between people. They're not only important and useful, they also make our life together vibrant and keep us agile.

Discover other personality differences – there are some more very interesting ones. Benefit from it if someone who's a completely different model gives you a perspective that you don't have. This strategy will extend your horizon potentially to infinity.

Enjoy your voyage of discovery!

Appendix

The test: introvert or extrovert?

If you would prefer to do this test online with automatic scoring, you will find it at www.leise-menschen.com/online-test/.

Tick all the statements that apply to you.

1 I quickly get impatient when I am talking to someone if they take too long to respond. ☐

2 I prefer to talk to one person rather than several. ☐

3 I find I can understand what I am thinking more easily if I talk to other people about it. ☐

4 I like my surroundings to be clean and tidy. ☐

5 I like to act quickly on a 'gut feeling' rather than thinking about things for a long time. ☐

6 If I'm really tired, I most like to be on my own. ☐

7 People who talk quickly wear me out. ☐

8 I have very personal, particular tastes. ☐

9 I avoid large crowds of people if I can. ☐

10 I normally find small talk easy, even with people I don't know. ☐

11 If I spend a long time with people I often get tired or even irritable. ☐

12 Other people usually pay attention to me when I speak. ☐

13 If I have visitors at home who stay for a long time, I expect them to help out. ☐

14 I prefer to work at a project in small sections rather than spending a long time on one piece. ☐

15 Sometimes I am very exhausted after a lot of conversations or loud ones. ☐

16 I do not need a lot of friends. Instead, I attach importance to genuine, reliable friendships. ☐

17 I don't spend a long time thinking about what is in other people's minds. ☐

18 It matters to me to get enough sleep. ☐

19 I find new places and surroundings exciting. ☐

20 I find sudden disturbances and unexpected situations a strain. ☐

21 I believe people often think I am too calm, boring, distant or shy. ☐

22 I like watching closely and I have an eye for detail. ☐

23 I'd rather talk than write. ☐

24 I brief myself carefully before making a decision about something. ☐

25 I am slow to spot tension between people. ☐

26 I have marked aesthetic sensibilities. ☐

27 I sometimes find reasons for going to some party or some other social occasion. ☐

28 I am relatively quick to trust people. ☐

29 I like thinking things over and getting to the bottom of them. ☐

30 I avoid speaking to large audiences if I can. ☐

31 Listening is not one of my greatest strengths. ☐

32 I often let other people's expectations put me under too much pressure. ☐

33 I can usually take personal attacks in good sport. ☐

34 I get bored quickly. ☐

35 If there is something special to celebrate, I'm happy for it to be on a large scale: a proper party or a meal with a lot of people. ☐

Now assess the statements you ticked:

- Introvert statements: 2, 6, 7, 9, 11, 15, 16, 20, 21, 22, 24, 27, 29, 30, 32.
- Extrovert statements: 1, 3, 5, 10, 12, 14, 17, 19, 23, 25, 28, 31, 33, 34, 35.
- Statements 4, 8, 13, 18 and 26 are nothing to do with introversion or extroversion and are there for one reason only: to stop you dropping into an answering routine.

What does your result look like?

- You are an introvert if you have ticked at least three more introvert statements than extrovert statements. The more introvert statements you ticked, the more markedly introverted you are. This book will tell you how to identify your needs and work to your strengths. Be sure to keep it with you!

- If you ticked roughly the same number of introvert and extrovert statements, i.e. no more than two statements different. You are in the intermediate zone between introvert and extrovert and as a so-called 'centrovert' or 'ambivert' you can get on well with both personality types. Your behaviour is particularly flexible. This book will show you above all something about the repertoire of your introverted side – in other words about the side that is probably less obvious to you.

- You're an extrovert if you ticked at least three more extrovert statements than introvert statements. The more statements you have agreed with, the more marked is your extroversion . This book will show you what makes introverts tick – and you will also come to see how you differ from them as an extrovert . You will understand a lot of people around you better and be able to get on with them better.

Notes

¹ Another subject which people I talk to frequently bring up is how to build and maintain contacts from the introvert's and extrovert's point of view. There is a detailed chapter on this subject for introverts in Loehken (2014). Extroverts will easily find information elsewhere, because most books on the subject assume an ideally extrovert personality – in most cases implicitly.

² Brian Little calls this part of the development of our personalities the 'free trait theory' (Little et al. 2007)

³ David Brooks (2011) summarizes the latest research results by saying that the unconscious makes up the bulk of the psyche and is where most decisions and the most impressive thought processes happen.

⁴ For more details on biological differences see Loehken (2014).

⁵ For examples see Cain (2011, p. 231). Here let it be once again expressly stated that we are all a mixture of introvert and extrovert characteristics. Not every extrovert likes gambling and even introverts will take business risks. Here we are talking about general tendencies with a wide range of variations.

⁶ More details and research deductions are very clearly summarized in Nettle (2009).

⁷ This distribution is also advantageous in terms of evolution. You will find a general summary in Cain (2011, p. 227 ff.) and a more precise research approach in Nettle (2006).

⁸ Further to the subject of self-monitoring are the interesting remarks by Snyder (1984), particularly the self-monitoring scale.

⁹ See Susan Cain's description of her extrovert husband (Cain, 2011, p. 240)

¹⁰ This long-term study comprised five volumes. Terman's colleague Melita Oden published the last volume, which is particularly interesting from the point of view of career development, after his

death: Terman, Lewis M. (Ed.) (1959), *The Gifted Group at Mid-Life*. Stanford: Stanford University Press. The study was continued and has now covered eight decades.

[11] Source: Erich Feldmeier, at: geistundgegenwart.de/2013/01/aaron-swartz-nachruf.html

[12] Eysenck (1973) attributed this characteristic to extroverts.

[13] Florian Werner (2012) published a good book on shyness. If you are interested in the science, look also at the work of American neurologist Louis A. Schmidt: http://www.science.mcmaster.ca/psychology/schmidt/

[14] A psychologist would say that the personality trait of introversion or extroversion does not correlate with the struggle for power.

[15] This association between personal characteristics and situation is described from a scientific point of view by Daniel Nettle (2009).

[16] The title of the article is 'Typisch: Warum wir immer anders und doch dieselben sind' ['Typical: Why we are always different and yet the same.']. You can find it at: http://www.geistundgegenwart.de/2012/12/erleben-und-persoenlichkeit.html

[17] There are relevant studies in Cain (2011, p. 164 and p. 170).

[18] You will find more details about these associations between social environment and biological development very well articulated in Hüther (2013, p. 26ff.).

[19] This flexibility goes beyond personality and is something different from the extrovert strength of the same name.

[20] The study was carried out with more than 2,800 breast cancer patients. See Kroenke et al. (2006).

[21] This fact is particularly striking in especially successful environments, e.g. as future social elites grow up. If you would like to investigate this further, see Hartmann (2004) or Friedrichs (2008).

[22] Read more at: http://smallbusiness.foxbusiness.com/starting-a-business/2011/06/13/why-co-founding-business-can-decimate-friendships/

[23] Steven Reiss (2010, p. 168ff.) coined this term with reference to the philosopher George Ramsay, who described the principle of self-hugging back in 1843 in a book about the key to happiness.

[24] If you are an introvert and want to deliver a presentation in accordance with your personality, Loehken (2014) may help you.

[25] For further details see Little (2000) and Little and Joseph (2007).

[26] This is the definition of free traits from Little (2000, p. 92f.): 'culturally scripted patterns of conduct carried out as part of a person's goals, projects, and commitments, independent of that person's 'natural' inclinations'.

[27] If you are interested in the details of this moving story, you will find them in Viktor Frankl's book *Man's Search for Meaning: An Introduction to Logotherapy* (Frankl 2009).

[28] Geier (2013) wrote an excellent biography of the famous brothers – one an introvert and the other an extrovert – it is very readable and gives an excellent impression of the times and the two personalities.

[29] Grotehusmann (2012) works mainly in the field of learning for exams and the personality-friendly acquisition of knowledge for different types of learners.

[30] You will find a separate section on business travel for introverts in general in Loehken (2014).

[31] For more detail, see Reiss (2010) or go online at www.reissprofile.eu.

[32] If you prefer the learner's perspective, I recommend the excellent book by Sabine Grotehusmann (2012). She also incorporates introvert and extrovert traits into her learning strategies.

[33] Pieper, D. (2013) '*Reformbaustelle Schule: Unsere Lehrer müssen besser werden*', *Spiegel Online*, 12 March 2013 Spiegel Online, 12 March 2013.

[34] If you are unsure, ask someone in the audience whom you trust to take particular note of the speed at which you speak. Extroverts in particular sometimes go off at a breakneck pace (introverts as well, but for different reasons: they speed up when they're nervous).

[35] The World Economic Forum and the Boston Consulting Group produced a study on this subject in 2011: http://www.bcg.de/documents/file69643.pdf

[36] If you want to know more about the fundamental requirements of corporate management, start with Malik (2009) or Maxwell (2012).

[37] These studies can be found in Barrick et al. (2001) and Kaplan et al. (2008).

[38] This study can be found in Grant et al. (2011).

[39] For example, Lehky (2011), Maxwell (2012), Assig and Echter (2012), Schüller (2012), Sprenger (2012), Groth (2013) and Su et al. (2013).

[40] The focus here is on the differences in communication with introverts and extroverts. If you are interested in diversity management from the economic point of view, a good starting point would be Jensen-Dämmrich (2011).

[41] For more about handling resistance from the communication point of view, read Sternberg (2011).

[42] Gloger (2013) describes the demands of 'Generation Y' in a detailed review. Schüller (2014) shows the requirements on companies.

[43] Link to press release: http://www.gallup.com/strategicconsulting/160901/pressemitteilung-zum-gallup-engagement-index-2012.aspx

[44] Recent research results are unanimous in this. For more detail see the review by Leffers (2012).

[45] Lehky (2011, p. 90 ff.), with reference to the *Harvard Business Manager*, Issue 2/2010, special issue on 'Motivation') offers a comprehensive list of all motivating factors. You will also find information in Leffers (2012), who cites a number of recent studies.

[46] This is shown by the results of Depue and Fu (2013) – as is the importance of external incentives and rewards for extroverts as a motivating factor.

[47] You will find a description of the various areas of conflict through which managers have to navigate in the excellent book by Groth (2013) and the article by Grote and Kauffeld (2007).

[48] For a readable and extensive discussion of the subject of resilience, see Maehrlein (2012).

[49] Rößler (2013) emphasizes the value of 'nay-sayers' in teams.

[50] The Gallup Engagement Index 2012 shows a high correlation between emotional attachment to a company and the possibility of expressing ideas and suggestions: 85 per cent of employees with an emotional attachment feel free to voice their opinions in such areas, but only 9 per cent of emotionally detached ones do. See: http://www.gallup.com/strategicconsulting/160901/pressemitteilung-zum-gallup-engagement-index-2012.aspx.

[51] Nöllke (2011) provides an illustrative introduction to management bionics – he reveals scientifically-based parallels between good management and cultivating a garden.

[52] Seßler (2010) and Pflug (2013) show the connection between the organization of the brain, emotions and purchase decisions. Köhler (2010) compares the sales relationship to the love relationship in his classic work.

[53] For more about loyalty and willingness to make recommendations see Schüller (2012, p. 91ff).

[54] Pink (2013a) cites several studies that unanimously prove this.

[55] You will find the basis for this assumption in Boaz et al. (2010) and in Pink (2013a, p. 83ff.).

[56] You can find more details and the basics of status communication in Tannen (1995) and – in the field of improvisational theatre – in Johnstone (1989). Tannen describes status communication as 'vertical communication' and separates it from the supportive 'horizontal communication' which is geared towards encounters on equal terms and serves group cohesion. Aron (2010) offered an excellent overview of the two forms of communication. Instead of vertical and horizontal communication, she talks of 'ranking' and 'linking'. Knaths (2007), Schmitt and Esser (2009) and Modler (2012) show applications, examples and strategies.

[57] There are numerous books which deal with the differences between male and female communication. I have now become

very cautious and consider it possible that the real differences in communication behaviours can be attributed to personality differences such as power seeking, competitiveness or introversion/ extroversion and less to gender-specific characteristics. The latter may be described logically as behaviours which certain cultures ascribe to the genders; these behaviours are considered appropriate and are taught from childhood and would be part of social 'second nature'. A power-conscious woman in Saudi Arabia has fewer roles available to her than a power-conscious French woman to live out this facet of her personality. What is more, a woman from the conservative upper class may well live out options which are different from those of the daughter of a liberal family of teachers or a traditional working class family. E.g. Carothers and Reis (2012) deliver a critical debate between gender and personality.

[58] The following remarks relate to our western European culture. Cultural differences in status communication are therefore excluded. In Japan, for example, people stand relatively far apart and tend to avoid physical contact. An example from conversation is that in many southern European countries, interruptions are accepted as part of normal communication much more than in eastern Asia.

[59] A good and even historical example of failure to assert an equal footing is the neck massage which the German Chancellor Angela Merkel was given in 2006 during the G8 summit by the then US President George W. Bush. She should have stood up! But take a look for yourself: http://www.youtube.com/watch?v=5dfrHT8o-0A

[60] It can be a test of courage for reticent people to sit directly at the conference table in bigger meetings. Practise it!

[61] A telling example is the powerful drug baron Gustavo Fring from the American TV series *Breaking Bad*. The actor Giancarlo Esposito speaks quietly in this role – and what he says leaves a lasting impression in his cinematic environment.

[62] This active attention is significantly different from criticism made from the low status position, e.g. complaining or passive non-compliance.

[63] Another consequence of this behaviour is not relevant to status but is nevertheless important: if you voluntarily give something away, you

feel particularly good. The World Giving Index of the British Charities Aid Foundation is an example of the proof of this. You can find the latest index from the end of 2012 at https://www.cafonline.org/PDF/WorldGivingIndex2012WEB.pdf .

[64] An exception to this rule would be something like an urgent interruption which demands attention, such as a sudden news flash or a physical disruption such as a power cut.

[65] You can read about the situations and exceptions in Schmitt and Esser (2009, p. 64 and p. 121 ff).

[66] Remember that even a movement of the corner of the mouth is still a movement – and it should be defined, i.e. should have a beginning and an end.

[67] I have left out the specific cases where status symbols are a cover-up for a lack of self-confidence and respect.

[68] If you are interested in more about this topic, read Szeliga (2011) or Titze and Patsch (2012).

References and bibliography

Ancowitz, N. (2010) *Self-Promotion for Introverts. The Quiet Guide for Getting Ahead.* New York: McGraw Hill

Aron, E. (2010) *The Undervalued Self.* New York, Boston, London: Little, Brown and Company

Aron, E. (1999) *The Highly Sensitive Person: How to Thrive when the World Overwhelms you.* 6th edn. London: Thorsons

Assig, D. & Echter, D. (2012) *Ambition. Wie Große Karrieren Gelingen.* [*Ambition. How Great Careers are Achieved.*] Frankfurt, New York: Campus

Barrick, M. R., Mount, M. K. & Judge, T. A. (2001) 'Personality and performance at the beginning of the new millennium: what do we know and where do we go next?' *International Journal of Selection and Assessment* 9, 1–2 (March/June 2001), pp. 9–30

Beck, M. (2004) *Das Polaris-Prinzip.* [*The Polaris Principle.*] Munich: Integral Verlag

Benien, K. (2003) *Schwierige Gespräche Führen.* [*Conducting Difficult Interviews.*] Reinbek: Rowohlt

Benun, I. (2010) *Jetzt Hört Ihr Mal Zu! Erste Hilfe für Schüchterne, Verunsicherte und Zurückhaltende.* [*Now Just Listen! First Aid for Shy, Insecure and Reserved People.*] Weinheim: Wiley

Boaz, N., Murnane, J. & Nuffer, K. (2010) 'The Basics of Business-to-Business Sales Success'. *McKinsey Quarterly*, May 2010, available with free registration at: http://www.mckinseyquarterly.com/The_basics_of_business-to-business_sales_success_2586

Brooks, D. (2011) *The Social Animal.* New York: Random House

Cain, S. (2011) *Quiet. The Power of Introverts in a World that Can't Stop Talking.* New York: Crown Publishing Group

Calendreau, L. et al. (2006) 'Extracellular hippocampal acetylcholine level controls amygdala function and promotes adaptive conditioned emotional response'. *The Journal of Neuroscience*, 27, December, 26(52), pp. 13556–13566. Link: http://www.jneurosci.org/content/26/52/13556.full

Carothers, B. J. & Reis, H. T. (2012) 'Men and women are from earth: examining the latent structure of gender'. *Journal of Personality and Social Psychology*. doi: 10.1037/a0030437

Cohen, D. & Schmidt, J. P. (1979) 'Ambiversion: characteristics of midrange responses on the introversion-extraversion continuum'. *Journal of Personality Assessment*, 43(5): pp. 514–516

Dembling, S. (2012) *The Introvert's Way. Living a Quiet Life in a Noisy World*. New York: Perigee Trade

Depue, R. A. & Fu, Y. (2013) 'On the nature of extraversion: variation in conditioned contextual activation of dopamine. Facilitated affective, cognitive, and motor processes'. *Frontiers in Human Neuroscience*, 7:288. Link: http://www.frontiersin.org/Human_Neuroscience/10.3389/fnhum.2013.00288/abstract

Dodge, K. A. (2006) 'Emotion and social information processing'. In J. Garber & K.A. Dodge (Ed.) *The Development of Emotion Regulation and Dysregulation*. Cambridge: Cambridge University Press, pp. 159–181.

Etrillard, S. (2013) *Mit Diplomatie zum Ziel. Wie gute Beziehungen Ihr Leben leichter machen*. [*Getting to your Goal with Diplomacy. How Good Relationships make your Life Easier*.] Offenbach: GABAL

Eysenck, H. (1947/2012) *Dimensions of Personality*. New Brunswick, London: Transaction Publishers

Eysenck, H. (1973) *Eysenck on Extraversion*. London: Crosby Lockwood Staples

Eysenck, H. (1971) *Readings in Extraversion-Intraversion: Bearings on Basic Psychological Processes*. New York: Staples Press

Frankl, V. E. (2009) *…trotzdem Ja zum Leben sagen: Ein Psychologe erlebt das Konzentrationslager*. [*Man's Search for Meaning: An Introduction to Logotherapy*. Available in translation] Munich: Kösel

Friedman, H. & Martin, L. (2011) *The Longevity Project. Surprising Discoveries for Health and Long Life from the Landmark Eight-Decade Study*. London: Penguin

Friedrichs, J. (2008) *Gestatten Elite. Auf den Spuren der Mächtigen von Morgen.* [*With your Permission: Elite. On the Trail of Tomorrow's Power Holders.*] Munich: Heyne

Geier, M. (2013) *Die Brüder Humboldt. Eine Biographie.* [*The Brothers Humboldt. A Biography.*] 2nd edition. Reinbek bei Hamburg: Rowohlt

Gerbrecht, S. & Gloger, S. (2013) "Durch Wirkung bewegen. Führen mit Charisma'. ['Motivating through impact. Leading with charisma'.] In: *managerSeminare* 178, January 2013, pp. 60–66

Gloger, A. (2013) 'Das Ende des Vorgesetzten' ['The end of the boss'] In: *managerSeminare* 183, March 2013, pp. 24–30

Grant, A. (2013a) 'Rethinking the extraverted sales ideal: The ambivert advantage'. *Psychological Science* 24:6, pp. 1024–1030. Link: http://www.management.wharton.upenn.edu/grant/Grant-AmbivertAdvantage_PsychScienceForthcoming.pdf

Grant, A. (2013b) 'Rocking the boat but keeping it steady: The role of emotion regulation in employee voice'. *Academy of Management Journal.* vol. 56, no. 61703–1723

Grant, A., Gino, F. & Hofmann, D. (2011) 'Reversing the extraverted leadership advantage: The role of collective employee proactivity'. *Academy of Management Journal* 54:3, pp. 528–550

Grote, S. & Kauffeld, S. (2007) 'Stabilisieren oder dynamisieren: Das Balance-Inventar der Führung (BALI-F)'. ['Stabilizing or dynamizing: the balance inventory of management (BALI-F)'.] In J. Erpenbeck & L. von Rosenstiel (Ed.): *Handbuch Kompetenzmessung: Erkennen, verstehen [sic!] und bewerten [sic!] von Kompetenzen in der betrieblichen, pädagogischen und psychologischen Praxis.* [*Handbook of Competence Measurement: Recognizing, Understanding and Evaluating Competences in Business, Educational and Psychological Practice.*] 2nd Edition. Stuttgart: Schäffer-Pöschel, pp. 317–336

Grotehusmann, S. (2012) *Der Prüfungserfolg. Die optimale Prüfungsvorbereitung für jeden Lerntyp.* [*Success in Exams. The Optimum Preparation for Every Type of Learner.*] 2nd edition. Offenbach: Gabal

Groth, A. (2013) *Führungsstark im Wandel. Change Leadership für das mittlere Management*. [*Strong Management under Change. Change Leadership for Middle Management*.] 2nd, revised edition. Frankfurt a.M.: Campus

Hamer, D. & Copeland, P. (1998) *Living with Our Genes*. New York: Anchor Books

Hartmann, M. (2004) *Elitesoziologie. Eine Einführung*. [*Elite Sociology. An Introduction*.] Frankfurt a.M.: Campus

Helgoe, L. (2010) 'Revenge of the Introvert'. *Psychology Today* 9/2010. Link: http://www.psychologytoday.com/articles/201008/revenge-the-introvert

Helgoe, L. (2008) *Introvert Power. Why Your Inner Life Is Your Hidden Strength*. Naperville: Sourcebooks

Hüther, G. (2013) *Was wir sind und was wir sein können. Ein neurobiologischer Mutmacher*. [*What We Are and What We Can Be. A Neurobiological Encouragement*.] Frankfurt a.M.: Fischer Taschenbuch

Jánszky, S. G. & Jenzowsky, S. A. (2010) *Rulebreaker. Wie Menschen denken, deren Ideen die Welt verändern*. [*Rulebreakers. How People Whose Ideas Change the World Think*.] Vienna: Goldegg

Jensen-Dämmrich, K. (2011) *Diversity-Management: Ein Ansatz zur Gleichbehandlung von Menschen im Spannungsfeld zwischen Globalisierung und Rationalisierung?* [*Diversity Management: An Approach to Equal Treatment of People in the Field of Tension between Globalization and Rationalization*.] Munich, Mehring: Rainer Hampp Verlag

Johnson, D. et al. (199) 'Cerebral blood flow and personality: A positron emission tomography study'. *American Journal of Psychiatry* 156, pp. 252–257. Link: http://ajp.psychiatryonline.org/article.aspx?articleid=173270

Johnstone, K. (1989) *Impro: Improvisation and the Theatre*. London: Methuen Drama

Jung, C.G. (1992) *Psychological Types*. London: Routledge

Kagan, J. (2004) *The Long Shadow of Temperament*. Cambridge, Massachussetts: Harvard University Press

Kahnweiler, J. B. (2009), *The Introverted Leader. Building on Your Quiet Strength*. San Francisco: Berrett-Koehler

Kaplan, S. N., Klebanov, M. M. & Sorensen, M. (2008) 'Which CEO characteristics and abilities matter?' In: Swedish Institute for Financial Research Conference on the Economics of the Private Equity Market 2008. Link: faculty.chicagobooth.edu/steven.kaplan/research/kks.pdf

Kelly, E. L. & Conley, J. (1987) 'Personality and compatibility: A prospective analysis of marital stability and marital satisfaction'. In: *Journal of Personality and Social Psychology*, 52(1), pp. 27–40. Link (option to buy): http://psycnet.apa.org/index.cfm?fa=buy. optionToBuy&id=1987-15348-001

Keltner, D. (2009) *Born to Be Good. The Science of a Meaningful Life*. New York, London: W.W. Norton & Company

Kimich, C. (2012) 'Verhandlungstango – Tanz auf dem Vulkan oder Schweben übers Parkett' ['The Negotiation Tango – Dancing on a volcano or floating across the parquet'.] In: H.U.L. Köhler (Ed.) *Die besten Ideen für erfolgreiches Verkaufen*. [*The Best Ideas for Successful Selling*.] Offenbach: GABAL, pp. 160–170 (GSA Top Speakers Edition, Volume 3)

Knaths, M. (2007) *Spiele mit der Macht. Wie Frauen sich durchsetzen*. [*Power Games. How Women Assert Themselves*.] Hamburg: Hoffmann und Campe

Köhler, Hans Uwe L. (2010) *Verkaufen ist wie Liebe. Nutzen Sie Ihre emotionale Intelligenz*. [*Selling is like Love. Use Your Emotional Intelligence*.] 16th edition. Regensburg: Walhalla und Praetoria

Kroenke, C. H., Kubzansky, L. D., Schernhammer, E. S., Holmes, M. D. & Kawachi, I. (2006) 'Social networks, social support, and survival after breast cancer diagnosis'. In: *Journal of Clinical Oncology* 24:7, pp. 1105–1111. Link: http://jco.ascopubs.org/content/24/7/1105.full

Kullmann, K. (2012) 'Die Kraft der Stillen' ['The Power of the Quiet People'] Cover story in: *Der Spiegel*, No. 34, pp. 102–110. Link: http://wissen.spiegel.de/wissen/image/show.html?did=87818628&aref=image052/2012/08/18/CO-SP-2012-034-0102-0110.PDF&thumb=false

Leffers, J. (2012) 'Geld allein ist ein zu schwacher Motor'. ['Money alone is not a sufficiently powerful motor'] Spiegel Online Link:

http://www.spiegel.de/karriere/berufsleben/mitarbeiter-motivation-geld-allein-ist-ein-zu-schwacher-motor-a-816970.html

Lehky, M. (2011) *Leadership 2.0. Wie Führungskräfte die neuen Herausforderungen im Zeitalter von Smartphone, Burnout & Co. managen* [*Leadership 2.0. How Executives Manage the New Challenges in the Age of Smart Phone, Burnout & Co*] Frankfurt, New York: Campus

Little, B. R. (2000) 'Free traits and personal contexts: Expanding a social- ecological model of well-being'. In W. Walsh et al. (Ed) *Person-Environmental Psychology. New Directions and Perspectives*. 2nd edition. New York: Guilford, pp. 87–116

Little, B. R. & Joseph M. F. (2007) 'Personal projects and free traits: mutable selves and well beings'. In: B.R. Little et al. (Ed.) (2007) *Personal Project Pursuit. Goals, Action, and Human Flourishing*. Mahwah/New Jersey, London: Lawrence Erlbaum pp. 375–400

Loehken, S. (2014) *Quiet Impact*. London: Hodder & Stoughton

Loehken, S. (2012) 'So fördern Sie die leisen Leister' ['How to develop quiet performers'] In: *managerSeminare* 169, April, pp. 70–75

Loehken, S. (2010) 'Unter Extros. Erfolgsstrategien für introvertierte Persönlichkeiten'. ['Among extroverts: Success strategies for introvert personalities.] In: J. Löhr (Ed.) *Die besten Ideen für ein estarke Persönlichkeit.* [*The Best Ideas for a Strong Personality.*] Offenbach: GABAL, pp. 231–246 (GSA Top Speakers Edition, Volume 1)

Lucas, R.E. & Diener, E. (2000) 'Cross-cultural evidence for the fundamental features of extraversion'. In: *Journal of Personality and Social Psychology* 79:3, pp. 452–468

Maehrlein, K. (2012) *Die Bambus-Strategie. Den täglichen Druck mit Resilienz meistern.* [*The Bamboo Strategy. Mastering Daily Pressure with Resilience.*] Offenbach: GABAL

Malik, F. (2009) *Managing Performing Living: Effective Management for a New Era.* University of Chicago Press

Maxwell, J.C. (2012) *Developing the Leader Within You.* Thomas Nelson Publishing

Mehl, M. R., Vazire, S., Holleran, S. E. & Clark, C. S. (2010) 'Eavesdropping on happiness: Well-being is related to having less small talk and more substantive conversations'. In: *Psychological Science* 21, pp. 539–541

Modler, P. (2012) *Das Arroganz-Prinzip. So haben Frauen mehr Erfolg im Beruf.* [*The Arrogance Principle. How Women can have More Successful Careers.*] Frankfurt a.M.: Fischer

Mummendey, H.D. (1983) 'Sportliche Aktivität und Persönlichkeit: Versuch einer Tertiäranalyse' ['Sporting activity and personality: An attempt at a tertiary analysis'] In: *Sportwissenschaft* [*Sports Science*] 13, pp. 9–23. Link: http://pub.uni-bielefeld.de/luur/download?func=downl oadFile&recordOId=1782504&fileOId=2313864

Nelson, B. (2005) *1001 Ways to Reward Employees.* Workman Publishing

Nettle, D. (2006) 'The evolution of personality variation in humans and other animals'. In: *American Psychologist* 61:6, pp. 622–631

Nettle, D. (2009) *Personality: What Makes You the Way You Are* Oxford: OUP

Nöllke, M. (2011) *In den Gärten des Managements. Für eine bessere Führungskultur.* [*In the Gardens of Management. For a Better Management Culture.*] Planegg nr. Munich: Haufe

Olsen L.M. (2002) *The Introvert Advantage. How to Thrive in an Extrovert World.* New York: Workman Publishing

Pflug, K. (2013) *Praktische Verkaufspsychologie. Mit psychologischem Wissen leichter mehr Erfolg in Vertrieb und Marketing.* [*Practical Sales Psychology: Be more Successful more Easily in Sales and Marketing with Psychological Knowledge.*] Berlin: epubli

Pink, D. (2013a) *To Sell Is Human. The Surprising Truth about Persuading, Convincing, and Influencing Others.* Edinburgh, London: Canongate.

Pink, D. (2013b) 'Why extroverts fail, Introverts flounder and you probably succeed'. *Washington Post*, 28 January. Link: http://www. washingtonpost.com/national/on-leadership/why-extroverts-fail-introverts-flounder-and-you-probably-succeed/2013/01/28/bc4949b0-695d-11e2-95b3-272d604a10a3_story.html?hpid=z11

Pink, D. (2011) *Drive. The Surprising Truth About What Motivates Us.* New York: Canongate

Prochnik, G. (2010) *In Pursuit of Silence. Listening for Meaning in a World of Noise.* New York: Doubleday

Reiss, S. (2010) *Das Reiss Profile. Die 16 Lebensmotive. Welche Werte und Bedürfnisse unserem Verhalten zugrunde liegen,* [*The Reiss Profile. The 16 Basic Desires. The Values and Needs Underlying our Behaviour,*] 2nd edition. Offenbach: GABAL

Ridgeway, E. (2010) 'Why introverts can be great leaders'. In: *CNN,* 9 December

Roming, A. (2011) 'Die Stillen im Lande'. ['The quiet people here'.] In: *Psychologie Heute* [*Psychology Today*], Year 38, No. 1, pp. 20–27

Rößler, A. (2013) 'Teams brauchen nicht nur Ja-Sager' ['Teams don't just need yes-men'.] In: business-wissen.de. Link: http://www.business-wissen. de/arbeitstechniken/kritisches-denken-teams-brauchen-nicht-nur-ja-sager/

Ruttkowski, W. (2012) *Typen und Schichten. Zur Einteilung des Menschen und seiner Produkte.* [*Types and Social Strata. Classifying People and Their Products.*] Hamburg: Igelverlag (first edition 1978)

Schäfer, L. (2012) *Emotionales Verkaufen. Was Ihre Kunden wirklich wollen.* [*Emotional Selling. What your Customers Really Want.*] Offenbach: GABAL

Scheuermann, U. (2013a) *Wenn morgen mein letzter Tag wär – so finden Sie heraus, was im Leben wirklich zählt.* [*If Tomorrow were my Last Day – How to Discover what Really Matters in Life.*] Munich: Knaur

Scheuermann, U. (2013b) *Wer reden kann, macht Eindruck – wer schreiben kann, macht Karriere. Das Schreibfitnessprogramm für mehr Erfolg im Job.* [*Good Speakers Make an Impression – Good Writers Make Promotion. The Writing Fitness Programme for More Success in your Job.*] 2nd, updated edition. Vienna: Linde

Scheuermann, U. (2012) *Schreibdenken. Schreiben als Denk- und Lernwerkzeug nutzen und vermitteln.* [*Thinking in Writing. Using and Communicating Writing as a Thinking and Learning Tool.*] Leverkusen, Berlin: Verlag Barbara Budrich

Schmitt, D. P. (2008) 'Big five traits related to short-term mating: From personality to promiscuity across 46 Nations'. In: www.epjournal.net. Link: http://www.epjournal.net/wp-content/uploads/ep06246282.pdf

Schmitt, T. & Esser, M. (2009) *Status-Spiele. Wie ich in jeder Situation die Oberhand behalte. [Status Games. How I can Keep the Upper Hand in Every Situation.]* Frankfurt a.M.: Scherz

Schüller, A. M. (2014) *DasTouchpoint-Unternehmen. [The Touchpoint Company.]* Offenbach: GABAL

Schüller, A. M. (2012) *Touchpoints. Auf Tuchfühlung mit dem Kunden von heute. [Touchpoints. Up Close to the Customers of Today.]* Offenbach: GABAL

Seßler, H. (2011) *Limbic Sales. Spitzenverkäufe durch Emotionen. [Limbic Sales. Top Selling through Emotions.]* Freiburg: Haufe Lexware

Snyder, M. (1984) *Public Appearances, Private Realities: The Psychology of Self-Monitoring.* New York: W.H. Freeman

Sprenger, R. K. (2012) *Radikal führen. [Radical Leadership.* Available in translation] Frankfurt, New York: Campus

Stafford, T. (2013) 'What makes us extroverts and introverts?' 17 July. Link: http://www.bbc.com/future/story/20130717-what-makes-someone-an-extrovert

Sternberg, L. (2011) *Führungskommunikation zwischen Konsens und Dissens. Führung, Kommunikation und Beratung. [Management Communication between Consensus and Dissention. Leadership, Communication and Consultancy.]* Berne: Peter Lang (Europäische Hochschulschriften) [(European University Publications)]

Su, A.J. & Wilkins M.M. (2013) *Own the Room: Discover your Signature Voice to Master your Leadership Presence.* Boston Harvard Business Review Press 2013

Szeliga, R. (2011) *Erst der Spaß, dann das Vergnügen. Mit einem Lachen zum Erfolg [First the Fun, then the Pleasure. Succeeding with Laughter]* Munich: Kösel

Tannen, D. (1995) 'The power of talk: Who gets heard and why'. In: *Harvard Business Review* 9/10, pp. 138–148

Thorne, A. (1987) 'The press of personality: A study of conversation between introverts and extraverts'. In: *Journal of Personality and Social Psychology* 53:4, pp. 718–726

Titze, M. & Patsch, I. (2004) *Die Humor-Strategie. Auf verblüffende Weise Konflikte lösen.* [*The Strategy of Humour. Resolving Conflicts in an Astonishing Way.*] Munich: Kösel

Werner, F. (2012) *Schüchtern. Bekenntnis zu einer unterschätzten Eigenschaft.* [*Shy. Committing to an Underestimated Quality.*] Zurich: Nagel und Kimche

Zack, D. (2012) *Netzwerken für Networking-Hasser.* [*Networking for Networking Haters.*] Offenbach: GABAL

Zeldin, T. (1999) *Der Rede Wert. Wie ein gutes Gespräch Ihr Leben bereichert.* [*Worth Talking About. How a Good Conversation Enriches Your Life.*] Munich: Malik

Online resources

geistundgegenwart.de

This is a blog by Gilbert Dietrich, coach by trade, but also head of the Human Resources department of a web company. Dietrich deals with exciting issues of personality psychology which he talks about in clear terms, on the basis of deep knowledge and with a focus on real life.

hsperson.com

Psychologist Elaine Aron is an expert in high sensitivity. There is an English test on her website which you can use to find out whether you are a highly sensitive person.

introvertday.org and personic.de/blog.html

Felicitas Heyne, likewise a psychologist, has declared 2 January to be 'World Introvert Day'. There are some contemporary resourrces in English on her website about introversion and extroversion, including an eBook which can be downloaded free. Felicitas Heyne also writes about introversion and extroversion in her blog.

leise-menschen.com/leise-texte

There are a lot of my own texts and media publications about introverts and extroverts on my website.

psychologytoday.com/blog/the-introverts-corner

Sophia Dembling writes this blog, 'The introvert's corner', in the American journal *Psychology Today* (English). You will find a lot of intelligent pieces about introverts and extroverts there.

thepowerofintroverts.com

Susan Cain's website and blog.

youtube.com/user/LeiseMenschenTV

My YouTube channel with all past (and future) videos from the 'noisy-quiet sofa' series. Also includes plenty of material about introverts and extroverts for all those who would rather listen and look than read.

Index

Ackstaller, Susanne, 5
adaptability, 90–2, 207
aggression, 29–30, 204, 229
analytical thinking, 15–16, 205, 229
anxiety, 24–5, 228
assertiveness, 40–1
attention
  to detail, 26–7
  to others, 249–56

Baumeister, Roy, 52
biological factors, xvii–xviii, 7, 25
body/spirit relationship, 132–3, 136–7
brain structures, 3–4
Brooks, David, xix, 53, 158

Cain, Susan, 21, 25, 141, 217
calmness, 14–15, 205, 229, 243
carelessness, 24–5
caution, 9–10
centroverts, 117–23, 206–8
childhood, 50–7
clothing choices, 5
communication, 10–22, 25–36, 269
  for managers, 164–75, 184
  in politics, 108
  in selling, 198, 200–1, 210–12
  social media, 59–63
  status, 217–34, 261–5
community, status in, 218–24
community principle, 50–2, 56

concentration, 11–12
conflict avoidance, 35–6, 205, 228
conflict management skills, 21–2
confrontation, 224–34, 261–3
contact avoidance, 34–5, 61, 206, 228
contact stimulation, 73
courage, 10

Dembling, Sophia, 11, 74
Dietrich, Gilbert, 43
distraction, 32–3, 62
diversity, 165–71
dopamine, 5, 6, 73
drive, 15–16, 203

emotional warmth, 16–17, 203, 249–56
emotions, 6, 200–1
empathy, 21–2, 205, 229
employment security, 183–91
endurance, 131, 135
energy management, 97
energy and status, 245–9
enthusiasm, 10–11, 202–3
extroverts
  benefits of being around introverts, 66–7
  body/spirit relationship, 132–3
  compatibility with introverts, 41–2
  as customers, 196–7, 208–12
  differences from introverts, 127–53

employment security for, 184–91
endurance, 131
hurdles, 23–38
introvert characteristics, 42–3
in introvert professions, 95–6, 97, 98–105
leadership skills, 160–3
learning, 52–5, 147–51
management of, 166–9, 172–4, 179–81, 184–9
as managers/executives, 155–7, 159–65, 170–1, 175, 181–3, 190–1
motivation of, 177–83
myths, 39–43
receptivity to stimuli, 6, 33, 53, 73, 118, 131, 148–9
reward orientation, 149–50
as salespeople, 196, 202–4, 211–12
and social media, 59–60, 62–3
sport, 129, 130–3
status, 229–34, 240, 244–5, 248–9, 255–6, 260
strength training, 131–2
strengths, 9–23
successful, xxii–xxiii
teamwork with introverts, 66–7, 74–81, 84–5, 132
understanding of introverts, 67–72

fear, 206
Feynman, Richard, 91, 100
fixation, 32–3, 61
flexibility, 11–12, 92–3, 203
flight, 29–30, 61, 228

focus, 26–7
force, overpowering, 35–6, 230
Frankl, Victor, 91
free trait theory, 90–2, 96
friendship, 70–3

Grant, Adam, 118, 159, 201, 207
Grotehusmann, Sabine, 110–12

Humboldt, Alexander von, 95–6, 97, 98–9
Hüther, Gerald, 51
hypersensitivity, 4

impatience, 27–8, 62, 229
impulsiveness, 30–1, 62, 229
independence, 16–17
inner status, 221–3, 234
inside-out learning, 142
intellectualization, 30–1
intrinsic characteristics, 94–113
introverts
    benefits of being around extroverts, 66–7
    body/spirit relationship, 136–7
    community principle, 50–2, 56
    compatibility with extroverts, 41–2
    as customers, 196, 204, 208–11
    differences from extroverts, 127–53
    employment security for, 184–91
    endurance, 135
    extrovert characteristics, 42–3
    in extrovert professions, 96–7, 106–13
    hurdles, 23–38

leadership skills, 160–3
learning, 55–6, 142–6
management of, 155–7, 166–9,
    172–4, 179–81, 184–9
as managers/executives, 159–65,
    170–1, 175, 181–3, 190–1
motivation of, 177–83
myths, 39–43
risk aversion, 96–7
safety considerations, 144–5,
    183
as salespeople, 196–7, 204–6,
    212
sensitivity to stimuli, xx, 3–4,
    27–8, 73, 118, 142–4
socializing, 73–4
and social media, 59–62
sport, 134–7
status, 228–9, 231–4, 239–40,
    243–4, 247–8, 253–5, 259–60
strength training, 135–6
strengths, 9–23
successful, xxii–xxiii
teamwork with extroverts, 66–7,
    74–81, 84–5, 134, 136, 137
understanding of extroverts,
    67–72

Kant, Immanuel, 74
Kimich, Claudia, 199–200
Kura, Lilian, 103–4

Lammert, Corinna, 146
leadership skills, 160–3
learning, 52–7, 139–52
level-headedness, 208

listening skills, 12–13, 200–1,
    204–5, 229
Little, Brian, 90, 96

management, 155–93, 218–24
meaningful life, xx–xxi, 89–115,
    268
mediation, 207
Merkel, Angela, 92
motivation, 176–83

nature/nurture debate, xix
noisy–quiet sofa, 85
Nöllke, Dr Mattthias, 102–3

outer status, 221–3, 234
outside-in learning, 147–8
overstimulation, xx, 3–4, 27–8, 73,
    118, 142–4

passivity, 28–9, 61, 228
physical exercise, 129–39
presentation skills, 12–13

Reiss motivation profile, 115,
    176–7
reward orientation, 149–50
risk, 4–5, 82, 96–7

safety considerations, 4–5, 29, 82,
    96–7, 144–5, 183
Schäfer, Lars, 200–1
Scheuermann, Ulrike, 20, 142
Schmitt, Tom and Michael Esser,
    221–2, 226, 234, 260
self-avoidance, 34–5, 62

self-awareness, 50–1
self-centredness, 31–2, 204
self-denial, 31–2
self-dramatization, 28–9, 204
self-hugging, 69, 165
self-presentation, 256–60
selling, 195–215
situation, 42–3
social accessibility, 39–40
social communities, 64–7
social environment, xviii–xix, 49–53
socializing, 73–4
social media, 59–63
solitude, 74
space and status, 235–40
speaking
   preference for, 19–20, 203
   skills, 230
   as status signal, 241–2
speed, 14–15
spontaneity, 17–19
sport, 129–39
status communication, 217–34, 261–5

status, zones, 234–60
stimulation, 73, 118, 230
   extroverts, 6, 33, 53, 73, 131
   introverts, xx, 3–4, 27–8
   in learning, 142–4, 148–9
strength training, 131–2, 135–6
stressful situations, 224–7
substance, 10–11
superficiality, 26–7, 62
Swartz, Aaron, 19

teamwork, 66–7, 74–81, 84–5, 132, 134, 136, 137, 151, 268–9
tenacity, 17–19, 205, 229, 243
time and status, 241–5

under-stimulation, 6, 33, 53, 73, 118, 131, 148–9

versatility, 207

writing, preference for, 19–20